ASSESSING WRITING TO SUPPORT LEARNING

In this book, authors Murphy and O'Neill propose a new way forward, moving away from high-stakes, test-based writing assessment and the curriculum it generates and toward an approach to assessment that centers on student learning and success. Reviewing the landscape of writing assessment and existing research-based theories on writing, the authors demonstrate how a test-based approach to accountability and current practices have undermined effective teaching and learning of writing. This book bridges the gap between real-world writing that takes place in schools, college, and careers and the writing that students are asked to do in standardized writing assessments to offer a new ecological approach to writing assessment.

Murphy and O'Neill's new way forward turns accountability inside out to help teachers understand the role of formative assessments and assessment as inquiry. It also brings the outside in, by bridging the gap between authentic writing and writing assessment. Through these two strands, readers learn how assessment systems can be restructured to become better aligned with contemporary understandings of writing and with best practices in teaching. With examples of assessments from elementary school through college, chapters include guidance on designing assessments to address multiple kinds of writing, integrate reading with writing, and incorporate digital technology and multimodality. Emphasizing the central role that teachers play in systemic reform, the authors offer sample assessments developed with intensive teacher involvement that support learning and provide information for the evaluation of programs and schools.

This book is an essential resource for graduate students, instructors, scholars and policymakers in writing assessment, composition, and English education.

Sandra Murphy is Professor Emerita at University of California, Davis, USA.

Peggy O'Neill is Professor of Writing at Loyola University Maryland, USA.

ASSESSING WRITING TO SUPPORT LEARNING

Turning Accountability Inside Out

Sandra Murphy and Peggy O'Neill

To Kathryn,
I've enjoyed learning
so much from you over the
years.
Peggy O'Neill

Routledge
Taylor & Francis Group

NEW YORK AND LONDON

Cover image: © Getty Images

First published 2023
by Routledge
605 Third Avenue, New York, NY 10158

and by Routledge
4 Park Square, Milton Park, Abingdon, Oxon, OX14 4RN

Routledge is an imprint of the Taylor & Francis Group, an informa business

ISBN: 978-1-032-28289-3 (hbk)
ISBN: 978-1-032-26809-5 (pbk)
ISBN: 978-1-003-29614-0 (ebk)

DOI: 10.4324/9781003296140

Typeset in Bembo
by Apex CoVantage, LLC

CONTENTS

ACKNOWLEDGMENTS

We are deeply grateful to the teachers, researchers, authors, reviewers, and friends who contributed to the spirit and substance of this book.

We are grateful to the following organizations for permission to reprint copyrighted work:

> The University of California Office of the President granted permission for Figure 4.1.
>
> The National Writing Project granted permission to reprint material for Figure 4.2.
>
> The National Center on Education and the Economy granted permission for Figure 4.3.
>
> Utah State University Press granted permission to reprint material for Figure 4.4.
>
> The California Writing Project granted permission to reprint material for Figures 5.1 and 5.2.

AUTHOR BIOGRAPHIES

Sandra Murphy is professor emerita at the University of California, Davis. She has published several books and chapters on the teaching and assessment of writing. She co-chaired the Steering Committee to develop the 2011 framework for the National Assessment of Educational Progress in Writing and served as a work group member to develop the Common Core State Standards for English Language Arts & Literacy in History/Social Studies, Science, and Technical Subjects.

Peggy O'Neill is professor of writing at Loyola University Maryland where she has served as the director of composition, chair of the writing department, and associate dean. She has published several books, book chapters, and journal articles on teaching and assessing writing and has served on many committees for the National Council of Teachers of English as well as other organizations. She served as co-editor for the *Journal of Writing Assessment*, 2011–2014.

LIST OF FIGURES

1

WHY DO WE NEED TO REMODEL OUR ACCOUNTABILITY AND ASSESSMENT SYSTEMS AND WHY NOW?

As any house renovator knows, home remodeling can be costly, time-consuming, and messy. Still, there is no doubt that remodeling is worth the effort. For many people, the home is the center of their personal and financial world. People choose to renovate for many reasons—to increase their comfort and enjoyment of their home, to fix safety issues, to add functional upgrades such as space, a modern kitchen, or a deck for outdoor entertaining, to make the home more efficient by adding insulation, or replacing new windows and outdated water and heating systems. Making smart decisions about upgrades can have a long-term effect on the home's worth both in terms of market value and in terms of personal safety and comfort.

In this book, we argue that we need to remodel our assessment and accountability systems—that is, evaluate them, consider alternatives, and take calculated risks in removing outdated features, fixing what's broken so it is better, more functional, and more likely to support the well-being of the educational system as a whole. While comparing house renovations to renovating educational assessment and accountability systems might seem something of a stretch, it has helped us think about ways we need to reconstruct our current systems, remaking them from the ground up, preserving their best features, and discarding those that are outdated, dysfunctional, and beyond repair. This is hard work in house renovation, and it is even harder work when dealing with complex social systems.

We focus specifically on two elements of the educational system—accountability and assessment—as they relate to writing. We argue the test-based approach to accountability undermines the teaching and learning of writing that students need in the 21st century and that current assessment procedures are out of sync with contemporary theories of writing and learning.

DOI: 10.4324/9781003296140-1

While writing assessment is only a part of the larger structure of our account-ability and educational systems, we focus on it here because writing is a funda-mental skill within the classroom that remains essential long after one's formal education comes to an end. It facilitates communication, reflection, and expres-sion, and it serves as "a gateway for success in academia, the new workplace, and the global economy, as well as for our collective success as a participatory democ-racy" (National Writing Project & Nagin, 2006, p. 2). Today writing is more important than ever before for academic success, career advancement, and civic engagement as documented in a long list of reports and studies conducted by various groups from government agencies to academic researchers. The National Commission on Writing for American Schools and Colleges (2003), for example, concluded, "Writing today is not a frill for the few, but an essential skill for the many" (n.p.). Brandt (2005) summed up the role of writing in the contemporary workplace this way:

> *Writing is at the heart of the knowledge economy.* Knowledge-intensive companies account for more than 40% of new employment growth during the past 50 years (Stewart, 1997, p. 41). Some analysts estimate that knowledge, most of it codified in writing, now composes about three fourths of the value added in the production of goods and services (Neef, 1998, p. 4), making it more valuable than land, equipment, or even money.
>
> *(p. 166, emphasis in original)*

The knowledge economy is, according to Brandt (2015), "an economy based not in the manufacturing of things but in the manufacturing of services—knowledge, ideas, information, news," and it requires effective writing skills. Brandt explains that in this type of economy, the role of writing and texts has shifted:

> texts serve as a chief means of production and a chief output of production, and writing becomes a dominant form of manufacturing. . . . As the nature of work in the United States has changed—toward making and managing information and knowledge in increasingly globalized settings—intense pressure has come to bear on the productive side of literacy, the writing side (Brandt, 2004; Drucker, 2003).
>
> *(Brandt, 2015, p. 3)*

More recent reports continue to identify soft skills—that is, those skills not considered technical or vocational, such as written communication—as desired by employers. For example, the Association of American Colleges and Universities (AACU) 2018 employment report, "Fulfilling the American Dream: Liberal Education and the Future of Work," based on a survey of hiring managers and executives, identified written communication as among the skills and knowledge areas of "greatest importance to both business executives and hiring managers when hiring" (AACU, 2018, p. 11).

This finding is consistent with the AACU 2015 employment report, which concluded that there is wide agreement among employers about the value of writing. Employers said that "[w]hen hiring recent college graduates . . . they place the greatest priority on a demonstrated proficiency in skills and knowledge that cut across majors," and written communication is one of "the most highly valued of the seventeen skills and knowledge areas tested" (AACU, 2015, p. 4). In addition,

> Underscoring the importance they place on written communication skills when hiring, four in five employers also say they would be more likely to consider an individual as a job candidate if he or she had completed multiple courses that require significant writing assignments.
>
> *(AACU, 2015, p. 7)*

Similarly, according to a survey conducted by the National Association of Colleges and Employers (2017), 95.9% of employers rated communication, both oral and written, as essential for college graduates to be career ready. The report also indicated that only 41.6% of recent graduates demonstrated proficiency in the necessary communication skills (2017).

Recognizing the need for more attention to writing in the curriculum, the National Commission on Writing (2003) called for a "writing revolution." Arguing that writing is "the neglected 'R'" in education, the Commission identified a need for, among other things, a K–college writing agenda for the nation. This agenda included making writing a priority in all aspects of education including curriculum, policy, and funding. For example, the group specified (1) more time on writing in all classrooms; (2) writing across the curriculum programs; (3) better preparation for all faculty members in writing pedagogy; (4) writing assessment that is fair and authentic and aligns with best practices; and (5) support for technology for both teachers and students. The Commission published its first report in 2003, with a series of other reports appearing in the following years, including *Writing: A Ticket to Work . . . Or a Ticket Out* (2004); *Writing: A Powerful Message From State Government* (2005); and *Writing and School Reform* (2006). Given the continued, and as Brandt (2015) argues, the increasing demand for effective writing abilities in contemporary society, it is clear that the "writing revolution" has not occurred.

Why hasn't the revolution happened if we know that effective written communication—broadly defined—is needed now more than ever? What impact have educational assessment practices and accountability policies had on writing instruction in K–college? What can we do to improve writing assessment and, in turn, enhance writing instruction?

This text is our attempt to address those questions. Our particular focus here is on writing assessment, K–college, and the impact it can have on teaching and learning. Creating writing assessments that support learning (assessments that are fair, authentic, and aligned with best practices) is only one of the challenges facing the writing revolution, but it is certainly a good place to start.

We shape our discussion around several interrelated claims:

- That standardized exams in combination with high-stakes accountability policies have negatively impacted education generally, and have distorted writing curriculum and instruction in particular;
- That assessment practices should be aligned with current understandings of the nature of writing as a complex cognitive and socially situated meaning-making activity that varies in significant ways across contexts and purposes for writing;
- That assessment practices should support learning and be aligned with current cognitive and social understandings of the nature of learning;
- That teachers and students should be at the center of our efforts to reshape the assessment system.

Before delving into these topics in more detail in this and subsequent chapters, we begin by acknowledging our limitations and clarifying terms.

Our goal in this text is to take an expansive view of writing assessment research—from elementary through college classrooms and beyond—to consider how we can improve student writing by turning accountability assessment inside out. Because of that scope, we have had to set some other boundaries. We focus primarily on the United States, in part because education and writing are situated activities and cultural differences make a difference in teaching, learning, and educational policy. However, we do include some research from the United Kingdom and other primarily English–speaking countries that seemed to fit our context. We do not include much on the research specific to English Language Learners and other forms of linguistic diversity. While we realize these are important issues for both teaching and assessing writing, it would require another text to do these topics justice given the wealth of research specific to teaching and assessing students who are ELL.

The following brief primer on basic assessment terminology will no doubt be a review for many readers, but we want to support a shared understanding of categories and terminologies associated with assessment.

What do we mean by assessment?

While definitions of assessment may not seem important, they are. Because assessment has been coopted by the accountability agenda, we need to reconsider all that is included in the concept if we are going to recapture the potential for it to improve teaching and learning. In general, to assess means to evaluate, to judge, or to estimate the amount, quality, or value of something or someone. In education, assessment is also used to refer to *the instrument* we use for evaluation, such as a survey, test, or an examination, as well as to *the process* of evaluating the learner, teacher, school, or program. The process of writing assessment has included a wide range of formal and informal methods, such as multiple-choice questions, brief constructed responses, observations, running records, essay exams, and collections of work (such as portfolios). Assessment results can be expressed in qualitative and/or quantitative ways. In general, however, assessment is a sampling used to make inferences about students' competencies.

Although the issue has been hotly debated, it is fair to say that the preferred method among writing assessment scholars is some form of direct (performance) assessment, that is, a sampling that actually requires students to write. The sampling could be at the classroom level, where a teacher assigns a diagnostic essay as a means of determining students' current writing competency as she plans the year's activities. Or, it might involve a standardized essay prompt that all incoming first-year college students complete for a placement test to determine which course they will enter. In both examples, performance on the writing task doesn't represent the students' writing abilities in response to every possible purpose, audience, or genre. The evaluators make inferences, to some extent, about a student's potential performance in other situations from the sample. But even if multiple writing samples are solicited, they cannot represent every writing situation. Madaus (1994) explains assessment this way:

> But strip away the linguistic veneer and, regardless of what noun we choose—assessment, exhibitions, examinations, portfolios, or just plain test—all types of evaluation rest on the same basic technology. That is we elicit a small sample of behavior from a larger domain of interest . . . to make inferences about a person's probable performance relative to the domain. Then, on these inferences, we classify, describe, or make decisions about individuals or institutions.
>
> *(p. 77)*

The *Standards for Educational and Psychological Testing* (AERA et al., 2014), published by the professional organizations that represent a wide variety of assessment professionals, acknowledges that "assessment" and "test" are often used synonymously (p. 216). Assessment, as Madaus (1994) explains, serves to evaluate, measure, and document student learning, growth, skills, needs, and/ or achievement. Sometimes, the purpose of an assessment may be less formalized, such as when a teacher evaluates students' progress as part of the regular classroom activity to determine if they understand a particular concept before moving on to the next activity; sometimes the purpose is more formalized, such as when a district requires a final exam to determine if a student is prepared for the next level of education or a college uses a test score to place students into the curriculum.

Because assessment can encompass so much, we usually refer to different types. Assessment *for* learning is described as *formative*; assessment *of* learning as *summative*. While this distinction is not always so clear-cut in practice, it is useful in considering different theories and methods, especially as related to writing development. For example, formative assessment occurs when a teacher comments on a draft in progress and aims to help the writer revise and develop the ability to critique her own writing. Or, as in the earlier example, it occurs when a teacher assigns a diagnostic task to get a sense of where students are to plan future learning opportunities. Summative assessment may occur when the teacher grades the student text after the student has revised and edited earlier drafts. However, when a teacher comments on a graded text, she could, in some ways, be doing both: the summative act is the grade, while the comments serve a formative function if they aim to help the writer with future writing tasks. The teacher may also adapt future teaching or assignments based on students' performance on the writing task.

Another way of thinking about assessment is *classroom-based* versus *large-scale*. Both of these kinds of assessment can be summative or formative, formal or informal, and standardized or teacher designed. They can be embedded in the curriculum or done outside of it. Classroom-based assessments, whether formative or summative, are often designed by the teacher, but not always. For example, a teacher may use (or be required to use) a final exam not designed by her but by a testing or textbook company. This exam may function as part of the course grade but also can be linked to an accountability system, and it may carry another stake, such as determining whether the student can progress to the next level. Other teachers may design their own end-of-course exam or may work with colleagues to design a common final exam or assessment. Likewise, formative assessments might be teacher-designed or standardized. A teacher may collect a quickwrite at the end of a class to get a sense of students' understanding of the concepts covered in a class discussion or give a quiz to see if students understand the main points of a reading assignment. Both of these kinds of activities tend to be teacher designed, although they may be standardized through curricular materials provided to the teacher. Other formative assessments are more clearly standardized, for example, practice tests that are provided by a testing company or the district to determine if students need additional support before the formal assessment. Whether teacher-designed or standardized, classroom-based assessments are integrated into the regular class activities, typically administered and evaluated as part of those activities.

In contrast to classroom-based assessments are those labeled large-scale. These assessments extend beyond the single classroom with results reported to governing bodies and are typically mandated by a program, institution, district, or state. They are not usually part of the routine classroom activity. While not always the case, these assessments are typically standardized tests, performances, or activities.

Sometimes, classroom-based and large-scale assessments can overlap. For example, an essay assignment can be part of the classroom-based assessment of a student, but it can move beyond the classroom to become part of a large-scale program or school assessment. In this case, the large-scale use may not have a direct impact on the individual student but be considered an indicator for the program's effectiveness.

Other ways of thinking about assessments are based on their consequences. Most often, we use *high stakes* and *low stakes* to describe this aspect of assessment. High stakes, as the term implies, means that the results are used to make important decisions about test-takers that have significant consequences. For example, graduation exams are considered high stakes because a student cannot graduate without passing the exams. These exams are considered summative, although they may serve a secondary, formative purpose, for example, if a student fails and information is shared about the student's performance so teachers can provide remediation or support. Placement exams may be considered high stakes if the results channel students into non-credit courses, but low stakes if all of the placement options earn credit toward graduation and fulfill the writing requirement. The results of the exams, whether framed as high or low stakes, also may inform instruction for future students or influence professional development for teachers.

Low-stakes assessments are the opposite of high stakes: there is little serious consequence based on the results. For example, a teacher may use a practice test in class to help students get a better sense of the expectations on the test that will "count." In large-scale assessment, the assessment results might not have any real consequence for the student, but the school or district could use the aggregated results to get a sense of the performance of the students as a group. This is how the National Assessment of Educational Progress (NAEP) is framed: the results don't have a direct consequence to the students, schools, or districts, but they provide information about educational progress across the country that may influence educational policies when considered with other data. In colleges and universities, exams such as the College Learning Assessment, a standardized, performance-based exam of critical thinking developed by the Council for Aid to Education, may be given to a sample of graduating students as part of an institution's accreditation assessment program with no consequences to the particular students taking the exam. The institution might use the results as evidence of learning or in revising the curriculum in conjunction with other information, but the test results alone don't lead to an important consequence.

The distinctions between high- and low-stakes assessments, however, are often not so clear-cut. For example, the consequences of an assessment may vary across the stakeholders. A student may not have a high-stake consequence riding on the results of the assessment, but the teachers in that student's school may if the district uses the aggregated results to make decisions about teachers' performance or staffing at the school. Perception of the consequences also complicates discussions of high- and low-stakes assessments. If stakeholders—or at least some of them—perceive the assessment to be high stakes, then it will be approached this way and can result in the negative consequences associated with high-stakes testing. Teachers, for instance, who believe that the results of a mandated assessment will impact their teaching assignments may feel the pressure associated with high-stakes assessment even if the test is low stakes for the test takers. Likewise, students may consider the consequences significant even if policymakers or teachers don't. Schools may require the administration of practice tests modeled on the required mandated test, and based on the results, students may be designated for remediation or have classes such as art or music replaced by those geared specifically to the test. This might be considered low stakes by personnel at the district level but high stakes to many of the other stakeholders who experience the consequences directly. An urban elementary teacher provided an example in a recent survey conducted by the National Council of Teachers of English (NCTE):

> My district often uses mock tests that are supposed to imitate the state exam. These tests are slapped together by the district office and are not checked for reliability or validity. However, these exams are used to place students in mandatory tutoring. (Even though subjects tested were not necessarily covered in class yet.) Admin relied more on these test scores than teacher observation and assessments. Thus placing many students in tutoring who didn't need to be there.
>
> *(2016, p. 10)*

This teacher did not seem to think the stakes were low. Instead, she explained that the mock test undermined teachers' judgement and led to unnecessary tutoring, which required taking time away from other activities for the student.

This brief review of basic concepts illustrates the role of context in understanding definitions of familiar assessment terms, such as high-stakes, low-stakes, classroom-based, and large-scale, and the ways these definitions can shift depending on particular situations and uses. In the section that follows, we consider the impact of high-stakes assessment policies on teaching and learning. High-stakes policies have consequences for schools, students, and teachers, including at the state level: "public reporting of test results, prevention of grade-to-grade promotion and high school graduation, and possible takeover of schools that continue to demonstrate low levels of student performance" (Vogler, 2002, p. 39).

How have high-stakes accountability policies impacted writing curriculum?

Scholars who investigate the impact of testing on teaching and learning look at the effects on teachers and students, in classrooms, schools, and districts, and speak to the health of the general ecology of education in our society. In the field of language testing and the educational measurement literature generally, the impact of testing is associated with the terms "consequential validity" (Messick, 1989, 1996), "measurement-driven instruction" (Popham, 1987), "curricular alignment" (Madaus, 1988b; Smith, 1991a), "washback" (Alderson & Wall, 1993; Hamp-Lyons, 2000), "backwash" (Hughes, 1989), and "impact" (Wall, 1997). According to Wall (1997), "washback" is "frequently used to refer to the effects of tests on teaching and learning," while "impact" refers to "any of the effects that tests may have on individuals, policies or practices, within the classroom, the school, the educational system, or society as a whole" (p. 291). Our particular focus here is on the impact of tests on teaching and learning and, in particular, the teaching and learning of writing, although we address as well the broader impact of top-down accountability systems on individuals and the educational system.

In the last 30 years or so, our assessment system has been coopted by the accountability agenda. Accountability dominates educational policy in many ways, and its consequences are felt by students and teachers. Whenever we offer writing assessment workshops or conference sessions, the discussions among teacher participants, K–college, quickly turn to formalized, mandated, standardized assessments—whether those tests are related to the Common Core, state mandates, composition placement, graduation exams, or district requirements. Educators, students, and the public have come to equate assessment with top-down, standardized accountability systems linked to federal, state, district, or institutional requirements. Other kinds of more "voluntary" tests, such as the SAT and ACT for college admissions, Advanced Placement, or International Baccalaureate exams for college credit, and MCAT, LSAT, or GRE tests for graduate education, also garner attention and influence what and how students learn. While these tests are not focused exclusively on writing assessment, they no doubt impact the teaching and learning of student writing from K–college, and high-stakes policies add fuel to the fire.

As early as 1985 Madaus observed that although state-level policymakers had initially turned to test results for information about at-risk students, they soon realized that test results could also be used to drive or implement policy. Warning about the potentially negative impact of using tests in this way, Madaus reasoned such high-stakes tests would influence "how teachers teach and students learn" (1988a, p. 30). Describing what he called an "inherent weakness in measurement driven instruction," he explained how tests can narrow the curriculum to the detriment of other skills not on the tests. He traced the increase of high-stakes, state-mandated testing programs (at the time from one in 1960 to 34 by 1985) and argued that using high-stakes tests for accountability purposes "corrupts the test's ability to serve as a valid indicator of the knowledge or skill it was originally intended to measure" 1988a, p. 30). His warnings appear to have largely been ignored by policy makers in subsequent years. For example, Stecher and Barron (1999) report that during the '80s and early '90s, there was a "dramatic increase in state's use of tests as educational policy tools" (p. 1). By 1992, "40 states used test scores for accountability purposes" (p. 2). Au and Gourd (2013) report, "by 2000 every US state but Iowa had administered a state-mandated test" (p. 14).

Early concerns about the negative washback of high-stakes standardized tests on writing centered on multiple-choice tests. For example, in an extensive qualitative study of the impact of testing in Arizona, Smith (1991b) observed that when the date of the district's multiple-choice test neared, teachers shifted from teaching the writing process to "worksheets covering grammar, capitalization, punctuation and usage" (p. 10). Smith explains that data from interviews revealed that "teachers believe that scores are used against them," and they "determine to do what is necessary to avoid low scores" (p. 8). A key finding in a study conducted by Smith et al. (1990) was that schools neglect material that external tests do not include in high-stakes environments. According to Shepard and Dougherty (1991), such schools neglect writing, "concentrating instead on . . . recognition of errors in spelling, usage, punctuation" (p. 3). Similarly, analyses of surveys distributed to teachers in California revealed that when California switched from an exam that assessed multiple genres of writing to a strictly multiple-choice exam, teachers "spent less time teaching actual writing and more time teaching grammar and usage" (Murphy, 2003). Studies of the impact of high-stakes, multiple-choice "writing" tests suggest that when such tests are employed, "actual writing begins to disappear from the curriculum," and "the curriculum begins to take the form of the test" (Murphy, 2008, p. 36).

While early concerns about unintended consequences focused on multiple-choice tests, several studies have investigated the impact of high-stakes, single-sample direct assessments of writing. Several report distortions of teaching and the curriculum. For example, Madaus (1988a) describes the impact of a compulsory examination called the Irish Primary Certificate that was a requirement for graduation and used for competency testing in Ireland from 1943 to 1967. One part of the exam required students to write an essay on a topic that changed from year to year: "A bicycle ride, 1946; A day in the bog, 1947; A bus tour, 1948" (p. 37). Because teachers felt the pressure of the stakes, their teaching of writing was "inordinately skewed toward test preparation" (p. 36). They "taught generations of Irish children to memorize a series of stock sentences that could be used with any prompt (e.g., "I awakened early, jumped out of bed and had a quick breakfast. My friend was coming to our house at nine o'clock as we were going for a—*fill in the prompt*—"). Madaus explains the implications:

> As a result of this type of test preparation, a high score on the writing exam was no longer a valid indicator of well-developed writing skills, but only of the student's ability to memorize, recall, and use the stock responses with that year's prompt. The IPC changed teaching, and the ensuing test taking strategies drilled into students vitiated the validity of inferences made from the exam about students' ability to write.
>
> *(1988a, p. 37)*

In a more recent study, Hillocks (2002, 2003) investigated five state writing assessments and their impact on the teaching of writing. In two of the states that assessed persuasive writing, he found that students were asked to write about "an issue about which they may or may not be informed" and that prompts provided "no information about the issues, no data, and no other help"(2003, p. 11). He also found that many teachers relied on formulaic writing:

> [W[hen teachers are under pressure to raise school scores . . . teachers prepare their students to pass the tests. They can see that no real thinking is required by examining the scoring guides. They also see that it must be organized. Our interviews with teachers and administrators in Texas and Illinois revealed that very high percentages concentrated on formulaic writing, primarily the five-paragraph theme (nearly 55% in Texas and 72% in Illinois). Furthermore, interviews with administrators indicate that such formulaic writing has become district-wide policy. One elementary school principal spoke of the faculty's consideration of bringing the rudiments of the five paragraph theme into the kindergarten curriculum by teaching youngsters to say they have three reasons for so and so. A third-grade teacher in the same district told me that, for her class, the formula involves the use of *first, next, last* as a way of ensuring three-body paragraphs, and she said, "we pound it, pound it, pound it!" And no teachers interviewed in this district talked about teaching students how to develop the substance of an argument.
>
> *(2003, p. 17)*

Hillocks (2003) was particularly critical of the tests that relied on impromptu persuasive tasks because they "actively work against" the kind of "critical thinking involved in real persuasive writing" (p. 20). He concluded that these types of tests are "encouraging teachers and students to believe that critical thinking and argument involve no more than asserting unsupported opinions, to believe that they have made a case when they have only blethered" (Hillocks, 2003, p. 20). In other words, the very concept of argumentative writing—the construct of the writing that the test purported to assess—was compromised based on the decisions the teachers, schools, and districts made in response to the assessment system.

The studies conducted by Madaus (1988b), Madaus and Greaney (1985), and Hillocks (2002, 2003) suggest that when a single kind of writing is assessed in a large-scale assessment with high stakes attached, whether it is a particular genre or a five-paragraph theme, teachers may resort to a formula for writing. These findings give cause for concern because recent analyses of how writing has been assessed in the states have indicated that most direct assessments (assessments that require actual writing) hold students accountable for only one writing type (Beck & Jeffery, 2007; Jeffery, 2009). The problem with a single sample assessment is that the assessment provides no information about how a student might perform given other genres. And if teachers narrow their curriculum to focus on a single genre because it's on the test, student writers will have few opportunities to learn how writing varies across genres, purposes, situations, and discourse communities. Similarly, Mislevy (2013) points out that when we standardize the time for writing (as is routinely done in large-scale writing tests), "we forgo the opportunity to obtain evidence about students' capabilities to write at different lengths and their capacities to write and revise over time" (Mislevy, 2013, p. 52). Research comparing the effects of testing across states indicates that the formats of writing assessments influence both what teachers teach and how they teach it. For instance, O'Neill et al. (2005) found that teachers in Kentucky, where a portfolio assessment program was in place, were more likely to allow several days for writing and to require more drafts. In contrast, teachers at the time in Georgia, where a single sample was assessed and 90 minutes were allowed for writing, were more likely to assign single-draft short pieces of writing and to require that the writing be turned in on the same day. In sum, when the assessment is narrowed to a single sample of writing written under a standardized (and usually abbreviated) time frame, student writers are denied opportunities to show what they can do with other genres or within other time frames.

It's not unreasonable to suggest that teachers feel pressure to teach to the test, especially if high stakes are attached. And in fact, over many years, studies have provided evidence that teachers do shift their instruction to emphasize what's on the test (e.g., Au, 2007; Corbett & Wilson, 1991; Firestone & Mayrowetz, 2000; Firestone et al., 2000; Jones et al., 1999; Jones & Johnston, 2002; McNeil, 2000; Scherff & Piazza, 2005; Stecher & Barron, 1999; Stetcher et al., 1998; Stetcher et al., 2000). Some researchers see a directly proportional relationship between the stakes of a test and the strength of washback—the higher the stakes, the more forceful the impact (e.g., Alderson & Wall, 1993; Alderson & Hamp-Lyons, 1996; Shohamy et al., 1996). In a meta-analysis of 49 studies about the impact of high-stakes testing, Au (2007) found that high-stakes testing effects not only what is taught but how it is taught. He explained that most of the tests he investigated

> have the predominant effect of narrowing curricular content to those subjects included in the tests, resulting in the increased fragmentation of knowledge forms into bits and pieces learned for the sake of the tests themselves and compelling teachers to use more lecture-based teacher-centered pedagogies.
>
> *(p. 264)*

In "a significant minority of cases," however, some types of high-stakes tests "led to curricular content expansion, the integration of knowledge, and more student-centered cooperative pedagogies" (p. 258). Au observed that "the nature of high-stakes-test-induced curricular control is highly dependent on the structures of the tests themselves" (p. 258). Au concluded, "Combined, these findings indicate that high-stakes testing exerts significant amounts of control over the content, knowledge forms, and pedagogies at the classroom level" (p. 264).

Research on high-stakes writing assessments clearly shows that such tests do influence instruction (e.g., Dappen et al., 2008; Escamilla et al., 2003; Hillocks, 2002; Luce-Kapler & Klinger, 2005; Messenheimer & Packwood, 2002; Vogler, 2002). When actual writing is included in the test, some effects of the assessments appear to be positive. For example, studies have shown that teachers are likely to *increase* the time spent on writing in the curriculum when actual writing is required (e.g., Almasi et al., 1995; Koretz et al., 1996; Koretz & Hamilton, 2003; Murphy, 2003; Stetcher et al., 1998; Vogler, 2002). For example, in his study of the Massachusetts Comprehensive Assessment system, Vogler found that teachers were "making changes in their instructional practices," with "notable increases in . . . use of rubrics or scoring guides, [and] writing assignments" (p. 1). Vogler also notes, "Teachers . . . decreased the use of multiple-choice and true-false questions, textbook-based assignments, and lecturing" (p. 1). In sum, if little actual writing is already included in the curriculum, the assessment can influence teachers to include more writing. In contrast, when the so-called writing tests are of the high-stakes, multiple-choice variety, studies show that teachers spend more time on basic skills, vocabulary lists, and the like (Shepard & Dougherty, 1991) and less time on actual writing (Murphy, 2003; Smith, 1991b). The common thread through all of this research is that districts, schools and teachers are influenced by high-stakes tests. While effects can sometimes be positive, for writing, the big problem is that effects can be negative, even when actual writing samples are collected, if the tests promote formulas for writing such as the five-paragraph theme, as Hillocks' (2002) study of the Texas and Illinois writing assessments revealed. Like Hillocks, Jones (2007) reports that Florida's 45-minute writing assessment led teachers to emphasize formulaic writing, in this case what they called the "3-point-five essay," an essay in which students make three points in five paragraphs (p. 71). Readers will no doubt recognize the familiar outline of the five-paragraph theme. When teachers emphasize a single formula of this kind for writing, students miss opportunities to develop rhetorical knowledge, that is, understanding the varying demands of context across a range of texts and writing situations, including various purposes and audiences for writing.

Koretz (2017) provides an example of a somewhat different, but similarly disturbing unintended consequence of high-stakes testing. He argues that the Kentucky Instructional Results Information System (KIRIS) was a "particularly influential program" and yet had deleterious effects for overall education because the rewards and sanctions were focused on sorting students into "large bins" with the mandate to get all students into the proficient bin (pp. 26–27). As a result, educators focused on moving students into the proficient category, but neglected them when they arrived at or exceeded this marker, giving little attention to the complex reasons why students might not make it to the proficient category. Like several of the other assessment scholars cited previously, Koretz

(2017) acknowledges some of the positive effects of high-stakes accountability systems like KIRIS—such as reporting scores for subpopulations and mandating that school systems offer rigorous curricula to all students—and he acknowledges the good intentions of many who supported these test-based accountability approaches to education reform. Yet, in his view as an assessment expert for more than 30 years, the negative impacts of the test-based accountability approach to reform far outweigh the benefits. Koretz concludes that the continued reliance on test-based accountability flies in the face of what prominent measurement researchers and scholars have been telling us for decades (Koretz, 2017).

Koretz cites an important early developer of standardized tests, Lindquist, who in 1951 issued the warning against using test scores by themselves to evaluate students and teachers (p. 39). Linquist said:

> The widespread and continued use of a test will, in itself, tend to reduce the correlation between the test series and the criterion series [the later behavior outside the testing situation, that is our real concern] for the population involved. Because of the nature and potency of the rewards and penalties associated in actual practice with high and low achievement test scores of students, the behavior measured by a widely used test tends in itself to become the real objective of instruction, to the neglect of the different behavior with which the ultimate objective is concerned.
>
> *(as cited in Koretz, 2017, p. 39)*

In spite of the early warnings of assessment scholars such as Lindquist (1951), Madaus (1988a), and Corbett and Wilson (1991)—and the empirical evidence that supports them—test-based accountability not only became more pervasive, it reached a whole new level when it moved into federal policy through No Child Left Behind in 2002. This federal law required states to test all students in certain grade levels and subjects (reading and math) in order to demonstrate annual yearly progress. According to Koretz (2017), high-stakes accountability systems were the beginning of the "era of pay-and-punish" approach to education with states meting out "concrete sanctions and rewards, including money, for test scores" (p. 26).

Test-based accountability relies on a few basic assumptions, as Koretz (2017) explained, and as Hillocks (2002) noted specifically in reference to writing. One assumption is that test scores are valid indicators of student learning. In this thinking, improvements in test scores mean that students have improved. A second assumption is that the harder the test, the more the students will be learning. Another is that teaching to the test is a good thing (assuming, of course, that the tests are good tests). And the overall rationale behind the test-based approach to reform is the assumption student achievement will improve when teachers, schools, and districts are held accountable for student achievement, particularly in terms of improvement on the tests. These assumptions, however, have been challenged by educational scholars.

Educators and advocates such as Graves (2002), Kohn (2000), Ohanian (1999), and organizations such as Fair Test: The National Center for Fair and Open Testing and Rethinking Schools have long argued against the use of standardized tests to make high-stakes decisions. Even before the implementation of NCLB, Hillocks put the issue this way:

> At the center of the K-12 testing fury is the myth that testing alone is able to raise standards and the rates of learning. Certainly, testing assures that what is tested is taught, but tests cannot assure that things can be taught well.
>
> *(2002, p. 204)*

In the test-based accountability context, assessment is intended to promote change and improvements in educational systems. But as the research reviewed earlier indicates, there is growing evidence that the use of high-stakes assessment for accountability has not delivered on its promises. Test-based reform and high-stakes assessments with rewards and punishments do not improve teaching and learning (Koretz, 2017; Nichols & Berliner, 2007; Ravitch, 2010, 2012). Instead, evidence shows that using high-stakes testing not only narrows the curriculum, but also it encourages cheating and stimulates excessive test prep. These and other forms of collateral damage overwhelm any positive effects that may be associated with the accountability movement and threaten the construct validity of the test results (Berliner, 2011).

Research also shows how the negative consequences of testing can be exacerbated for minority students. In relationship to diversity and equity, Garcia and Pearson (1994) discuss the ways testing has been used to promote or maintain racism through the development of assessments as well as their use: "In general, educational assessment has not been friendly to students from diverse cultural, linguistic, and economic backgrounds. The documentation on this point is clear for formal tests" (p. 377). Schmidt and Camara (2004) report the existence of "persistent score differences among racial groups" for a variety of standardized tests (p. 189). Across standardized admission tests, the "largest gaps" appear "between white and African-American test takers, followed by Hispanic test takers" (p. 192). Several scholars (e.g., White & Thomas, 1981; Ball, 1997, 1999; Agnew & McLaughlin, 1999, 2001; Kelly-Riley, 2011; Poe et al., 2014; Gere et al., 2021) have explored the link between writing assessments and students from underrepresented groups. For example, Gere et al. (2021) challenge "standard language ideologies" found in "many of the policies and publications that guide writing instruction and assessment" (p. 386) and call upon the field to "revise aspects of assessment that contribute to unjust outcomes for students" (p. 386). They focus in particular on "assessing writing in terms of a privileged dialect" and conclude, "Through writing assessment, linguistic prejudices played a structural role in reinforcing social prejudices" (p. 388).

Many students and teachers recognize the limitations and negative impact of standardized tests that have high stakes attached.

What students say about standardized tests

- I know a lot of people that don't test well, so that's not the best way to show people you understand . . . (as cited in Northwest Evaluation Association, 2014, p. 17)
- These tests are an enormous waste of 17 hours of my time. The only thing accomplished by these tests will be the standardization and institutionalization of what we focus on in school. By forcing the schools to conform to the arbitrary standards set by the test, the creativity and innovation of what and how we learn will be eliminated in the pursuit of high test scores. I am glad I will be out of high school by the time MCAS counts toward graduation, because I will hopefully be able to avoid the sterilization it will force upon my school and others like it. (as cited in Nichols & Berliner, 2007, p. 55)
- As I learned of my results, they didn't surprise me. I aced everything overall in the English department. After all the practicing and studying who wouldn't. TAAS is just a big hype that teachers in high school teach. The test doesn't really prepare me for college like I thought it would. (as cited in Blalock & Haswell, 2003, n.p.)
- Overall I feel this wasn't a good educational experience for me at all. As for another comment I feel the TAAS test is kind of worthless because there is no way that test prepares you for college. This test has no relation to the future. I think the students in high school need to be better prepared for the shock they will face their freshman year in college. (as cited in Blalock & Haswell, 2003, n.p.)
- Every year after that it was the same thing, teachers would get sample writing prompts and make us practice every day. I never really saw the point in TAAS testing. It was like every year day in day out all we would do was prepare for what was going to be on the TAAS test. To me that does not seem very beneficial considering that the TAAS is not very practical and most of the stuff on it we do not use in day to day living. (as cited in Blalock & Haswell, 2003, n.p.)
- Since [state accountability] tests do not impact us at all, it seems silly that it takes so much of our time. (as cited in Northwest Evaluation Association, 2014, p. 13)
- No one learns from state tests. It's testing what you know. You're not learning anything from it. (as cited in Northwest Evaluation Association, 2014, p. 13)
- It [Georgia high school graduation test in writing] really isn't judging them on their writing ability it judges them on their test taking ability test. (as cited in O'Neill, 2001)

What teachers say about the impact of standardized tests

- We are losing 3 days of instructional time. Students are very stressed. (as cited in O'Neill et al., 2005, p. 98)
- Oh yes, it's caused panic. Soon we'll be teaching directly to the test I'm afraid. The ESL [English as a second language] students I teach sit for 2-hour periods and stare at their papers: a form of child abuse. (as cited in O'Neill et al., 2005, p. 98)
- The [XXX] Reading Assessment has pigeonholed many of my students as struggling readers, when they are not. Years of stress over this exam causes them to believe that they cannot read and snowballs into general academic failure. Approximately 10% of my level 1 and 2 readers are actually reading below grade level. (as cited in NCTE, 2016, p. 10)
- I feel depressed every time test scores come out. (as cited in Filkins, 2015)
- The EOC test for my at-risk sophomores is just one more nail in the coffin. They already hate school; why not add failure to the list? (as cited in Filkins, 2015)
- Each year when our school's results are released, I see the disappointment in the eyes of my administrators and colleagues. They wonder why our scores aren't higher and what we are doing . . . or aren't doing . . . in the English department to get those scores where they need to be. (as cited in Filkins, 2015)
- We only teach to the test even at second grade, and have stopped teaching science and social studies. We don't have assemblies, take few field trips, or have musical productions at grade levels. We even hesitate to ever show a video. Our second graders have no recess except for 20 minutes at lunch. (as cited in Nichols & Berliner, 2007, p. 138)
- The overemphasis on testing has led many teachers to eliminate projects and activities that provide students with an opportunity to be creative and imaginative, and scripted curriculum has become the norm in many classrooms. There is nothing creative or imaginative about filling in a bubble sheet for a multiple-choice test. Students are so tired of prepping for and taking standardized tests that some have protested by dressing up like zombies to protest—and thousands of families are opting their children out of taking high-stakes exams. (as cited in Strauss, 2014)
- Our school raised its APO by 14 points last year. Focus has been on maintaining this mundane surge of our students' ability to work with the letters A–E. Instead of promoting higher learning, critical thinking, and preparation for the real world, students are focused to be good test-takers. (as cited in O'Neill et al., 2005, p. 98)
- The data that we get back from the standardized tests is NOT useful because of the curve, cut scores, etc. Those calculations take away from the ability of a teacher/parent to help a child improve. (as cited in NCTE, 2016, p. 7)

Like Ravitch (2012), Koretz (2017), and others, policymakers are beginning to re-think the role of standardized assessment in education reform and accountability. The latest version of the Elementary and Secondary Education Act, Every Student Succeeds Act (ESSA), gives more decision-making authority to the states. The US Department of Education explains that

> ESSA . . . maintains the requirement that states administer to all students annual statewide assessments in reading/language arts and mathematics in grades 3–8 and once in high school, as well as assessments once in each grade span in science for all students and annual English language proficiency assessments in grades K–12 for all English learners. The law also includes important protections to ensure that all students are tested, offered appropriate accommodations when needed, and held to the same high standards.
>
> *(2017, para 6)*

However, ESSA also provides several "new flexibilities to help states develop innovative approaches to assessments and reduce unnecessary testing" (U.S. Department of Education, 2017, para 6). So, states have some flexibility in testing designs and requirements, and there is some evidence that the era of dependence on high-stakes testing may be waning. A report by the National Center for Fair and Open Testing (Fair Test), updated in May 2019, indicates that "the number of states requiring high school graduation exams in language arts has declined rapidly over the past few years" (para. 1). At the time the report was updated, "Only eleven states [had] graduation tests in place for the high school class of 2020, down from a high of 27 that had or planned such tests" (para. 1). According to another report from Fair Test, states have opportunities under the Innovative Assessment pilot program to "develop assessment systems that minimize standardized testing" and "enhance classroom-based, teacher-controlled, student-focused assessing" (National Center for Fair and Open Testing, 2016, para 1).

> In recent years school accountability appears to be somewhat less dependent on standardized tests, but they still play a significant role. Klein et al. (2017) report that the vast majority of states—more than 40—chose to stick with some kind of school ratings system that gives an overall grade to schools, such as "A" or "F," or to award schools a certain number of stars or points as a measure of quality.
>
> *(para 7)*

They also say that "ESSA also requires states to look beyond test scores in calculating those school ratings and consider some other factor that gets at school quality or student success" (para 8). Another bright spot is the increased use of student growth as an indicator in state accountability systems, instead of focusing only on proficiency. Edgerton (2019) points out that focusing on proficiency alone, as was the case during NCLB, "obscures the improvement that occurs below that level" (para 4).

Teacher accountability has also seen substantial changes as a result of ESSA. Writing for ASCD, Fennell (2016) reported that interventions "hung over schools like a guillotine if they didn't meet AYP" (the Adequate Yearly Progress requirement) during the NCLB years (p. 63). According to Close et al. (2019, September 23) under NCLB and Race to the Top:

> many states required that teachers be evaluated according to their students' test scores, often using value-added models (VAMs) which compared the growth of students' test scores with those of demographically similar students in other classrooms. If students' test scores did not show improvement over time, their teachers' professional files could be permanently flagged or they could often be denied merit pay, tenure, or continuing teacher contracts.
>
> *(p. 22)*

One fatal flaw of the NCLB policy, as Koretz (2017) explained, was that states and districts had access to appropriate tests for some of the teachers but not others, for example, teachers of students in untested grades or subjects. In some cases states or districts used the scores of teachers who had scores from appropriate tests to "evaluate" other teachers. Under ESSA, states regained "control over their teacher evaluation systems" (Close et al., 2019, p. 23). Data suggest that many states have backed off from high-stakes consequences based on students' scores. In 2019, Close et al. (2019) reported that 15 of 51 (29%) of the states "indicated they still encouraged the use of VAMs," but 23 of 51 (45%) indicated they no longer did (p. 23). Ten states encouraged "more local control," deferring to districts "to make their own teacher evaluation system and policy decisions" (p. 23). Other states endorsed using VAMs, "but only for informational and formative purposes" (Close et al., 2019, p. 24).

In this current climate, there seems some hope that we can make real changes that will improve our assessment and accountability systems. (Perhaps the recent impact of the pandemic will also prompt rethinking how we use testing, but it is unclear at this point what long-term impact the pandemic will have.) It will take time and be difficult. As educators, we all need to be ready to push policymakers to think about what really matters and how we can design assessments that encourage best practices and support learning. As writing and literacy teachers, we need to support policies that will help us move beyond the formulaic writing encouraged by standardized tests and help students become flexible, rhetorically sophisticated writers. If students are going to be ready for what comes next—college or career—they need experiences that help them learn how to analyze and adapt their writing to various audiences, purposes, and contexts. What they don't need is an over emphasis on a single formula for writing.

In the next chapter, we argue that any debates about assessment and pedagogy need to be grounded in established theory about assessment in general and writing assessment more specifically. We focus on three theoretical concepts that have become central to all assessment: consequential validity, with its implications for assessment design and validity arguments; construct validity, the degree to which an assessment addresses the theoretical domain to which it is related; and generalizability, the dependability of generalizations made from a person's observed score on a test (Shavelson et al., 1989). In Chapter 3 we describe how the constructs of writing and learning have evolved over time under the influence of sociocultural theory. We argue that writing is now viewed as a complex, socially situated activity, and that theories of learning have moved generally from a cognitive focus on the individual toward learning as a social and participatory process. We discuss, in Chapter 4, recommendations for redesigning and using assessments in ways that are aligned with contemporary views of the nature of writing and learning. We focus in particular on formative assessment practices and teaching strategies that engage students in self-assessment of their work. In Chapter 5 we discuss ways to build a writing assessment system that puts students and learning, and teachers and teaching, at the center of the educational system. In Chapter 6 we draw on the concept of ecosystems to argue that we need to take the interconnectedness of educational systems into account as we design assessments. Drawing on the concepts of ecology and ecological validity, we argue that we need to pay more attention to the impact of assessment policies in our K–16 systems and to the skills and understandings students will need to be successful writers for school, college, career, and civic engagement.

References

Agnew, E., & McLaughlin, M. (1999). Basic writing class of 93 five years later: How the academic paths of blacks and whites diverged. *Journal of Basic Writing, 18*(1), 40–54.

Agnew, E., & McLaughlin, M. (2001). Those crazy gates and how they swing: Tracking the system that tracks African-American students. In G. McNenny & S. H. Fitzgerald (Eds.), *Mainstreaming basic writers politics and pedagogies of access* (pp. 85–100). Lawrence Erlbaum.

Alderson, J. C., & Hamp-Lyons, L. (1996). TOEFL preparation courses: A study of washback. *Language Testing, 13*(3), 280–297.

Alderson, J. C., & Wall, D. (1993). Does washback exist? *Applied Linguistics, 14*(2), 115–129.

Almasi, J., Afflerbach, P., Guthrie, J., & Schafer, W. (1995). *Effects of a statewide performance assessment program on classroom instruction practice in literacy.* Reading Research Report 32. National Reading Research Center, University of Maryland.

American Educational Research Association, American Psychological Association, & National Council on Measurement in Education. (2014). *The standards for educational and psychological testing.* American Educational Research Association.

Association of American Colleges and Universities. (2015). *Falling short? College learning and career success.* www.aacu.org/leap/public-opinion-research/2015-survey-results

Association of American Colleges and Universities. (2018). *Fulfilling the American dream: Liberal education and the future of work.* www.aacu.org/sites/default/files/files/LEAP/2018EmployerResearchReport.pdf

Au, W. (2007). High-stakes testing and curricular control: A qualitative metasynthesis. *Educational Researcher, 36*(5), 258–267. https://doi.org/10.3102/0013189X07306523

Au, W., & Gourd, K. (2013). Asinine assessment: Why high-stakes testing is bad for everyone, including English teachers. *English Journal, 103*(1), 14–19.

Ball, A. F. (1997). Expanding the dialogue on culture as a critical component when assessing writing. *Assessing Writing, 4*(2), 169–202.

Ball, A. F. (1999). Evaluating the writing of culturally and linguistically diverse students: The case of the African American vernacular English speaker. In C. R. Cooper & L. Odell (Eds.), *Evaluating writing: The role of teachers' knowledge about text, learning, and culture* (pp. 225–248). National Council of Teachers of English.

Beck, S., & Jeffery, J. (2007). Genres of high-stakes writing assessments and the construct of writing competence. *Assessing Writing, 12*(1), 60–79.

Berliner, D. (2011). Rational responses to high stakes testing: The case of curriculum narrowing and the harm that follows. *Cambridge Journal of Education, 41*(3), 287–302.

Blalock, G., & Haswell, R. (2003). *Student views of TAAS.* http://comppile.org/TAAS/index.html

Brandt, D. (2004). Drafting US literacy. *College English, 66*(5), 485–502.

Brandt, D. (2005). Writing for a living. *Written Communication, 22*(2), 166–197.

Brandt, D. (2015). *The rise of writing: Redefining mass literacy.* Cambridge University Press.

Close, K., Amrien-Beardsley, A., & Collins, C. (2019). Mapping America's teacher evaluation plans under ESSA. *Phi Delta Kappan, 101*(2), 22–26. https://kappanonline.org/mapping-teacher-evaluation-plans-essa-close-amrein-beardsley-collins/

Corbett, H. D., & Wilson, B. (1991). *Testing, reform, and rebellion.* Ablex.

Dappen, L., Isernhagen, J., & Anderson, S. (2008). A statewide writing assessment model: Student proficiency and future implications. *Assessing Writing, 13*(1), 45–60.

Edgerton, A. K. (2019, September 23). The essence of ESSA: More control at the district level? *Phi Delta Kappan Online.* https://kappanonline.org/the-essence-of-essa-more-control-at-the-district-level/

Escamilla, K., Mahon, E., Riley-Bernal, H., & Rutledge, D. (2003). High-stakes testing, Latinos, and English language learners: Lessons from Colorado. *Bilingual Research Journal, 27*(1), 25–49.

Fennell, M. (2016, June). What educators need to know about ESSA. *Educational Leadership, 73*(9), 62–65.

Filkins, S. (2015). *NCTE assessment story project: What we have learned* [Conference Presentation] National Council of Teachers of English Annual Meeting.

Firestone, W. A., Camilli, G., Yurecko, M., Monfils, L., & Mayrowetz, D. (2000). State standards, socio-fiscal context and opportunity to learn in New Jersey. *Education Policy Analysis Archives, 8*(35), 1–25. https://doi.org/10.14507/epaa.v8n35.2000

Firestone, W. A., & Mayrowetz, D. (2000). Rethinking "high stakes": Lessons from the United States and England and Wales. *Teachers College Record, 102*(4), 724–749.

Garcia, G. E., & Pearson, P. D. (1994). Assessment and diversity. *Review of Research in Education, 20*, 337–392.

Gere, A., Curzan, A., Hammond, J. W., Hughes, S., Li, R., Moos, A., Smith, K., Van Zanen, K., Wheeler, K. L., & Zanders, C. J. (2021). Communal justicing: Writing assessment, disciplinary infrastructure, and the case for critical language awareness. *College Composition and Communication, 72*(3), 384–410.

Graves, D. (2002). *Testing is not teaching: What should count in education.* Heinemann.

Hamp-Lyons, L. (2000). Social, professional and individual responsibility in language testing. *System, 28*(4), 579–591.

Hillocks, G. (2002). *The testing trap: How state writing assessments control learning.* Teachers College Press.

Hillocks, G. (2003). How state assessments lead to vacuous thinking and writing. *Journal of Writing Assessment, 1*(1), 5–21.

Hughes, A. (1989). *Testing for language teachers.* Cambridge University Press.

Jeffery, J. (2009). Constructs of writing proficiency in U.S. state and national writing assessments: Exploring variability. *Assessing Writing, 14*(1), 3–24.

Jones, B. D. (2007). The unintended outcomes of high—stakes testing. *Journal of Applied School Psychology, 23*(2), 65–86.

Jones, B. D., & Johnston, A. F. (2002, April). *The effects of high-stakes testing on instructional practices* [Conference Session] Annual Meeting of the American Educational Research Association.

Jones, G. M., Jones, B. D., Hardin, B., Chapman, L., Yarborough, T., & Davis, M. (1999). The impact of high-states testing on teachers and students in North Carolina. *Phi Delta Kappan, 81*(3), 199–203.

Kelly-Riley, D. (2011). Validity inquiry of race and shared evaluation practices in a Large-scale, university-wide writing portfolio assessment. *Journal of Writing Assessment, 4*(1), 1–16. www.scholarship.org/uc/item/7m18h956.

Kohn, A. (2000). *The case against standardized testing.* Heineman.

Koretz, D. (2017). *The testing charade: Pretending to make schools better.* University of Chicago Press.

Koretz, D., Barron, S., Mitchell, K., & Stecher, B. (1996). *The perceived effects of the Kentucky instructional results information system.* RAND.

Koretz, D., & Hamilton, L. S. (2003). *Teachers' responses to high-stakes testing and the validity of gains: A pilot study.* CSE Report 610. Center for the Study of Evaluation, University of California.

Lindquist, E. F. (Ed.). (1951). *Educational measurement.* American Council on Education.

Luce-Kapler, R., & Klinger, D. (2005). Uneasy writing: The defining moments of high-stakes literacy testing, *Assessing Writing, 10*(3), 157–173.

Madaus, G. F. (1985, Winter). Public policy and the testing profession: You've never had it so good? *Educational Measurement: Issues and Practice, 4*(4), 5–11. https://doi.org/10.1111/j.1745-3992.1985.tb00294.x

Madaus, G. F. (1988a). The distortion of teaching and testing: High-stakes testing and instruction. *Peabody Journal of Education, 65*(3), 29–46.

Madaus, G. F. (1988b). The influence of testing on the curriculum. In L. N. Tanner (Ed.), *Critical issues in curriculum: Eighty-seventh yearbook of the national society for the study of education* (pp. 83–121). University of Chicago Press.

Madaus, G. F. (1994). A technological and historical consideration of equity issues associated with proposals to change the nation's testing policy. *Harvard Educational Review, 64*(1), 76–96. https://doi.org/10.17763/haer.64.1.4q87663r0j76rwv1

Madaus, G. F., & Greaney, V. (1985). The Irish experience in competency testing: Implications for American education. *American Journal of Education, 93*(2), 268–294.

McNeil, L. (2000). *Contradictions of school reform: Educational costs of standardized testing.* Routledge.

Messenheimer, T., & Packwood, A. (2002, April). Writing: The state of the state vs. the state of the art in English and American schools. *Reading: Literacy and Language, 36*(1), 11–15.

Messick, S. (1989). Validity. In R. L. Linn (Ed.), *Educational measurement* (3rd ed., pp. 13–103). Macmillan.

Messick, S. (1996). Validity and washback in language testing. *Language Testing, 13*(3), 241–256. https://doi.org/10.1177/026553229601300302

Mislevy, R. J. (2013). *Four metaphors we need to understand assessment.* Educational Testing Service. www.ets.org/Media/Research/pdf/mislevy_four_metaphors_understand_assessment.pdf

Murphy, S. (2003). That was then, this is now: The impact of changing assessment policies on teachers and the teaching of writing in California. *Journal of Writing Assessment, 1*(1), 23–45.

Murphy, S. (2008). Some consequences of writing assessment. In A. Havnes & L. McDowell (Eds.), *Balancing dilemmas in assessment and learning in contemporary education.* Routledge.

National Association of Colleges and Employers. (2017). *The key attributes employers seek on students' resumes.* www.naceweb.org/about-us/press/2017/the-key-attributes-employers-seek-on-students-resumes/

National Center for Fair and Open Testing. (2016). *Assessment matters: Constructing model state systems to replace testing overkill.* https://www.fairtest.org/sites/default/files/FairTest-Model-Assessment-Report-2016-INTRO.pdf

National Center for Fair & Open Testing. (2019). *Graduation test update: States that recently eliminated or scaled back high school exit exams.* www.fairtest.org/graduation-test-update-states-recently-eliminated

National Commission on Writing for America's Families, Schools and Colleges. (2003). *The neglected "r," the need for a writing revolution.* College Board.

National Commission on Writing for America's Families, Schools and Colleges. (2004). *Writing: A ticket to work . . . or a ticket out.* College Board.

National Commission on Writing for America's Families, Schools and Colleges. (2005). *Writing: A powerful message from state government.* College Board.

National Commission on Writing for America's Families, Schools and Colleges. (2006). *Writing and school reform.* College Board.

National Council of Teachers of English. (2016). *The assessment story project: What we learned from teachers sharing their experiences with literacy assessment.* https://cdn.ncte.org/nctefiles/assessment story project/2016assessmentstoryprojectreport.pdf

National Writing Project & Nagin, C. (2006). *Because writing matters: Improving student writing in our schools.* Jossey-Bass.

Nichols, S., & Berliner, D. C. (2007). *Collateral damage: How high-stakes testing corrupts America's schools.* Harvard Education Press.

Northwest Evaluation Association. (2014). *Make assessment matter: Students and educators want test that support learning.* NWEA and Grunwald Associates. www.nwea.org/content/uploads/2014/05/MakeAssessmentMatter_5-2014.pdf

Ohanian, S. (1999). *One size fits few: The folly of educational standards.* Heinemann.

O'Neill, P. (2001, November 15–18). *College snapshots: Perspectives on preparedness from first-year students and teachers* [Conference Presentation] NCTE Annual Convention.

O'Neill, P., Murphy, S., Huot, B., & Williamsom, M. (2005). What high school teachers in three states say about different kinds of mandated state writing tests. *Journal of Writing Assessment, 2*(2), 81–108.

Poe, M., Elliot, N., Cogan, Jr, J. A., & Nurudeen, Jr., T. G. (2014). The legal and the local: Using disparate impact analysis to understand the consequences of writing assessment. *College Composition and Communication, 65*(4), 588–611.

Popham, W. J. (1987). The merits of measurement-driven instruction. *Phi Delta Kappan, 68*(9), 679–682.

Ravitch, D. (2010). *The death and life of the great American school system: How testing and choice are undermining education.* Perseus Books Group, Basic Books.

Ravitch, D. (2012). *The teacher accountability debate.* Occasional Paper Series. https://edu cate.bankstreet.edu/occasional-paper-seriels/vol2021/iss27/4

Scherff, L., & Piazza, C. (2005). The more things change, the more they stay the same: A survey of high school students' writing experiences. *Research in the Teaching of English, 39*(3), 271–304.

Schmidt, A. E., & Camara, W. J. (2004). Group differences in standardized test scores and other educational indicators. In R. Zwick (Ed.), *Rethinking the SAT: The future of standardized testing in university admissions* (pp. 189–201). Routledge.

Shavelson, R. J., Webb, N. W., & Rowley, G. L. (1989). Generalizability theory. *American Psychologist, 44*(6), 922–932.

Shepard, L. A., & Dougherty, K. C. (1991, April). *Effects of high-stakes testing on instruction* [Conference session]. Annual meeting of the American Educational Research Association, ED 337 468.

Shohamy, E., Donitsa-Schmidt, S., & Ferman, I. (1996). Test impact revisited: Washback effect over time. *Language Testing, 13*(3), 298–317.

Smith, M. L. (1991a). Meanings of test preparation. *American Educational Research Journal, 28*(3), 521–542.

Smith, M. L. (1991b). Put to the test: The effects of external testing on teachers. *Educational Researcher, 20*(5), 8–11.

Smith, M. L., Edelsky, C., Draper, K., Rottenberg, C., & Cherland, M. (1990). *The role of testing in elementary schools.* Center for Research on Evaluation, Standards, and Student Testing, University of California.

Stecher, B. M., & Barron, S. L. (1999). *Quadrennial milepost accountability testing in Kentucky* (CSE Tech. Rep. 505). National Center for Research on Evaluation, Standards, and Student Testing and the Center for the Study of Evaluation. https://cresst.org/publications/cresst-publication-2877/

Stetcher, B. M., Barron, S. L., Chun, T., & Ross, K. (2000). *The effects of the Washington State education reform on schools and classrooms* (CSE Tech. Rep. 525). National Center for Research on Evaluation, Standards, and Student Testing. https://cresst.org/wp-content/uploads/TECH525.pdf

Stetcher, B. M., Barron, S. L., Kaganoff, T., & Goodwin, J. (1998). *The effects of standards-based assessment on classroom practices: Results of the 1996–97 RAND survey of Kentucky teachers of mathematics and writing* (CSE Tech. Rep. 482). National Center for Research on Evaluation, Standards, and Student Testing. http://cresst.org/publications/cresst-publication-2854/

Strauss, V. (2014). 11 problems created by the standardized testing obsession. *The Answer Sheet Blog.* https://wapo.st/3qLRTLw

U. S. Department of Education. (2017). *Every student succeeds act. Assessments under title 1, part a & title 1, part B: Summary of final regulations.* https://www2.ed.gov/policy/elsec/leg/essa/essaassessmentfactsheet1207.pdf

Vogler, K. E. (2002). The impact of high-stakes, state-mandated student performance assessment on teachers' instructional practices. *Education, 123*(1), 39–56.

Wall, D. (1997). Impact and washback in language testing. In C. Clapham & D. Corson (Eds.), *Encyclopedia of language and education* (Vol. 7, pp. 291–302). Kluwer Academic.

White, E. M., & Thomas, L. L. (1981). Racial minorities and writing skills assessment in the California state university and colleges. *College English, 43*(3), 276–283.

2

WHAT DO ASSESSMENT CONCEPTS TELL US ABOUT THE LIMITATIONS OF TRADITIONAL APPROACHES TO THE LARGE-SCALE ASSESSMENT OF WRITING?

Returning to our remodeling metaphor, we note that one of the critical moments in a renovation process occurs when contractors evaluate the real condition of the house. They get beyond the surface appearance and into the systems—the plumbing, electric, HVAC, even the foundations. Do the systems work? Are they up to code? What hidden problems do they discover—leaks, termites, botched repairs? As homeowners, contractors, and designers assess the situation, they need to address the problems discovered.

In this chapter we argue that we need to remodel our large-scale writing assessment systems because the foundations on which they rest are flawed, and they undermine the validity of test results and the decisions based on them. While we address other important measurement concepts, we focus on two aspects of validity: construct (how we define writing ability and the degree to which a test measures what we claim to be measuring) and consequence (how we take into account the effects of an assessment on curriculum, teachers, and students). These two concepts are at the heart of responsible assessment. We discuss overarching educational measurement concepts largely in the context of large-scale assessments, but we keep in mind that writing assessment touches on all aspects of teaching and learning, across disciplines, levels of education, and beyond:

> Writing assessment occurs for many different purposes. Teachers assess writing to monitor students' progress, inform instruction, provide feedback, and judge the effectiveness of their teaching. Students assess their own writing to appraise growth, determine strengths, and identify areas in need of further development. Peers assess each other's writing, providing feedback on what works and what still needs improvement. Schools assess writing to determine how many students meet local or state performance

DOI: 10.4324/9781003296140-2

standards and identify youths who need extra help. States and the federal government administer writing tests to measure American students' collective writing success, evaluating students' ability to effectively convey thoughts and ideas through writing across time. Employers assess writing to make decisions about whom to hire and promote.

(Graham et al., 2011b, pp. 11–12)

Reliability

While validity (which we discuss later) is considered the key concept in educational assessment, reliability is also important. Parkes (2007) reminds us that reliability is about "values of dependability, stability, accuracy, and consistency or precision" (p. 2). Reliability can take many forms. For example, test–retest reliability refers to consistency in results over replications of the same testing procedure over time. Interrater reliability refers to the degree to which different judges or raters agree in their judgments. Internal consistency reliability refers to the degree to which different test items that are intended to probe the same construct produce similar results. Alternate form reliability refers to the degree to which two forms of the same test produce comparable scores. The common thread here is the idea of consistency.

Parkes (2007) contends that reliability should be considered as an argument in which all of the available evidence and theories are weighed in light of the particular assessment and its uses. His approach acknowledges the need to understand reliability in terms of specific contexts and purposes and aligns with social perspectives on literacy. Professional organizations note that reliability requires gathering and documenting all of the available evidence and judgments about the levels of reliability appropriate for the intended uses and interpretations of the scores (AERA et al., 2014, p. 41). Typically, reliability is assessed with a reliability coefficient that indicates the amount of error in the scores. The *Standards* document notes that "no single, preferred approach to quantification of reliability/precision" exists and "[n]o single index adequately conveys all of the relevant information. No one method of investigation is optimal in all situations." Choices about estimation techniques and other factors "remain a matter of professional judgment" (AERA et al., 2014, p. 41).

Beyond relying on formulas and coefficients to express reliability, test developers use standardized processes and procedures for tasks and scoring to achieve acceptable levels of reliability. In writing, this most often translates into essay exams that require precisely formatted prompts, specific directions for test administration, detailed rubrics for scoring, consistent scoring procedures, and controlled testing environments. Moss (1994) describes the traditional psychometric approach to reliability as:

> operationalized by examining consistency, quantitatively defined, among independent observations or sets of observations that are intended as interchangeable—consistency among independent evaluations or readings

of a performance, consistency among performances in response to independent tasks, and so on.

(p. 6)

"In a typical psychometric approach to assessment," she explains, "each performance is scored independently by readers who have no additional knowledge about the student or about the judgments of other readers" (p. 7). Moss (1994) notes that inter-reader reliability may "drop below acceptable levels for consequential decisions about individuals or programs" when tasks "vary substantially from student to student and when multiple tasks are evaluated simultaneously" (p. 6). The alternative Moss (1994) explores is "a hermeneutic approach to assessment" that would involve:

> holistic, integrative interpretations of collected performances that seek to understand the whole in light of its parts, that privilege readers who are most knowledgeable about the context in which the assessment occurs, and that ground those interpretations not only in the textual and contextual evidence available, but also in a rational debate among the community of interpreters.
>
> *(p. 7)*

Although Moss's suggestion of a hermeneutic approach to reliability has been frequently cited in the literature, it hasn't had much of an impact on what happens in testing systems, especially mandated, large-scale tests, which rely on psychometric approaches.

As writing assessment scholars such as Huot (1990) and Williamson (1993) have pointed out, the quest for psychometrically reliable scores became the dominant factor in designing writing assessments. Williamson (2003) concluded that the history of writing assessment has been the "drive toward more reliable and efficient ways to measure educational achievement and writing ability" (p. 86). However, because writing assessment tasks are typically designed to promote psychometrically reliable scores, assessment results can lead to a very narrow representation of writing and limit the meaningfulness of the assessment results.

According to the *Standards* "the level of reliability/precision of scores has implications for validity," and reliability/precision data "bears on the generalizability or dependability of the scores and/or classifications of individuals derived for the scores" (AERA et al., 2014, p. 34). While reliability is treated separately from validity, in terms of gathering evidence and establishing standards of test development, it ultimately is part of the validation of an assessment.

Validity

Although there are debates about its scope and the methods for establishing it, validity is the core concept in educational assessment, as explained by practitioners and theorists alike. In our discussion, we draw on recent scholarship related to validity and educational assessment as well as the *Standards of Educational and Psychological Testing* (AERA et al., 2014). The "intent" of the *Standards* is to "promote the sound and ethical use of tests . . . and to provide a basis for evaluating the quality of testing practices" as well as "information to test developers, publishers, and users about key elements in a testing program that should inform the development, selection, and use of tests" (Plake & Wise, 2014, p. 4). For the most part, the *Standards* document is concerned with standardized educational and psychological tests.

Classroom assessment is intentionally excluded from the *Standards*, although classroom and large-scale assessments are not mutually exclusive as we explained in Chapter 1. Likewise, teachers are not specifically identified as the intended audience of the *Standards*, but many agree that "there are a number of features of the *Standards* with which all teachers should be familiar" (Wiliam, 2014, p. 29). The joint committee that drafted the most recent edition "felt classroom teachers would benefit from reading the *Standards* and that promoting assessment literacy for teachers was another important goal" of the document (Plake & Wise, 2014, p. 6).

One of our goals in this section is to help writing teachers K–college become more familiar with concepts in the *Standards* and related research, not only to inform their own practices but to better engage with the assessment systems that influence their work. Teachers, we argue, are at the center of assessment and accountability because they are the link between the day-to-day teaching and learning that happens in classrooms and the larger educational and accountability systems that frame education. Student learning, in large part, depends on the experiences students have in their classrooms with their teachers. Therefore, teachers need to be informed, engaged participants in education policy and decision making, including decisions about assessment and accountability.

For concepts such as validity, the *Standards* provides a "consensus" definition and "serves as a touchstone" obliging those who develop and use tests to acknowledge when they deviate from that definition (Shepard, 2016, p. 268). Validity "refers to the degree to which evidence and theory support the interpretation of test scores for proposed uses of the tests" and is "the most fundamental consideration in developing tests and evaluating" them (AERA et al., 2014, p. 11). To conduct a validation inquiry requires "accumulating relevant evidence to provide a sound scientific basis for proposed score interpretations." Once completed, the validation process does not decide the validity of the instrument— the test, or assessment—but rather the interpretation and use of the results because it is the uses and interpretations that are evaluated, "not the test itself." Therefore, assigning validity to the test is wrong: "It is incorrect to use the unqualified phrase 'the validity of the test'" (AERA et al., 2014, p. 11).

This doesn't mean that the test itself doesn't matter. There can be "bad" tests; however, what makes these tests bad is that they produce invalid results. For example, a test that claims to assess students' writing abilities but consists solely of multiple-choice items about language conventions, and does not require any writing, is theoretically flawed, and the results cannot, therefore, be considered valid. As we discuss in the next chapter, writing as a construct is much more than knowledge of language conventions. Writing requires production of text and is a complex cognitive activity that is contextually situated. A test may produce results that are valid if its sole purpose is to determine a student's knowledge of isolated language conventions, but if its aim is to determine the student's ability to produce standard, edited English prose, then the results would not be valid. And even if a writing assessment requires the production of a text, it would not produce valid results if the results were used to make generalizations about a student's ability to write across different contexts, purposes, and genres. A writing test designed to assess proficiency, for instance, that is based on a prompt that assumes knowledge of subject matter and understanding of a particular context for writing that is beyond the test taker's experience would not produce valid results.

There are many other ways that the form and content of an assessment may produce invalid results, including the way writing is defined by the test's content, the evaluation criteria and/or procedures, the administration and conditions for taking the test, or the mismatch of the content of the exam with the curriculum. Sometimes the problem may be more obvious, as with poorly designed prompts or multiple-choice tests, but sometimes the concerns can be less obvious, as with essays and portfolios. Validation addresses all aspects of the assessment to ensure that the interpretation and use of the results are justified based on theoretical and empirical evidence.

Validation as argument

Drawing on the work of earlier scholars, Kane (2006, 2016b), a leading voice in the validity debates, advocates an argument approach to assessment validation and identifies the kinds and extents of evidence needed to evaluate claims based on test scores. For example, tests might be designed to support decisions about test takers, such as admission or placement, by "providing information about test-taker attributes that are relevant to the decision" (Kane, 2013, p. 1). Or tests might be designed to provide information about test-taker abilities. A test of writing, for example, could be interpreted in terms of the test taker's ability to write effectively in a range of contexts, and the scores might be used by various institutions to make a variety of decisions. According to Kane (2016a), "There is broad agreement that the evaluation of interpretive claims is at the core of our notion of validity and that such claims need to be justified in some way" (p. 198). In building the justification—the validity argument—assessment developers and users must consider both theoretical and empirical evidence that explores various aspects of validity. Kane (2016b) summarizes the argument-based approach to validation as involving "two basic steps . . . a) specify the claims that are to be based on test scores, as an interpretation/use argument . . . and b) evaluate the plausibility of these claims using appropriate methods and evidence in a *validity argument*" (emphasis in original; p. 309).

The *Standards* states that the validation process begins with explicit statements of the proposed interpretation of the test results, the construct (such as writing ability) and the rationale for the relevance of the proposed scores in terms of the construct. The construct should be elaborated with descriptions of it and its scope. The assessment design should be analyzed in relation to the scope of the construct. Is only an aspect of writing ability—such as a student's ability to respond to a common-knowledge prompt, in a certain genre, in isolation without consulting other people or sources, in a prescribed amount of time—assessed in the test in question? This kind of assessment of writing is very limited in scope, considering the variety of ways that literacy experts define writing (see Chapter 3 for discussion of the various ways writing is defined). The interpretation and intended use of the scores should also be clearly articulated. For example, in a placement test, relevant questions include how does the test align with the curriculum? What theories of writing does it reflect and promote? How do the students perform in the course in which they are placed?

Types of evidence and the methods for collecting and analyzing that evidence can vary, depending on the particular assessment. Different types of evidence, as specified in the *Standards* (AERA et al., 2014), address different aspects of the assessment, such as its content, the cognitive processes accessed, structure of the assessment/tasks, relationships with criteria, and consequences of the test results. The relationships of the construct being assessed with conceptually-related constructs also needs to be considered. For example, reading may be considered a conceptually-related construct to writing because reading and writing are both aspects of literacy (see Chapter 3 where we discuss reading and writing specifically). If reading is involved in the writing task, then the interaction of reading with the student's writing performance would need to be explored: Did the student's ability to comprehend the text influence her writing? And if so, how? Technology provides another example of the need to gather evidence about ancillary concepts or abilities. If a writing assessment requires test-takers to use a particular word processing program to generate the text, then evidence about the influence of the technology on the writers' performances would need to be gathered. Did the students' ability to use the software and hardware impact the writing they generated? And if so, how? After the evidence is collected, it is integrated into "a sound validity argument" that draws on the "various strands of evidence" to create "a coherent account of the degree to which existing evidence and theory support the intended interpretation of tests scores for specific uses" (AERA et al., 2014, p. 21).

Validating an end-of-course exam, for instance, would require an explicit statement about the purposes of the exam and how the results are to be interpreted and used. Do passing scores demonstrate test takers' knowledge of the course content, achievement of course outcomes, and/or readiness for the next level of study in that field? What construct—domain, characteristic, or concept—is the test aiming to measure? Are the results being used to retain students, provide remediation, inform pedagogy, and/or provide professional development to teachers? What are the outcomes of these uses? Does the test actually distinguish those students who have mastered the content from those who haven't? Are all students who pass the exam prepared for the next level of study? Do students fail because they haven't learned the course content or achieved the outcomes, or are other factors interfering? Because validity is considered a unitary concept, all of the various sources of evidence need to be included, and the claims must be "critically evaluated" (Kane, 2016b, p. 309). The specific questions might be different for a test used for a different purpose such as placement, but the types of inquiry would be the same. Smith's (1993) research illustrates a comprehensive, ongoing validation inquiry into a composition placement exam that involved collecting a variety of evidence about it, including its alignment with the curriculum, conditions for administration, scoring procedures, and student performance in the various courses in which it placed them (O'Neill, 2003).

The consequential aspect of construct validity

Messick (1994b) defines validity as "an overall evaluative judgment of the degree to which empirical evidence and theoretical rationales support the adequacy and appropriateness of interpretations and actions based on test scores or other modes of assessment" (p. 5). He explains that the traditionally separate trio of validity concepts (content, criterion, and construct) failed to take into account "evidence of the value implications of score meaning as a basis for action and of the social consequences of score use" (1994b, p. 5). To address this limitation, he proposed a new unified and comprehensive theory of construct validity that addresses "both score meaning and social values in both test interpretation and test use." Messick (1994b) identified six aspects of construct validity: "content, substantive, structural, generalizability, external, and consequential" (p. 5). The consequences of test use are of particular interest here because of the growing body of research showing that large-scale assessment impacts curriculum, teachers, and students in various ways, some of which we reviewed in Chapter 1, and some we review in subsequent chapters. According to Messick (1996):

> The consequential aspect appraises the value implications of score interpretation as a basis for action as well as the actual and potential consequences of test use, especially in regard to sources of invalidity related to issues of bias, fairness, and distributive justice (Messick, 1980, 1989), as well as to washback.
>
> *(pp. 9–10)*

While there is general agreement about the centrality of validity in assessment, Kane (2016a) acknowledges that there is "less agreement about the role of consequences in test use in validity" (p. 198). In fact, the role and inclusion of consequential validity evidence in validity investigations has been hotly debated over the years. Some scholars (e.g., Popham, 1997; Mehrens, 1997; Shepard, 1997; Cizek et al., 2010) have argued against including consequences in determinations of validity. Popham, for example, argues that "Cluttering the concept of validity with social consequences will lead to confusion, not clarity" (1997, p. 9). Cizek et al. (2010) claim that "researchers and practitioners do not gather or report evidence on validity based on consequences because it is not possible to include consequences as a logical part of validation" (p. 739). Mehrens (1997) proposes narrowing and reserving the use of the term validity "for determining the accuracy of inferences about (an understanding of) the characteristic being assessed, not the efficacy of actions following assessment" (p. 18), and Shepard (1997) is concerned that "lumping our attention to the social consequences of test use with the concept of validity" may "muddy the validity waters" and actually lead to "less attention to the intended and unintended consequences of test use" (p. 13). Other scholars, however, have argued that consequences of test use *should* be included in investigations of validity. Linn (1997) explains that "since validity depends on the uses to which results are put, it needs to include an evaluation of the consequences of those uses" (p. 14).

As Slomp et al. (2014) explain, Messick's seminal (1989a) work became "a lightning rod within this debate" because Messick holds the position that "unintended consequences should be included within the validity framework" (p. 278). But that doesn't mean *all* unintended consequences should be considered equally. Messick explains that "a poor test may be associated with positive effects and a good test with negative effects because of other things that are done or not done in the educational system" (p. 2). He concludes that "washback is a consequence of testing that bears on validity only if it can be evidentially shown to be an effect of the test and not of other forces operative on the educational scene" (Messick, 1996, p. 2). Kane (2013) concurs with Messick. Although Messick's formulation limits "the scope of consequences for which test users and developers must be held responsible to issues that result from flaws in construct representation," Cronbach (1988) argues that if negative consequences are severe, they furnish cause to discontinue the use of a test whether the consequences are related to concerns about construct validity or not. Clearly, there is disagreement about including consequences in efforts to establish validity. However, there seems to be little disagreement over the necessity of investigating the consequences of tests (Tsagari, 2007). As Shepard notes, "this debate is not whether consideration of consequences is worthwhile but whether it should be an integral part of validity theory and practice" (1997, p. 5). All of the experts cited here appear to agree that the consequences should be investigated (Cronbach, 1988; Cizek et al., 2010; Kane, 2013; Popham, 1997; Mehrens, 1997; Messick, 1989a, 1989b; Shepard,

1997; Slomp et al., 2014; Tsagari, 2007). The *Standards* document indicates that validity inquiries need to consider both the intended and unintended consequences of assessments (AERA et al., 2014, p. 20).

Because validity is a unitary concept, all of the various sources of evidence need to be included. The consequences of test score interpretations and uses, according to Kane (2016a), are critical to validation. If all consequences are not considered, then validation tends to only examine the *intended* interpretations of results and their uses. The reality is, however, that not many test-based accountability programs systematically collect evidence of consequential validity (Cizek et al., 2010). According to Kane (2006), test-based accountability programs are flawed if they assume they will improve teaching and learning but fail to collect evidence to determine whether they do or not.

Following their investigation of consequential validity research on large-scale writing assessment in Canada, Slomp et al. (2014) noted that testing agencies and/or the governments that contracted them infrequently conduct or report research on consequential validity:

> Assessment stakeholders seem to embrace the idea of using tests to hold others accountable but fail to systematically address the one aspect of validity theory that turns that accountability mechanism back on ourselves: the implications of our assessment actions. . . . If the true goal of government-mandated, large-scale assessment programs is to improve systems of education, then it is only logical that the designers and users of these tests should examine and publicly report on the consequences that accrue as a result of the use of these tests.
>
> *(p. 298)*

Many assessment scholars argue that more attention should be given to consequences, especially unintended ones, given the influence of testing-based accountability systems, high-stakes assessments, and measurement-driven instruction. Moss (2016) contends that we need to "shift our focus from intended interpretations and uses of test scores to the actual interpretations and uses by professionals in educational contexts: teachers, school leaders, policy-makers and other stakeholders" where "validity questions are equally relevant" (p. 236). Citing a range of research studies, Moss (2016) argues that actual uses are "invariably shaped by local users' purposes" (p. 236). The local interpretations and uses may not align with the intended uses and, in fact, may undermine them.

Moss (2016) calls for an expanded view of validity theory "to address questions at the meta or organizational level, where myriad test-informed interpretations, decisions and actions routinely occur" (p. 237). To illustrate her position, Moss presents several examples from the accruing research on how test scores influence a wide range of decisions. A three-year study by Coburn et al. (2009), for instance, "traced the processes through which . . . decisions were made over time" (Moss, 2016, p. 239). The researchers found that decisions build through many small steps, and they noted that the implications of the test scores are interpreted in different ways by different decision-makers. According to Coburn et al. (2009), as reported by Moss, decision makers in the district made assumptions about the reasons for low test scores and then made decisions based on these assumptions without clear evidence that linked test performance to classroom practices. According to Moss (2016), "The validity issue for conceptual use concerns how local decision-makers connected the scores to local practices" (p. 240).

This kind of research, which involves a variety of methodologies and extends over multiple years, helps us to understand how test scores are interpreted and used. It details the impact on the individual test takers as well as on the schools and districts that are responsible for student performance on the mandated assessments at the center of the test-based accountability approach. For example, in his study of state-wide assessment of writing, Hillocks (2002) found that the accountability system influenced the ways administrators and teachers prepared students for the tests. His study compared the ways policies were enacted across states, as well as within states. He purposefully included schools with different socioeconomic statuses and geographic locations (urban, rural, and suburban) and documented the policies and practices in the various schools that were linked to the state testing requirements. By looking at a range of types of schools, Hillocks's study provided insight into how context influenced the ways administrators implemented testing-related activities in different kinds of schools.

Moss's (2016) call for more research at the organizational level echoes, in many ways, Haertel's (2013) proposal that validation research should be expanded:

> First, validation must attend to actual test use and its consequences, not just score meaning. Second, validation must attend to unintended as well as intended testing consequences. Third, validation must attend to indirect and direct testing effects.
>
> *(p. 1)*

Haertel, who explores how testing is supposed to improve schooling, focuses on seven uses of educational assessment, which he separates into direct and indirect actions. Direct actions, according to Haertel (2013), "encompass uses or interpretations that rely directly on the information that scores provide about the measured construct" (p. 2). For example, direct actions include instructional guidance, student placement and selection, comparisons among educational approaches, and educational management (Haertel, 2013, p. 2). Indirect actions are "less clear and not always explicit," Haertel contends, and "are mechanisms of action, leading to intended or unintended consequences, that do not depend directly on particular test scores," such as directing student effort, focusing the system, and shaping perceptions (p. 2).

To explain these concepts, Haertel (2013) uses a classroom spelling test, in which the teacher grades the test and records that score, as an example where the direct actions might include grading, providing diagnostic feedback to students on their performance, and informing future instruction. An indirect action of the weekly spelling test might be to encourage students to study. If we use the example from Hillocks's (2003) research, a direct action based on the assessment's results was to determine the instruction students needed in writing arguments; an indirect action of the assessment was the way teachers and district leaders focused the writing curriculum exclusively on the five-paragraph theme structure, eliminating or minimizing other concepts critical to persuasive writing, such as the need for sound evidence and reasoning. The focus on formulaic writing is a result of the format of the test, not of particular test scores. Haertel's point is that many of the decisions and actions that result from assessment programs, especially those that are unintended and indirect, are not articulated by test developers or users and, therefore, are not examined in the validation process, yet they can have a significant impact on teaching and learning, and teachers and students. The specific impacts can vary quite a bit, as Hillocks (2002) showed, based on the socioeconomic context of the schools and districts. Decisions such as those made at the district level to promote the five-paragraph essay at the expense of other approaches to teaching writing should be included when conducting a validation inquiry for a writing exam because these decisions are linked to the interpretation and use of assessment results and impact teaching and learning, even if those decisions resulted from a series of tangential, incremental decisions that occurred over time.

Researchers have argued that the stakes of an assessment are critical because the consequences of an assessment can undermine or distort its stated purpose and intended use even when the test seems well constructed. A growing body of research, some of it reviewed in Chapter 1, demonstrates the powerful—and in many cases negative—impact the test-based accountability movement has had on educational practices.

Goodwin (2014) and Koretz (2015) invoke Campbell's Law, to explain how such negative effects come about:

> The more any quantitative social indicator is used for social decision making, the more subject it will be to corruption pressures and more apt it will be to distort and corrupt the social processes it is intended to monitor.
>
> *(Campbell, 1976, p. 54)*

In other words, according to Goodwin (2014), "the higher the stakes attached to any measure, the less valid that measure becomes" (p. 78). The use of assessment results to reform education and hold educators "accountable" is a prime example of Campbell's Law: scores may go up, but that does not mean an improvement in learning. Instead, the reverse may be true.

According to Koretz (2015), test-based accountability is based on the "hope" for three types of responses—"that teachers will allocate more time to instruction, work harder, and find more effective ways to teach" (p. 5). The assumption is these activities will lead to higher scores, which are interpreted as improvement in learning. However, other ways of responding to raise test scores have also been documented: cheating, reallocation, and coaching (Koretz, 2015, p. 5). Reallocation involves shifting resources to what is emphasized on the test away from material or experiences not targeted by the test. For example, in Chapter 1 we reviewed research showing the distortion of the writing construct when the rewards and sanctions associated with high-stakes tests led teachers to shift from teaching the writing process to using worksheets on grammar and conventions. We reviewed other research showing that single-sample assessments may lead teachers to over-emphasize the type of writing that appears on high-stakes tests. In other words, if a particular kind of writing is *not* on the mandated assessment, a teacher or school (or district) may not address that kind of writing in teaching. This kind of reallocation can be a validity threat, as Madaus (1994) explained, because assessments "elicit a small sample of behavior from a larger domain of interest" (p. 77). We use the results "to make inferences about a person's probable performance relative to the domain," and then we "classify, describe, or make decisions about individuals or institutions" (p. 77). If the reallocation narrows the construct of writing—the domain being assessed—it limits the interpretation and use of the test scores. When that limitation is not acknowledged and taken into account in how the scores are interpreted and used, validity is threatened.

While reallocation involves more substantive efforts, coaching emphasizes less substantive material. Coaching includes a variety of responses, such as teachers using the format of the test's instructions or the scoring rubrics in instruction, which, according to Koretz (2015), is often considered "test preparation" (Koretz, 2015, p. 6). Test preparation could also include teaching time-management strategies or strategies for guessing. Coaching can also narrow the construct by limiting the students' exposure to other ways of encountering material. For example, if teachers use the exact prompt format from the assessment for all writing assignments so students are familiar with that form when they encounter it on the test, students may learn how to interpret that specific type of prompt and respond to it but not how to read and respond to other kinds of writing assignments. Or, if a teacher (or an entire school curriculum) focuses exclusively on the five-paragraph essay structure because that is what is assumed to score well on the assessment, as we explained in Chapter 1, students will not develop an understanding of other ways to organize and structure an essay, or, for that matter, other genres of writing. Kane (2015) argues that "the use of coachable instruments in high stakes accountability makes it almost inevitable that many forms of coaching and less legitimate forms of gamesmanship (e.g., outright cheating) would tend to increase" (p. 47). Hillocks's (2002, 2003) study provides multiple examples of how reallocation and coaching can play out in writing assessments across various sites in different states. At the college level, researchers have documented the real-location and coaching students experienced when they failed mandated writing exams, raising doubts about the way students are sorted based on the test results (e.g., Adams, 1993; Wolcott, 1994; Agnew & McLaughlin, 1999, 2001).

Other actions that threaten the validity of test scores include the use of rewards and sanctions because they encourage reallocation, coaching, and cheating. They span a range of practices affecting students, teachers, schools, and districts. For example, a school might throw a pizza party for students who pass a particular test or require Saturday school tutoring for those who fail or are in danger of failing a test. Sometimes students, schools, or districts, especially those who do poorly in the practice assessments or the actual assessments, might reduce or eliminate certain courses—those that are untested such as art, music, or even academic subjects such as science or social studies. For example, one experienced teacher and K–5 principal wrote about changes in kindergarten in his district:

> It seems that many school leaders have reasoned that if they push more reading and math lessons into kindergarten it will somehow translate into better test scores once the students get to third grade. This has resulted in a big reduction in the amount of time kindergarten students spend drawing, painting, cutting, pasting, and doing other things artistic.
>
> *(Sackstein, 2015)*

The elimination or de-emphasis of the arts in favor of subjects tested on the required tests goes far beyond kindergarten. In an overview of research on the impact of testing on the curriculum, David (2011) noted that during the era of NCLB, increases in the tested areas "were substantial: a 47 percent increase in language arts and a 37 percent increase in math," and in the same districts, there was "decreased time allotted to other subjects and activities, including science, social studies, art, music, physical education, and recess" (p. 2).

Some advocates of test-based reform argue that the problem is not the concept but rather the tests—better tests will be more likely to promote the positive consequences intended and minimize the negative ones. Hillocks (2002) concluded, for example, that the format of a writing test (multiple choice, impromptu essay exams, and/or portfolios) mattered the most in terms of its effects on teaching and learning. According to Hillocks (2002), the impromptu, timed standardized essay prompts had more deleterious effects on writing instruction than the mandated portfolios used in Kentucky and Oregon, regardless of the stakes attached to the assessment results. In practice, however, it is the combination of the test format and the stakes that influence how writing is understood by the teachers and students, which, in turn, influences the instructional practices used by teachers to improve scores.

For example, in her year-long study of one high school English department's experience with the writing portfolios mandated by the Kentucky Education Reform Act, Callahan (1997) found that some of the assessment system goals were achieved but that the pressure teachers experienced because of the accountability component of the assessment compromised other goals. The portfolio assessment "did change the amount and kind of writing produced" by their students—a positive outcome—but "it did not demonstrably alter the way student writing was understood or taught" (p. 295)—another important goal of the program. Spalding and Cummins (1998) concurred with Callahan. Based on their survey of first-year college students who graduated from Kentucky high schools, they reported many positive consequences associated with the portfolios, such as more writing, more writing across the curriculum, and use of writing process activities, which were some of the goals of the portfolio program. Ultimately, however, they concluded that the "accountability system, of which the KIRIS [Kentucky Instructional Results Information System] portfolio is a part, may be undermining some of the instructional improvements it was intended to achieve" (Spalding & Cummins, 1998, p. 191). For example, students did not identify audience and purpose as important factors in their response to a writing task, although addressing audience and purpose was a significant component of the scoring rubric and an important instructional goal of the program. While some of the benefits were realized, others were not, and it may have been the very basic structure of the test-based accountability approach that compromised some of the potential benefits.

This kind of research (Callahan, 1997; Spalding & Cummins, 1998) goes beyond looking at the content of the test, the scoring procedures, and the intended uses of the results to examine the experience of the assessment system by students, teachers, and administrators and the uses of the results in classrooms, schools, and districts. It should be considered validation inquiry, as Moss (2016) conceives it, because researchers who have investigated the actual consequences the assessment systems had on teaching and learning have found that in many cases the intended results were not only unfulfilled but that the assessment system also encouraged unintended, deleterious consequences that compromised the validity of the interpretation and use of the test results (Agnew & McLaughlin, 2001; Callahan, 1997; Hillocks, 2002; Spalding & Cummins, 1998).

The growing body of research on the consequences of large-scale, high-stakes writing assessments is not confined to the United States. For example, Slomp et al. (2014) developed a framework for collecting and analyzing consequential validity evidence. The framework helped them integrate previously disconnected investigations of large-scale writing assessment programs in Canada and to identify recurring themes and patterns. They report that Canadian large-scale assessment practices "constrained writing as a construct" by:

- ignoring emergent forms of digital writing and multiliteracies (Lotherington, 2004; Peterson et al., 2012);
- truncating the writing process, emphasizing only the final draft while ignoring process-oriented writing (Peterson et al., 2012; Slomp, 2005, 2008);

- focusing more on procedure (write X number of lines) than actual writing (Ricci, 2004);
- focusing on narrow/traditional constructs of writing (Hardy, 2010; Peterson & McClay, 2010; Slomp, 2005, 2008); and,
- ignoring the importance of multiple assessments over time, as well as differentiated forms of assessment (Peterson & McClay, 2010; Skerrett & Hargreaves, 2008).

(Slomp et al., 2014, p. 295)

They also found that the tests limited pedagogical diversity in the classrooms for the following reasons:

- failing to provide teachers with any new evidence about their students (Lam & Bordignon, 2001; Skwarchuk, 2004; Toohey, 2007);
- taking time away from teaching to focus on test-taking skills (Lam & Bordignon, 2001; Ricci, 2004; Skwarchuk, 2004; Slomp, 2005, 2008); and
- encouraging convergent thinking over divergent (creative) thinking (Ricci, 2004; Zheng et al., 2011)

(Slomp et al., 2014, p. 295)

In addition to limiting pedagogical diversity, their analysis indicated that the tests had negative impacts on students and their teachers. The tests:

- lacked cultural diversity and favored students who had knowledge of Canadian symbols, historical events, and artifacts (Doe et al., 2011; Kim & Jang, 2009);
- led to students' negative self-image as writers and lessened motivation to learn (Doe et al., 2011; Fox & Cheng, 2007; Kearns, 2011); and
- disempowered teachers while undermining their professional judgment (Skerrett, 2010; Skerrett & Hargreaves, 2008).

(Slomp et al., 2014, p. 295)

Results such as these highlight the importance of investigating the consequences of assessments. While some high-stakes writing assessments have appeared to have positive effects, such as increasing attention to writing in the curriculum and improving teachers' practices in positive ways (Callahan, 1999; Dappen et al., 2008; Parke et al., 2006), research also shows that the costs can outweigh the benefits.

Construct validity, underrepresentation, and evolution

A construct is "an attribute, proficiency, ability, or skill" that "is defined by established theories" (Brown, 2000, p. 9). Construct validity has been defined as the degree to which a test assesses the underlying theoretical construct it is intended to measure. According to Messick (1996), "a key issue for the content aspect of construct validity is the specification of the boundaries of the construct domain to be assessed" (p. 10). When the borders are too narrow, construct underrepresentation happens. For example, in an early discussion of construct validity, Camp challenged the use of indirect (multiple-choice) tests of writing on the grounds of construct underrepresentation, noting that such tests do not "evoke evidence of the students' ability to engage in complex performances" (Camp, 1993a, p. 184). Camp explains:

> Teachers and researchers in writing and writing instruction have argued that student writers should demonstrate their knowledge and skills not merely by recognizing correctness or error in text, as they do in multiple-choice tests of writing ability, but by engaging in the complex act of creating their own text.
>
> *(p. 187)*

According to Camp (1993b):

> The impromptu writing sample provides a demonstration of the writer's handling of both subskills for writing and the larger-order skills involved in actually composing text: generating and developing ideas, organizing, establishing connections within the text, and finding a tone and rhetorical stance appropriate to the topic and audience.
>
> *(p. 50)*

Camp also observed that using a writing sample in assessment "sends a clear message the writing performance is important, and that grammar and usage are not sufficient proxies for actual writing" (1993b, p. 50). In Chapter 1 we reviewed research showing that multiple-choice tests of writing led teachers to shift from teaching the writing process to using worksheets dealing with grammar, punctuation, and usage. In terms of Messick's unified theory of validity, such consequences would be considered threats to construct validity. Camp recognized, and construct validity requires, that the ways in which students complete a writing assessment should be consistent with what writing is understood to be if inferences are to be made about students' overall proficiency in writing.

The ultimate challenge of course, is that conceptualizations of writing have evolved. While writing was once characterized as a set of discrete skills, over time it came to be seen as a cognitive process operating in the production of a text, and still later, as a social, meaning-making activity that varies across contexts and purposes for writing (Camp, 1993b). Some scholars have suggested that these different views of the writing construct have led to different sorts of assessment. For example, Yancey (1999) describes three overlapping waves of assessment. The first wave focused on "indirect" multiple-choice tests of the sort challenged by Camp (1993b). Yancey describes an indirect test as "a test of something assumed to be related to the behavior, but not the behavior itself (e.g., items like comma usage questions and pronoun reference corrections)" (p. 486). The second wave foregrounded the holistically scored essay—the product resulting from a cognitive process. The third wave foregrounded portfolios, what Brossell (1986) character- ized as "multiple writing samples written on different occasions and in various rhetorical modes" (p. 179). The construct underlying Yancey's third wave clearly brings the social nature of writing into focus. We discuss the evolution of the writing construct in more detail in the next chapter because, as we have dem- onstrated here, the way the construct is defined has a profound impact on the validity of the test results.

Generalizability

The validity of the results of an assessment can be compromised when writing tasks and contexts are highly standardized as they are in traditional writing exams. Standardization creates an artificial environment that is not representative of writ- ing outside of the artificial testing context, a concern to which we will return in Chapter 6. A student may be able to write competently in testing conditions where tasks are standardized, the process is constrained, and other variables controlled as much as possible; however, it doesn't mean that the same student can write as well in different conditions. And, of course, students may perform well in less standardized conditions—e.g., in a classroom, in a community setting, or in a work environment— and not do well on the test. Both of these possibilities are problematic because the results of the assessment are not generalizable to other situations and tasks.

Kane (2013) explains that standardization of testing procedures, which is com- mon in large-scale high-stakes tests, can introduce systematic error:

> If performance does vary across task formats and we fix the task format in the test, then this difference between the universe of generalization and the target domain will introduce systematic error into estimates of the target score . . . the errors introduced by standardization constitute systematic errors associated with the underrepresentation of the target domain in the universe of generalization.
>
> (p. 30)

In other words, if performance varies across different task formats, as it does across different kinds or genres of writing, when we use a single format (or genre) in a test, we introduce systematic error that influences the accuracy of the measurement of the target domain.

Professional organizations have recognized that writing varies across situations in significant ways. The Writing Study Group of the NCTE Executive Committee, for example, described how writing varies according to its purpose:

> Writing is not just one practice or activity. A note to a cousin is not like a business report, which is different again from a poem. The processes and ways of thinking that lead to these varied kinds of texts can also vary widely, from the quick email to a friend to the careful drafting and redrafting of a legal contract. The different purposes and genres both grow out of and create varied relationships between the writers and the readers, and existing relationships are reflected in degrees of formality in language, as well as assumptions about what knowledge and experience are already shared, and what needs to be explained. Writing with certain purposes in mind, the writer focuses attention on what the audience is thinking or believing; other times, the writer focuses more on the information she or he is organizing, or on her or his own emergent thoughts and feelings. Therefore, the thinking, procedures, and physical format in writing are shaped in accord with the author's purpose(s), the needs of the audience, and the conventions of the genre.
>
> *(NCTE, 2016)*

Genres are socially constructed "typified rhetorical actions" (Miller, 1984). As Graham et al. (2016) point out, and research has revealed, "genres differ in terms of rhetorical structures, basic elements, and even the types of words students use" (p. 73). They note that research has also shown that "developing writers know more about some writing genres than others (Gillespie et al., 2013; Klein & Rose, 2010; Lin et al., 2007)" (Graham et al., 2016, p. 73). To the list of differences provided by Graham et al. (2016), we would add that genres differ in the processes writers use when they write. Consider, for instance, the difference between source-based writing and writing from personal experience. A source-based writing task requires different processes for gathering content. Beaufort (2008) notes that several studies in workplace writing show that processes vary depending upon the genre of the writing (e.g., Broadhead & Freed, 1986; Schumacher et al., 1989). Studies indicate that processes vary as well depending on situational variables such as the amount of time available (Beaufort, 1999; Couture & Rymer, 1993) and the "physical realities of the workplace" (Beaufort, 1999).

Genres also differ in the kinds of thinking they require. For example, Matsuhashi (1981, 1982) showed that the composing processes of writers were different when they were planning versus generalizing. Her observational data "suggest that students can report more efficiently than they can generalize" (Ruth & Murphy,

1988 p. 82). Ruth and Murphy (1988) observed that "evidence in the research literature suggests that narrative forms are mastered earlier and are acquired more easily than more abstract forms (Freedman & Pringle, 1980; Matsuhashi, 1981, Keech, 1982)" (p. 82). Clearly, some genres may be more difficult or mastered earlier than others depending on whether or when particular strategies for writing are taught. Early research on the effects of discourse and response mode on the measurement of writing proficiency indicates that "levels of performance vary on tasks presenting different writing purposes. . . . The findings suggest that generalizations about student writing competence must reference the particular discourse domain rather than the general domain of writing" (Quellmalz et al., 1982, pp. 255–266).

More recently, Bouwer et al. (2015), conducted a study designed to "(a) investigate and demonstrate the validity of inferences made on the basis of writing performance both within and across genres and (b) describe its implications for the assessment of writing proficiency" (2015, p. 84). To disentangle genre effects from topic effects, multiple tasks were collected for each of four different genres. The researchers concluded:

> Because the ability to write differs from genre to genre, generalizable inferences are not appropriate. In order to draw conclusions about writing in general, writing assessment should rather include multiple tasks in multiple genres rated by multiple raters.
>
> *(Bouwer et al., 2015, p. 98)*

The conclusion drawn by Bouwer et al. (2015) is supported by research. In their review of six studies involving high-stakes assessments, Graham et al. (2011a) report: "In each study, the writing quality scores for two or more genres of writing differed statistically for the tested students," indicating that "students' performance on one writing task is not identical to their performance on a different one" (p. 3). Further, in their review of five other studies involving high-stakes assessments, Graham et al. found that correlations between writing quality scores for different genres were small to moderate, leading them to conclude that "a single piece of writing on a high-stakes test is not an adequate measure of students' writing capabilities" (2011a, p. 3).

As Shavelson et al. (1989) explain, a score's "usefulness . . . largely depends on the extent to which it allows us to generalize accurately to behavior in some wider set of situations" (p. 922). In writing assessment, a single sample is clearly inadequate for drawing conclusions about overall writing proficiency. Research has revealed large task variances, which suggests that changes in the writing task will lead to changes in text quality (Brouwer et al., 2015). Put another way, research indicates that students perform better when writing to some tasks rather than others (Breland et al., 1987; Freedman, 1979; Kim et al., 2017) and when writing about subjects they know more about than others (e.g., Langer, 1983,

1984). They perform better on some genres or modes of writing than others (e.g., Bouwer et al., 2015; Crowhurst & Piche, 1979; Freedman & Pringle, 1980; Godshalk et al., 1966; Ingebrand, 2016; Moss et al., 1982; Pringle & Freedman, 1985; Van den Bergh et al., 2012: Veal & Tillman, 1971; Quellmalz et al., 1982), and they perform better when writing in some conditions (such as time for writing) than others (e.g., Cho, 2003; Polio et al., 1998; Herman et al., 1993).

Other research supports the position that multiple writing samples are needed to make reliable estimates of students' writing proficiency, although the precise numbers needed appear to vary for different populations of students and writing elements. For example, Huang (2008) found that three writing tasks scored by two raters were needed to provide a reliable estimate of the quality of typically developing high school seniors' writing, but that five tasks were needed to obtain a reliable estimate of the writing of at-risk students. Chen et al. (2007) found that depending upon the variance from student by rater interaction, "three to five essays" were "required to evaluate and make reliable judgment of student writing performance" of ninth grade students who read self-selected and assigned stories (p. 13). In their investigation of the writing of second and third grade struggling writers, Graham et al. (2016) found that 14 writing tasks would be required to obtain an acceptable level of reliability for total number of words, 8 writing tasks for vocabulary diversity, and 11 for writing quality (p. 78).

This brief look at the literature on generalizability suggests that a number of different variables may influence the generalizability of writing tasks, including the age and abilities of the writers as well as the conditions of the assessment. What is consistent, however, is the conclusion that more than one sample is needed. As Graham et al. (2011a) put it, "writing assessments need to be based on multiple writing samples, as students' performance . . . cannot be accurately reflected through a single piece of writing" (p. 27). Similarly, Schoonen (2012) concluded, "Using multiple tasks in the assessment seems inevitable to reach an acceptable level of generalizability" (p. 15). Likewise, Bouwer et al. (2015) argue, "Because the ability to write differs from genre to genre, generalizable inferences are not appropriate. In order to draw conclusions about writing proficiency in general, writing assessment should rather include multiple tasks in multiple genres" (p. 98). The results of these many studies support the idea that proficiency is to some degree context-bound, a circumstance that is, as Chalhoub-Deville says, "difficult to reconcile with the tester's need for score generalizability" (2003, p. 369). The results also support Anastasi's (1986) contention that "in order to identify broad traits, we have to assess individuals across situations and aggregate the results" (p. 9) and Cronbach et al.'s (1972) observation: "[T]he ideal datum on which to base [a] decision would be something like the person's mean score over all acceptable observations" (p. 15).

The research reviewed here has implications for validity. Messick explains that "the meaning of the construct is tied to the range of tasks and situations that it generalizes and transfers to" (Messick, 1994a, p. 15). And Koretz (2017) reminds us that "the items on a test matter *only to the extent that they allow us to predict mastery of the larger subject area from which they are sampled*" (p. 13; emphasis in original). Airasian and Madaus (1983) put the issue this way:

> Simply put, a test is a sample of behaviors from a domain about which a user wishes to make inferences. Test items are important only insofar as they permit the user to make valid inferences about the larger domain of interest.
>
> *(p. 104)*

If the domain is writing, then the test needs to adequately represent writing through sampling. If writing as a construct is not well represented in a test, then the results are not valid in terms of making broad and general statements about students' writing proficiency.

Multiple writing tasks, whether in the form of a portfolio or multiple essay exams, make assessment results stronger representations of a student's writing abilities. Portfolio advocates have long argued that the ability to include multiple samples, written in different genres for different purposes and audiences, in different contexts, using various processes allow for a more comprehensive picture of a student's writing abilities (e.g., Murphy & Smith, 1992; Yancey, 1992; Hamp-Lyons & Condon, 2000). As Greenberg (1992) concluded, "Portfolio evaluation is probably the most valid means of assessing writing available" because it allows for the assessment of "composing and revising across a wide range of communicative contexts and tasks (Camp 'The Writing Folder')," and is "more relevant to our theories about the construct of writing and to our classroom practices" than other writing assessment methods (pp. 15–16).

Taken together, the studies reviewed here show that traditional assessment practices can significantly lag behind best practices in assessment, a situation that gives cause for concern. For example, Jeffery (2009) points out that although state writing standards typically promote the importance of exposing students to a variety of written forms, "most direct writing assessments designed to measure student progress meeting these standards hold students 'accountable' for only one writing type" (p. 6). As Graham et al. say, "High-stakes writing assessment as currently conceptualized and conducted is not defensible" (2011a, p. 2).

Implications for rebuilding the system

A first step toward reforming the system would be to eliminate, wherever possible, the high stakes attached to so many of our tests. As the research reviewed thus far has revealed, high-stakes testing often leads to negative consequences to the curriculum. In many instances it has misled the public into believing schools are improving when in fact they have not (Koretz, 2017). Of course, there may always be high stakes attached to some tests, such as those used in making decisions about admission to college, but even this practice has begun to be challenged by well-respected universities and lawsuits. According to Camera (2019), Senior Education Writer for *World Report News*, "more than 1,000 four-year colleges and universities do not require applicants to submit an SAT or ACT score as part of its admissions process" (para 7). In other words, students have the choice of whether or not to submit test scores when they apply. Some of these institutions are highly selective, elite research universities known for their rigorous academic programs, universities such as the University of California Berkeley and the University of Chicago. For example, as of this writing, six of the nine undergraduate campuses of the University of California campus have gone test optional. Three of the UC campuses (Berkeley, Irvine, and Santa Cruz) decided not to accept test scores at all. In addition, a "first of its kind" lawsuit filed by Public Counsel and The National Center for Fair & Open Testing has challenged the use of ACT/SAT test scores in admission decisions on the grounds that they are "demonstrably discriminatory against the . . . least privileged students, the very students who would most benefit from higher education" (Camera, 2019, para 2). By 2020, 1,600 colleges were test-optional (Tate, 2020; Fair Test, 2021). Many of these colleges may have changed their admission policies in reaction to the challenges of taking the SATs and ACTs safely during the pandemic (Daniel, 2021). However, many others have moved toward more permanent revisions of their admissions policies, including the various campuses of the University of California system as noted earlier.

Using high-stakes tests to evaluate teachers has also been challenged. Koretz (2017) has documented the absurd practices undertaken in response to mandates to base evaluations on test scores, such as "evaluating teachers based on the performance of students they don't even teach, often in subjects they don't teach, and sometimes in different schools" (p. 3). Koretz also shows how draconian policies and the state tests required by NCLB led to the misclassification of some schools as "low-performing" and being then "subject to a series of escalating sanctions" when other highly respected tests such as NAEP and TIMSS indicated top levels of achievement. Koretz concludes:

> Test-based accountability has become an end in itself in American education, unmoored from clear thinking about what should be measured, how it should be measured, or how testing can fit into a rational plan for evaluating and improving our schools.
>
> *(2017, p. 5)*

Clearly, high stakes testing leaves much to be desired. According to Fair Test, a national organization for fair and open testing, high-stakes testing "is unfair to many students," "leads to increased grade retention and dropping out," "produces teaching to the test," "drives out good teachers," and "misinforms the public" (2007, pp. 1–2). These are all good reasons for eliminating high stakes. But in addition to eliminating the kinds of stakes that make tests ripe for manipulation, an equally important step toward reforming the system would be to design and develop assessments that produce valid results.

For writing assessments to produce valid results, the construct of writing needs to be adequately represented in the assessment. The challenge, of course, is that theories evolve. Kane (2013) explains that assessment practices also change as theories evolve:

> Theories are likely to develop and evolve over time, and since the interpretation of a theoretical construct depends on its defining theory, the interpretation of indicators of these constructs will develop and evolve with the theory. If the evidence for the theory increases, confidence in the theory as a whole, including confidence in the appropriateness of the indicators, is likely to increase. If the theory is extended to account for a wider range of phenomena, the interpretation also expands. The extension of the theory to new types of phenomena will necessarily require additional evidence to support the broader application of the theory.
>
> *(p. 41)*

Unfortunately, our assessment practices have not kept pace with the evolution of our theories of literacy. In the next chapter, we explore the theoretical construct of writing more fully and describe ways it has evolved and expanded through the influence of social perspectives on literacy. We argue that we need to remodel the assessment system so it is in line with current theories of literacy and promotes effective teaching practices. Remodeling the system requires starting with a robust construct of writing, one that takes the variability of writing across different contexts, conditions, and purposes into account.

References

Adams, P. D. (1993). Basic writing reconsidered. *Journal of Basic Writing*, *12*(1), 22–36.

Agnew, E., & McLaughlin, M. (1999). Basic writing class of '93 five years later: How the academic paths of blacks and whites diverged. *Journal of Basic Writing*, *18*(1), 40–54.

Agnew, E., & McLaughlin, M. (2001). Those crazy gates and how they swing: Tracking the system that tracks African-American students. In G. McNenny & S. H. Fitzgerald (Eds.), *Mainstreaming basic writers politics and pedagogies of access* (pp. 85–100). Lawrence Erlbaum.

Airasian, P. W., & Madaus, G. F. (1983). Linking testing and instruction: Policy issues. *Journal of Educational Measurement*, *20*(2), 103–118.

American Educational Research Association, American Psychological Association, & National Council on Measurement in Education. (2014). *The standards for educational and psychological testing*. American Educational Research Association.

Anastasi, A. (1986). Evolving concepts of test validation. *Annual Review of Psychology*. www.psycholosphere.com/Evolving%20concepts%20of%20test%20validation%20by%20Anastasi%202.pdf

Beaufort, A. (1999). *Writing in the real world: Making the transition from school to work*. Teachers College Press.

Beaufort, A. (2008). Writing in the professions. In C. Bazerman (Ed.), *Handbook of research on writing: History, society, school, individual, text* (pp. 221–235). Routledge.

Bouwer, R., Beguin, A., Sanders, T., & Van den Bergh, H. (2015). Effect of genre on the generalizability of writing scores. *Language Testing, 32*(1), 83–100.

Breland, H. M., Camp, R., & Jones, R. J. (1987). *Assessing writing skill*. Research Monograph No. 11. College Board.

Broadhead, G. J., & Freed, R. (1986). *The variables of composition: Process and product in a business setting*. Southern Illinois University Press.

Brossell, G. (1986). Current research and unanswered questions in writing assessment. In K. Greenberg, H. Wiener, & R. Donovan (Eds.), *Writing assessment: Issues and strategies* (pp. 168–183). Longman.

Brown, J. D. (2000). What is construct validity. *Shiken: JALT Testing & Evaluation SIG Newsletter, 4*(2), 8–12. https://hosted.jalt.org/test/PDF/Brown8.pdf

Callahan, S. (1997). Tests worth taking?: Using portfolios for accountability in Kentucky. *Research in the Teaching of English, 31*(3), 295–336.

Callahan, S. (1999). All done with the best of intentions: One Kentucky high school after six years of state portfolio tests. *Assessing Writing, 6*(1), 5–40.

Camera, L. (2019, December 10). Lawsuit against university of California system challenges SAT, ACT admissions requirement. *U.S. News*. www.usnews.com/news/education-news/articles/2019-12-10/lawsuit-against-university-of-california-system-challenges-sat-act-admissions-requirement

Camp, R. (1993a). The place of portfolios in our changing views of writing assessment. In R. E. Bennett & W. C. Ward (Eds.), *Construction versus choice in cognitive measurement: Issues in constructed response, performance testing, and portfolio assessment* (pp. 183–212). Lawrence Erlbaum.

Camp, R. (1993b). Changing the model for the direct assessment of writing. In M. Williamson & B. Huot (Eds.), *Validating holistic scoring for writing assessment* (pp. 45–78). Hampton Press.

Campbell, D. T. (1976). *Assessing the impact of planned social change*. Public Affairs Center, Dartmouth College.

Chalhoub-Deville, M. (2003). Second language interaction: current perspectives and future trends. *Language Testing, 20*(4), 369–383.

Chen, E., Niemi, D., Wang, J., Wang, H., & Mirocha, J. (2007). *Examining the generalizability of direct writing assessment tasks*. Report No. CSE. 718. National Center for Research on Evaluation, Standards, and Student Testing.

Cho, Y. (2003). Assessing writing: Are we bound by only one method? *Assessing Writing, 8*(3), 165–191.

Cizek, G. J., Bowen, D., & Church, K. (2010). Sources of validity evidence for educational and psychological tests: A follow-up study. *Educational and Psychological Measurement, 70*(5), 731–743.

Coburn, C., Toure, J., & Yamashita, M. (2009). Evidence, interpretation, and persuasion: Instructional decision making at the district central office. *Teachers College Record, 111*(4), 1115–1161.

Couture, B., & Rymer, J. (1993). Composing processes on the job by writer's role and task value. In R. Spilka (Ed.), *Writing in the workplace* (pp. 4–20). Southern Illinois University Press.

Cronbach, L. J. (1988). Five perspectives on validity argument. In H. Wainer & H. Braun (Eds.), *Test validity* (pp. 3–17). Erlbaum.

Cronbach, L. J., Gleser, G. C., Nanda, H., & Rajaratnam, N. (1972). *The dependability of behavioral measurements: Theory of generalizability of scores and profiles.* Wiley.

Crowhurst, M., & Piche, G. L. (1979). Audience and mode of discourse effects on syntactic complexity in writing at two grade levels. *Research in the Teaching of English, 13,* 101–109.

Daniel, M. (2021). *Test optional colleges: Lots of colleges NOT requiring SAT scores.* www.collegelifetoday.com/blog/tips/college-not-requiring-sat

Dappen, L., Isernhagen, J., & Anderson, S. (2008). A statewide writing assessment model: Student proficiency and future implications. *Assessing Writing, 13*(1), 45–60.

David, J. L. (2011). Research says . . ./high-stakes testing narrows the curriculum. *Educational Leadership, 68*(6), 78–80.

FairTest. (2007). *The dangerous consequences of high-stakes standardized testing.* www.fairtest.org/dangerous-consequences-highstakes-standardized-tes

FairTest. (2021). *1600+ accredited, 4-year colleges & universities with ACT/SAT-optional testing policies for fall, 2022 admissions.* www.fairtest.org/schools-do-not-use-sat-or-act-scores-admitting-substantial-numbers-students-bachelor-degree-programs

Freedman, A., & Pringle, I. (1980). *The writing abilities of a representative sample of grade 5, 8, and 12 students: The Carleton writing project (Part 2. Final report).* Carleton Board of Education. https://eric.ed.gov/?id=ED217413

Freedman, S. W. (1979). How characteristics of student essays influence teachers' evaluation. *Journal of Educational Psychology, 71*(3), 328–338.

Godshalk, F. I., Swineford, F., & Coffman, W. E. (1966). *The measurement of writing ability.* College Entrance Examination Board. https://doi.org/10.1002/1520-6807(196701)4:1<93::AID-PITS2310040126>3.0.CO;2-Y

Goodwin, B. (2014, March). Research says/better tests don't guarantee better instruction. *Educational Leadership, 71*(6), 78–80. www.ascd.org/el/articles/better-tests-dont-guarantee-better-instruction

Graham, S., Harris, K. R., & Hebert, M. (2011b). *Informing writing: The benefits of formative assessment.* Report from the Carnegie Corporation of New York. Alliance for Excellent Education.

Graham, S., Hebert, M., & Harris, K. R. (2011a). Throw em out or make em better? State and district high-stakes writing assessments. *Focus on Exceptional Children, 44*(1), 1–12.

Graham, S., Hebert, M., Sandbank, M. P., & Harris, K. R. (2016). Assessing the writing achievement of young struggling writers: Application of generalizability theory. *Learning Disability Quarterly, 39*(2), 72–82.

Greenberg, K. (1992). Validity and reliability issues in the direct assessment of writing. *Writing Program Administration, 16*(1–2 F/W), 7–22. http://associationdatabase.co/archives/16n1-2/16n1-2greenberg.pdf

Haertel, E. (2013). How is testing supposed to improve schooling? *Measurement, 11*(1), 1–18. https://doi.org/10.1080/15366367.2013.783752

Hamp-Lyons, L., & Condon, W. (2000). *Assessing the portfolio: Principles for practice, Theory and research.* Hampton Press.

Herman, J. L., Gearhart, J., & Baker, E. (1993). Assessing writing portfolios: Issues in the validity and meaning of scores. *Educational Assessment, 1*(3), 201–224.

Hillocks, G. (2002). *The testing trap: How state writing assessments control learning.* Teachers College Press.

Hillocks, G. (2003). How state assessments lead to vacuous thinking and writing. *Journal of Writing Assessment, 1*(1), 5–21.

Huang, J. (2008). How accurate are ESL students' holistic writing scores on large-scale assessments? A generalizability theory approach. *Assessing Writing, 13*(3), 201–218.

Huot, B. (1990). The literature of direct writing assessment: Major concerns and prevailing trends. *Review of Educational Research, 60*(2), 237–263.

Ingebrand, S. W. (2016). *The development of writing skills: The use of genre-specific elements in second and third grade students' writing* [Doctoral Dissertation, Arizona State University]. https://core.ac.uk/download/pdf/79584998.pdf

Jeffery, J. (2009). Constructs of writing proficiency in U.S. state and national writing assessments: Exploring variability. *Assessing Writing, 14*(1), 3–24.

Kane, M. T. (2006). Validation. In R. L. Brennan (Ed.). *Educational measurement* (4th ed., pp. 17–64). Praeger.

Kane, M. T. (2013). Validating the interpretations and uses of test scores. *Journal of Educational Measurement, 50*(1), 1–73.

Kane, M. T. (2015). Adapting accountability systems to the limitations of educational measurement. *Measurement, 13,* 44–48. https://doi.org/10.1080/15366367.2015.10 16336

Kane, M. T. (2016a). Explicating validity. *Assessment in Education: Principles, Policy & Practice, 23*(2), 198–211.

Kane, M. T. (2016b). Validity as the evaluation of the claims based on test scores. *Assessment in Education: Principles, Policy & Practice, 23*(2), 309–311.

Kim, Y. G., Schatschneider, C., Wanzek, J., Gatlin, B., & Al Otaiba, S. (2017). Writing evaluation: Rater and task effects on the reliability of writing scores for children in grades 3 and 4. *Reading and Writing: An Interdisciplinary Journal, 30*(6), 1287–1310. https://doi.org/10.1007/s11145-017-9724-6

Koretz, D. (2015). Adapting measurement to the demands of test-based accountability: Focus article. *Measurement, 13*(1), 1–25. https://doi.org/10.10801/15366367.2015.1 000712

Koretz, D. (2017). *The testing charade: Pretending to make schools better.* University of Chicago Press.

Langer, J. (1983). *Effects of topic knowledge on the quality and coherence of informational writing.* ED 234 418. https://files.eric.ed.gov/fulltext/ED234418.pdf

Langer, J. (1984). The effects of available information on responses to school writing tasks. *Research in the Teaching of English, 18*(1), 27–44.

Linn, R. L. (1997). Evaluating the validity of assessments: The consequences of use. *Educational Measurement: Issues and Practice, 16*(2), 14–16.

Madaus, G. F. (1994). A technological and historical consideration of equity issues associated with proposals to change the nation's testing policy. *Harvard Educational Review, 64*(1), 76–96. https://doi.org/10.17763/haer.64.1.4q87663r0j76rwv1

Matsuhashi, A. (1981). Pausing and planning: The tempo of written discourse production. *Research in the Teaching of English, 15*(2), 113–134.

Matsuhashi, A. (1982). Explorations in the real-time production of written discourse. In M. Nystrand (Ed.), *What writers know: The language, process and structure of written discourse* (pp. 269–290). Academic Press.

Mehrens, W. A. (1997). The consequences of consequential validity. *Educational Measurement: Issues and Practice, 16*(2), 16–18.

Messick, S. (1989a). Meaning and values in test validation: The science and ethics of assessment. *Educational Researcher, 18*(2), 5–11.

Messick, S. (1989b). Validity. In R. L. Linn (Ed.), *Educational measurement* (3rd ed., pp. 13–103). Macmillan.

Messick, S. (1994a). The interplay of evidence and consequences in the validation of performance assessments. *Educational Researcher, 23*(2), 13–23.

Messick, S. (1994b). *Validity of psychological assessment: Validation of inferences from person's responses and performances as scientific inquiry into score meaning.* Research Report. ERIC No. ED 380496. Educational Testing Service.

Messick, S. (1996). *Validity and washback in language testing.* Research Report. ERIC No. ED403277. Educational Testing Service.

Miller, C. (1984). Genre as social action. *Quarterly Journal of Speech, 70*(2), 151–167.

Moss, P. A. (1994). Can there be validity without reliability? *Educational Researcher, 23*(2), 5–12. https://doi.org/10.3102/0013189X023002005

Moss, P. A. (2016). Shifting the focus of validity for test use. *Assessment in Education: Principles, Policy & Practice, 23*(2), 236–251.

Moss, P. A., Cole, N. S., & Khampalikit, C. (1982). A comparison of procedures to assess written language skills at grades 4, 7, and 10. *Journal of Educational Measurement, 19*(1), 37–47.

Murphy, S., & Smith, M. A. (1992). *Writing portfolios: A bridge from teaching to assessment.* Pippin Publishing Limited.

National Council of Teachers of English. (2016). *NCTE Beliefs about the teaching of writing.* https://ncte.org/statement/teaching-writing/

O'Neill, P. (2003). Moving beyond holistic scoring through validity inquiry. *Journal of Writing Assessment, 1*(1), 47–65.

Parke, C., Lane, S., & Stone, C. (2006). Impact of a state performance assessment program in reading and writing. *Educational Research and Evaluation, 12*(3), 239–269.

Parkes, J. (2007). Reliability as argument. *Educational Measurement: Issues and Practice, 26*(4), 2–10.

Plake, B. S., & Wise, L. L. (2014). What is the role and importance of the revised AERA, APA, NCME Standards for Educational and Psychological Testing? *Educational Measurement: Issues and Practice, 33*(4), 4–12.

Polio, C., Fleck, C., & Leder, N. (1998). If only I had more time: ESL learners' changes in linguistic accuracy on essay revisions. *Journal of Second Language Writing, 7*(1), 43–68.

Popham, W. J. (1997). Consequential validity: Right concern—wrong concept. *Educational Measurement: Issues and Practice, 16*(2), 9–13.

Pringle, I., & Freedman, A. (1985). *A comparative study of writing abilities in two modes at the grade 5, 8, and 12 levels.* Ministry of Education. https://eric.ed.gov/?id=ED258202

Quellmalz, E. S., Capell, F. J., & Chou, C. (1982). Effects of discourse and response mode on the measurement of writing competence. *Journal of Educational Measurement, 19*(4), 241–258. https://doi.org/10.1111/j.1745-3984.1982.tb00131.x

Ruth, L., & Murphy, S. (1988). *Designing writing tasks for the assessment of writing.* Ablex.

Sackstein, S. (2015, August 9). The arts: One more victim of common core testing—part 2. *Education Week.* www.edweek.org/education/opinion-the-arts-one-more-victim-of-common-core-testing-part-2/2015/08

Schoonen, R. (2012). The validity and generalizability of writing scores: The effect of rater, task and language. In E. van Steendam, M. Tillema, G. Rijlaarsdam, & H. van den Bergh (Eds.), *Measuring writing: Recent insights into theory, methodology and practice* (pp. 1–22). Koninklijke Brill NV.

Schumacher, G. M., Scott, B. T., Klare, G. R., Cronin, F. C., & Lambert, D. A. (1989). Cognitive processes in journalistic genres. *Written Communication, 6*(3), 390–407.

Shavelson, R. J., Webb, N. W., & Rowley, G. L. (1989). Generalizability theory. *American Psychologist, 44*(6), 922–932.

Shepard, L. A. (1997). The centrality of test use and consequences for test validity. *Educational Measurement: Issues and Practice, 16*(2), 5–8, 13.

Shepard, L. A. (2016). Evaluating test validity: Reprise and progress. *Assessment in Education: Principles, Policy & Practice, 23*(2), 268–280. https://doi.org/10.1080/0969594X.2016.1141168

Skerrett, A. (2010). "There's going to be community. There's going to be knowledge": Designs for learning in a standardized age. *Teaching and Teacher Education, 26,* 648–655.

Skerrett A., & Hargreaves, A. (2008). Student diversity and secondary school change in a context of increasingly standardized reform. *American Education Research Journal, 45*(4), 913–945.

Slomp, D. H., Corrigan, J. A., & Sugimoto, T. (2014). A framework for using consequential validity evidence in evaluating large-scale writing assessments: A Canadian study. *Research in the Teaching of English, 48*(3), 276–302.

Smith, W. L. (1993). Assessing the reliability and adequacy of using holistic scoring of essays as a college composition placement technique. In M. Williamson & B. Huot (Eds.), *Validating holistic scoring for writing assessment: Theoretical and empirical foundations* (pp. 142–205). Hampton Press.

Spalding, E., & Cummins, G. (1998). It was the best of times: It was a waste of time: University of Kentucky students' view of writing under KERA. *Assessing Writing, 5*(2), 167–200.

Tate, E. (2020). *1,600 colleges are now test-optional: How many will go back?* www.edsurge.com/news/2020-09-25-1-600-colleges-are-now-test-optional-how-many-will-go-back

Tsagari, D. (2007). *Review of washback in language testing: How has it been done? What more needs doing?* https://files.eric.ed.gov/fulltext/ED497709.pdf

Van den Bergh, H., Maeyer, S., Van Weijen, D., & Tillema, M. (2012). Generalizability of text quality scores. In E. Van Steendam, M. Tillema, G. Rijlaarsdam, & H. van den Bergh (Eds.), *Measuring writing: Recent insights into theory, methodology and practice* (Vol. 27, pp. 23–32). Brill. https://doi.org/10.1163/9789004248489_003

Veal, L. R., & Tillman, M. (1971). Mode of discourse variation in the evaluation of children's writing. *Research in the Teaching of English, 5*(1), 37–45.

Wiliam, D. (2014). What do teachers need to know about the new standards for educational and psychological testing? *Educational Measurement: Issues and Practices, 33*(4), 29–30.

Williamson, M. M. (1993). An introduction to holistic scoring: The social, historical and theoretical context for writing assessment. In M. Williamson & B. Huot (Eds.), *Validating holistic scoring for writing assessment: Theoretical and empirical foundations* (pp. 1–44). Hampton Press.

Williamson, M. M. (2003). Validity of automated scoring: Prologue for a continuing discussion of machine scoring student writing. *Journal of Writing Assessment, 1*(2), 85–104.

Wolcott, W. (1994). A longitudinal study of six developmental students' performance in reading and writing. *Journal of Basic Writing, 13*(1), 14–40. https://doi.org/10.37514/JBW-J.1994.13.1.05

Yancey, K. B. (Ed.). (1992). *Portfolios in the writing classroom: An introduction.* National Council of Teachers of English.

Yancey, K. B. (1999). Looking back as we look forward: Historicizing writing assessment. *College Composition and Communication, 50*(3), 483–503.

Zheng, Y. Klinger, D. A., Cheng, L., Fox, J., & Doe, C. (2011). Test-takers' background, literacy activities, and views of the Ontario Secondary School Literacy Test. *Alberta Journal of Educational Research, 57*, 115–136.

3
HOW HAVE THEORIES OF WRITING AND LEARNING EVOLVED?

As we explained in our introduction to Chapter 2, remodeling a house requires renovators remove old, dysfunctional, and outdated parts of the structure. Remodeling also demands recognition of the impact of new technologies—including changes in materials, equipment, functions, and uses, as well as a sense of how these may be evolving. As we consider how to renovate and rebuild our writing assessment system, we want to think about not just meeting our current needs but creating an assessment system that will serve us well into the future. We need to use knowledge gleaned from theories, research, and practice, and address what that knowledge reveals about the limitations of current practices in assessment of writing.

In this chapter we examine theories of writing and learning and consider the influence of sociocultural theories on our understanding of writing and learning to write. We review research on writing and learning and argue that we need to build assessments aligned with what we now know about best practices in teaching. To do this, we are mindful of the advice of Adler-Kassner and Wardle (2015), in their useful collection *Naming What We Know: Threshold Concepts of Writing Studies*. They advise:

> If we want to positively impact the lives of writers and writing teachers, we must do a better job of clearly stating what our field knows and helping others understand how to use that knowledge as they set policy, create programs, design and fund assessments, and so on.
>
> *(p. 7)*

To this end, we draw on the rich history of research in literacy, writing, and learning to argue for a complex view of writing, and we discuss its implications

DOI: 10.4324/9781003296140-3

for teaching, learning, and assessment. As we have explained in Chapter 2, a complex view of writing raises critical issues for assessment, since the validity of any assessment ultimately rests on its alignment with the theoretical construct it purports to measure (Williamson, 1993; Messick, 1989).

Over the past several decades, researchers and scholars have developed a substantial body of work that has explored writing as a construct, showing that writing is quite complex. In this chapter, we present a working framework for thinking about writing constructs and the teaching, learning, and assessment of writing that draws on this work. Writing, unsurprisingly, resists a simple or single definition, or for that matter, a single theoretical perspective. In fact, there are multiple theoretical perspectives on writing, and they are moving targets that are still evolving.

To describe the multifaceted nature of writing, we organize related conceptualizations of writing into two broad descriptive categories, one emphasizing individual perspectives and the other social ones, and describe how they have evolved over time. The borders of these categories are not firm or stable; in fact, in action, they are fluid and changing, sometimes overlapping, sometimes operating in tandem. Like Law (2007), we acknowledge that it is impossible to map what we are studying precisely and definitively because what we are attempting to map is "a slippery phenomenon," one that changes "its shape" and is "fuzzy around the edges" (p. 598). The collection of conceptualizations we discuss does not represent a complete description of writing. We highlight these particular conceptualizations in our discussion because they are reflected in teaching practices and because they raise significant issues about current assessment practices. The conceptualization of writing makes a difference in how it is taught and assessed. As Ivanic (2004) explains, different "configurations of beliefs and practices in relation to the teaching of writing . . . lead to particular forms of situated action, to particular decisions, choices and omissions" (p. 220).

In the *individual* category in our working framework, writing is characterized as the embodied act of a writer. Here the focus is on the knowledge and skills that an individual acquires over time as well as the process an individual uses when writing. In the *social* category, writing is viewed as a social achievement that is "made and sustained through human relationships" and by "organized practices through which the activity of writing takes its meanings" (Bazerman et al., 2018, p. 9). Based on the work of social and cultural anthropologists, sociologists, educational ethnographers, sociolinguists and linguists, as well as composition theorists and educators, a *social* perspective defines reading and writing "as social and cultural practices" (Bloome & Katz, 1997, p. 206). As Bloome and Katz (1997) explain, this view of literacy invariably involves social relationships:

> Any time people are involved in reading or writing, they are constructing at least two sets of social relationships. They are establishing social relationships between themselves as readers and author(s) and they are establishing

social relationships among the people present in the reading or writing event itself.

(p. 206)

In addition to focusing on social relationships, a social perspective on literacy focuses attention on the varying demands of different contexts of participation, including contexts in the worlds of work and daily life, as well as "students' acculturation into disciplinary and subject-based discourses and genres" in the world of academia (Lea & Street, 2006, p. 369). The social also draws attention to the "situated power relations involved in writing" (Kamberelis & De La Luna, 2004, p. 240).

In the last several decades, the educational field at large has grown much more focused on the social aspects of literacy. Among others, scholars such as Broadfoot (1996), Cope and Kalantzis (1993), Gipps (1999), Street (1995), and Bazerman and Prior (2004) have transformed our view of writing and how to teach and assess it. While writing was once viewed as if it were a set of discrete skills, contemporary theories now characterize it as a socially mediated process that varies in important ways across different cultures, discourse communities, contexts, and purposes for writing.

Borrowing a metaphor from Yancey's 1999 essay, we think of these categories as something like waves, although not necessarily as waves that have arrived and receded in sequence. Rather, each wave, whenever it arrives, builds and contributes to what we know about writing and learning to write, leaving behind valuable insights as it is overtaken, absorbed, and transformed by new waves. In our discussion of conceptualizations of writing, we explain how social ways of viewing writing have led the field to reconsider and revise theories that cast writing as a purely individual endeavor.

In developing our framework, the work of several scholars in particular influenced our thinking about ways to categorize what we know about writing. For example, Lea and Street (1998, 2006) describe three conceptualizations of literacy, one that reflects a focus on writing as an *individual* activity and two that reflect a focus on the *social*. The first, "study skills," reflects an *individual perspective* and casts literacy as "a set of atomized skills which students have to learn and which are then transferable to other contexts" (Lea & Street, 1998, p. 158). The second, "academic socialization," sees the task of teachers as inducting "students into a new 'culture,' that of the academy" (1998, p. 158). The third, called "academic literacies," "treats reading and writing as social practices that vary with context, culture, and genre" (Lea & Street, 2006, p. 368).

Presenting an elaborate and complex framework for thinking about literacy, Ivanic (2004) describes a multilayered view of different aspects of language that includes text, cognitive processes, events, and sociocultural and political contexts. She then sorts beliefs about writing and learning to write into categories of "discourses," that is, "constellations of beliefs about writing, beliefs about learning to write, ways of talking about writing, and the sorts of approaches to teaching and assessment which are likely to be associated with these beliefs" (Ivanic, 2004, p. 224). Ivanic's six discourses include skills, creativity, process, genre, and social practices discourses, as well as a sociopolitical discourse. Her framework attends to aspects of writing that emphasize both the *individual* and the *social context*. Each of these different conceptualizations has implications for policies, teaching programs, and assessments.

While we rely on the work of these scholars in developing our own approach, we also incorporate recent research on the teaching of writing in our discussion. Researchers and scholars have defined writing theoretically in very different ways that have evolved, generally moving from a focus on individual writers and the characteristics of their texts and processes toward a focus on the social context in which writing occurs. Over time, writing has been viewed and taught, among other things, as a set of skills, as a product, as a process, as creative expression, as purposeful communication, as reading and writing (and speaking and listening) woven together, as an element of multimodal literacy, and as socially constructed. In reality, writing is all of these things. But each perspective provides a somewhat different, but nonetheless important, lens for thinking about how we might design more effective writing programs and assessments.

Conceptions of writing: shifting toward the social

Writing as a set of skills

According to Ivanic (2004), "skills approaches" to teaching "focus on the autonomous linguistic 'skills' of correct handwriting, spelling, punctuation and sentence structure" (p. 227). As she explains:

> Underlying a great deal of policy and practice in literacy education is a fundamental belief that writing consists of applying knowledge of a set of linguistic patterns and rules for sound-symbol relationships and sentence construction. At its most extreme, this is a belief that writing is a unitary context-free activity, in which the same patterns and rules apply to all writing.
>
> *(p. 227)*

Although a purely skills approach to teaching writing has well-known limitations as a stand-alone theoretical construct for teaching, it does offer ways to break down the text into smaller units—such as sentences and paragraphs—in order to make rhetorical moves more visible and accessible to novice writers. Focusing on rhetorical moves as opposed to grammar, correctness, and conventions represents a shift toward a social perspective on writing. The shift can be seen in how some scholars now define "skills" and "knowledge." As noted earlier, a narrow view of skills might focus only on "autonomous linguistic skills." A more expansive social-contextual view of skills would include the ability to draw on social-contextual aspects of knowledge, including genre knowledge, rhetorical knowledge, and discourse community knowledge (Beaufort, 2007) in making choices about what language to use. This view situates decisions about correctness, for example, in relation to the audience, context, and genre. Although skills approaches once favored autonomous skills, the shift toward social perspectives on writing has made it clear that writing, as Beaufort says, "is a complex cognitive and social activity" that involves both "mental processes" as well "contextual knowledge" (2007, p. 8).

Writing as a product

The focus on writing as a product is often associated with the traditional modes of discourse (narration, description, exposition, and argument). As Durst and Newell (1989) explained, the modes came to be seen as static structures, perhaps because "influential 19th century rhetoricians (e.g., Bain, 1866; Wendell, 1891) were interested primarily in the study of classical texts," an emphasis that "directed attention to the form and logic of the written product rather than the processes involved in its creation" (Durst & Newell, 1989, p. 376).

A focus on writing as a product also goes hand in hand with the skills approach to teaching described by Ivanic (2004). According to Ivanic, the "skills discourse of writing . . . focuses on the product" and is linked to "a belief that writing is a unitary, context-free activity, in which the same patterns and rules apply to all writing" and "the belief that writing is a set of text-types" (pp. 226–227). The writing as a product perspective leads to a focus on form, particular patterns of organization, syntactical and grammatical structures, correctness, accuracy, and control, which by the way, are features of the text that can be analyzed—and for that matter, easily scored.

While the writing as product perspective appears to have had wide influence in assessment circles, there are other, more social-contextual ways to analyze texts that resonate with an assessment as inquiry approach. For example, arguing that "texts are indexical—pointing to the context in which they have concrete meanings and function," Kamberelis and De La Luna (2004) explain that "paying careful attention to the formal (and semiotic) properties of texts can tell us a lot not only about the internal organization of the texts themselves but also about their authors, contexts of use, audiences, and so on" (p. 241). Research on intertextuality also reflects a shift toward social-contextual perspectives. For example, commenting on different levels of intertextuality, Bazerman (2004b) points out, "By using certain implicitly recognizable kinds of language, phrasing and genres, every text evokes particular social worlds where such language and language forms are used" (p. 87).

Writing as a process

The idea of writing as a process took the field of writing studies by storm during the 1970s and 80s. From this perspective, writing consists of composing processes in the writer's mind, and their practical realization in text. Early on, Murray (1972) described the writing process itself in three stages: prewriting, "everything that takes place before the first draft"; writing, "the act of producing a first draft"; and rewriting, a "reconsideration of subject, form, and audience" (p. 4). Later on, Flower and Hayes (1981) described writing as a recursive cognitive process of *planning*, taking into account the writing assignment and information from long-term memory; *translating*, which generates text in light of the plan for the text; *reviewing* the text produced so far, which includes revising and editing; and *monitoring*, which entails metacognitive processes that coordinate the planning, translating, and reviewing processes.

Various scholars critiqued early writing process models, some because statements about the process might be considered to be universal and invariant, that is, to apply in all or most writing situations. As Olsen (1999) explains, "process theorists assume that we can somehow make statements about the process that would apply to all or most writing situations" (p. 7). Other scholars critiqued cognitive process models because of their lack of attention to emotional and social aspects of writing, their neglect of genres, and their singular focus on the individual. For example, Cooper (1986) writes that "the belief on which [the cognitive process model] is based—that writing is thinking and, thus, essentially a cognitive process—obscures many aspects of writing we have come to see as not peripheral" (p. 365).

While early research on writing as a process focused on the development of a model of the cognitive writing process employed by an individual, the turn toward the social in more recent research and scholarship suggests that "writing as process" might just as well be categorized as both cognitive and social-contextual. Several writing researchers have demonstrated that processes vary across genres and tasks (e.g., Matsuhashi, 1981; Witte & Cherry, 1994; Schumacher et al., 1989) and from writer to writer depending on "a writer's resources (i.e., working memory, genre knowledge, topic knowledge, and linguistic proficiency)" (Van den Bergh et al., 2016, p. 57). And as Deane and his colleagues (2008) have recently pointed out, "Each genre—indeed every occasion for writing—presents specific, problem-solving challenges to the writer" (p. 16). They propose that "each stage in the writing process is sensitive to purpose, genre, and context," and say that "it is impossible to speak of the writing process in generic terms without considering the specific demands imposed by a particular purpose, audience, and context" (Deane et al., 2008, p. 31).

Writing as creativity

As in early conceptions of writing as product and process, writing creativity has typically been treated as an individual endeavor. According to Ivanic (2004), creativity is concerned with both mental processes and features of the text. The focus, however, unlike the writing-as-product view, is more on the text's content and style than its linguistic form. From this perspective, she says, writing is viewed as "a valuable activity in its own right: the creative act of an author, with no social function other than that of interesting or entertaining a reader" (Ivanic, 2004, p. 229). In the field of education, Britton (1970) identified a similar category, "poetic writing," for creating poems and narratives for aesthetic purposes. Creativity is also clearly linked to invention and the idea of an "inspired, autonomous author" (Howard, 1999, p. 57), an idea that permeates composition pedagogy. As Bawarshi (2003) points out, "Invention heuristics such as freewriting, brainstorming, clustering, and mapping locate the writer as the primary site and agent of invention" (p. 4). Similarly, Perl and Egendorf (1986) focused on the individual writer and treat the writing as the source of "creativity discovery":

> If writing is made possible by the discovery of what one wants to say, it is just as true that discoveries come about through the writing itself. Thus *writing* is what makes discovery possible by creating the possibilities for discovery.
>
> *(pp. 258–259; emphasis in original)*

More socially oriented theorists have qualified the view of the writer as an "originating consciousness" (Crowley, 1990, p. 16). Tracing changes in views of invention, Bawarshi (2003) acknowledges that invention emerges from the writer, but he also argues that it is nonetheless influenced by the social sphere, in particular, by genres:

> [G]enres function as sites of action in which writers acquire, articulate, and potentially resist motives to act . . . genre is a social motive and a rhetorical instantiation of that motive. Genre is what it allows us to do, the potential that makes the actual possible, the concept and its practice, the "con-" and the "-text" at the same time.
>
> *(p. 45)*

Bawarshi says that when writers write, they write within a genre, and since writing varies from situation to situation, students need the ability to analyze and determine the rhetorical strategies for writing within genres. Other scholars point to collaborative activity as a generative mechanism for creativity. For example, Robinson (2001) suggests that creativity springs not solely from qualities of the individual:

> Creativity is not purely an individual performance. It arises out of our interactions with ideas and achievements of other people. It is a cultural process. Creativity prospers best under particular conditions, especially where there is a flow of ideas between people who have different sorts of

> expertise. It requires an atmosphere where risk-taking and experimentation are encouraged rather than stifled.
>
> *(p. 12)*

Similarly, LeFevre (1987) describes the social and interactional aspect of invention, what she calls "the ecology of invention—the ways ideas arise and are nurtured or hindered by interaction with social context and culture" (p. 126).

Writing as expression

In James Britton's framework, a focus on the individual can be seen in his category of expressive writing for the self, to explore ideas, feelings, opinions, etc. (1970; Britton et al., 1975). As Durst (2015) explains, Britton "focused on how individuals used language . . . to comprehend experience and make sense of the world" (p. 388). In Britton's view, expressive writing was closely linked to Vygotsky's notion of inner speech, a medium for thought that is a precursor to and provides substance for verbal thought. Expressive writing was viewed as "the form of language in which we 'first-draft' our tentative or speculative ideas. In other words, it is an essential mode for learning—for the tentative exploration of new areas of knowledge" (Durst, 2015, p. 26). According to Pelz (1982), the primary aim of expressive writing is exploratory. It "is writing in which persons seek to probe their experience, to reflect upon it, with the intentions of discovering and developing their attitudes, beliefs, feelings and ideas about experience." Although trusted friends and colleagues may serve as a secondary audience for such writing, the primary "audience for such writing is the author of it" (Pelz, 1982, p. 4).

While Britton's notion of writing as expression clearly focuses on the individual, as a whole, Britton's framework spans several of the perspectives we have characterized separately here. For example, as we have noted earlier, his "poetic" category is linked to the category we call "writing as creativity," a category that emphasizes the creative role of the individual. In fact, poetic writing is often called creative writing. However, while expressive and poetic writing in Britton's framework emphasize the role of the individual, his category of transactional writing shifts the focus to the social context and what happens via communication between writers and readers. Transactional writing includes "expository and persuasive kinds of writing," in other words, writing to inform or persuade a reader (Durst & Newell, 1989, p. 378).

Conceptions of writing: emphasizing the social context

In the preceding section, we describe conceptualizations of writing that focus on the internal knowledge, skills, creativity, and processes of the individual and note how they have been influenced, reshaped, and revised in response to research on how writing and individual processes vary across different social contexts and discourse communities. In this section, we describe conceptualizations that see writing primarily as a socially situated activity. Following Perry's (2012) example, we use the term *sociocultural* to refer to a collection of related theories. As she explains, major theoretical perspectives within this collection include, for example, "literacy as a social practice," "multiliteracies," "multiple literacies," and "critical literacy" (Perry, 2012, p. 50).

While the theories and framework dimensions under our own broad "social context" umbrella in this next section are diverse, they share a common focus in their emphasis on the influence of social and cultural contexts in which literacy is practiced. Understanding writing in its fullest sense, especially the sociocultural aspects of it, is necessary if we are going to create learning opportunities that reflect the complexity of writing and assessments that represent the full range of students' writing competencies.

Writing as a socially constructed and situated activity

As explained earlier, while theories of writing that focus on skills and processes privilege cognitive understandings, that is, what's happening in the mind, more socially based theories foreground what's happening or has happened in the social context. We consider writing to be "socially constructed" in at least two senses: (1) writing is a socially embedded activity constructed and shaped by the events and communicative purposes in which writing plays a part, and (2) writing is sometimes literally produced by individuals working collaboratively.

From a social constructivist or sociocultural perspective, reality and meaning are constructed through human activity. Writing is thus shaped by the events, situations, and communicative purposes in which it plays a part. The outcomes of that shaping are patterned ways of accomplishing purposes in texts, in other words, genres. Whether one begins with Miller's (1984) emphasis on genre as social action, or the systemic linguistics approach of the Australian genre theorists (Halliday & Martin, 1993; Cope & Kalantzis, 1993), research on writing has emphasized the extent to which writing genres are context specific and socially situated (Applebee, 2005; Bazerman, 2004a; Cope & Kalantzis, 1993). Devitt (1993) explains that genres are not just socially situated but that they help create the situation: "Genre not only responds to but also creates recurring situations" (p. 577). These social perspectives on writing challenge the view of writing as a generic set of skills as well as the idea that statements about "the" writing process might be considered universal or invariant. They challenge process approaches to the teaching of writing that emphasize expression of self on the grounds they privilege students who come from a background in which self-expression is encouraged and who have had more opportunities for reading and travel. Proponents of genre studies suggest that a better way to teach writing would be to make features of genre more explicit to students (Bawarshi, 2003; Derewianka, 1990).

Social perspectives on writing also challenge the idea that writing is purely an individual endeavor. Although writing may be characterized as an individual endeavor in school, particularly since it often serves to demonstrate what individual students have learned, in reality, as Prior (2006) explains:

> teachers in schools are always coauthors (often dominant ones) in students' writing as teachers take up many roles in the authorship function (deciding to write, setting deadlines, specifying style and topic, structuring the writing process, offering specific words and phrases).
>
> *(p. 58)*

And in the world outside the classroom, collaborative writing is common. In a review of research on this kind of writing, Beaufort (2008) points out that, "Collaborative writing is not just a division of labor; rather, it entails interactive cognitive processes among writers, editors, and managers (p. 230). Lunsford and Ede (1994) go so far as to say:

> After a lengthy research project and eight years of study, we feel confident in saying that the traditional model of solitary authorship is more myth than reality, that much or most of the writing produced in professional settings in America is done collaboratively, and that, in fact, much of what we call "creative" writing is collaborative as well, though it almost always flies under the banner of single authorship.
>
> *(p. 418)*

Researchers (e.g., Allen, 1993; Dorff & Duin, 1989; Dyson, 1993; Cross, 1994; Locker, 1992; Witte & Haas, 2001; Winsor, 1996) have documented various kinds of collaboration in writing in academic and non-academic settings. As for policy, an important impetus for encouraging both the teaching and the assessing of collaborative activities comes from the need for employees who can work productively in group settings in professional and service-oriented work settings (Baron, 1990). As Baron notes, "Whether in fast-food restaurants, industrial settings, or research laboratories, people do not work in isolation. They depend on each other for ideas, implementation, follow-through, and well being" (1990, p. 254).

Writing as communication to accomplish a purpose

One of Britton's three categories, transactional writing, focuses on what happens in the situational context when there is communication between writers and readers. Writers intend to affect readers and, sometimes collaterally, they are able to make something happen in the world. Among discourse theorists, D'Angelo's approach is perhaps most closely linked to the idea of writing for a purpose.

D'Angelo (1980) begins with the writing situation, which includes the writer, the writer's purpose, the reader/audience, and the occasion (the circumstances, e.g., idea, problem, event, or question) that motivated the person to write. D'Angelo then classifies kinds of writing in terms of purpose—the change the writer wants to bring about in the reader (the effect on the reader the writer wants to have). In D'Angelo's framework, the purpose of informative writing is to inform or instruct. The purpose of persuasive discourse is to convince or persuade. The purpose of literary discourse is to entertain or please with an aesthetic purpose. The purpose of expressive discourse is to express strong feeling and emotion. Generally speaking, the idea that writing is done to have an effect on readers puts this conceptualization of writing squarely under the "social" umbrella.

Writing as integrated with reading, speaking, and listening

While writing has often been treated as a "stand-alone" activity in the curriculum, in reality, reading and writing are always closely intertwined. For example, in an elaboration of her transactional theory, Rosenblatt (1989) explained that "reading is an integral part of the writing process" (p. 166). She identified two types of "authorial" reading. In the first, more inner-oriented kind, authors test words as they appear on the page "not just for how they make sense with the preceding text but also against something more demanding: whether the emerging meaning serves or hinders the purpose." In the second kind of authorial reading, writers read the text "through the eyes of potential readers (i.e., tries to judge the meaning *they* would make)" (Rosenblatt, 1989, p. 167). In later work, authorial reading has been linked to the quality of the written product (Breetvelt et al., 1996).

Reading is also intertwined with writing when writers work with sources. Hayes (1996) notes that reading for writing is not just about gathering topic knowledge: "Readers may form at least three different representations when they read: a representation of the topic discussed, a representation of the writer's persona, and a representation of the text as a spatial display" (pp. 18–19). Each of these representations could ultimately play a role in the development and functioning of the student's own text. In other words, when writers are composing from sources, they read for comprehension, and they use reading strategies to select and evaluate information from source documents. They form judgments about the writer's persona and credibility, so how they interpret what they read influences what they write.

Research at several grade levels has shown that literacy skills can be enhanced by connecting reading and writing, for example, in elementary school (Graves, 1983; Calkins, 1983; Tierney & Leys, 1984), in middle school (Atwell, 1987; Reif, 1992; Taylor & Beach, 1984), in high school (Strickland & Strickland, 1993, 1996), and in college composition (Carillo, 2015). Writing scholars also argue that writing can support reading. For example, citing several studies that support the claim that writing enhances a reader's sense of the author's craft, Tierney and Leys (1984) conclude that:

> [S]tudents involved in a rich writing curriculum develop a keen sense of why something they are reading was written, as well as its strengths and weaknesses. Furthermore, unlike students who receive little time to write, the students who write frequently and discuss their writing will approach reading with what might be termed the "eye of a writer."
>
> *(p. 19)*

Speech can also play a central role in writing, whether in collaborative composing, in boss-to-secretary-style of dictation, or in the more contemporary case of speech-to-text software. Voice recognition programs now allow individual writers to literally speak the composing process. In classrooms, as Dyson's (1993) work shows, children use their rich cultural traditions and both oral and written language to accomplish social work—to enact identities and engage their audiences—as they write. Speaking also plays a role in writers' processes of writing when they talk through ideas (as in "Let me run this by you"), discuss a draft in process with a peer or teacher, or collaborate with others. In fact, conferencing with writers, a staple of many teachers' pedagogy, is grounded in the idea that talking about writing is an effective way to help writers develop and to improve a draft (Glenn & Goldthwaite, 2014; Williams, 2014). Writing center pedagogy, of course, is firmly grounded in talk through peer tutorials where "tutors are educated, interested readers/writers who play the role of an engaged and supportive, yet simultaneously critical audience for texts" (Hobson, 2001, p. 166). Tutors use "active listening techniques" such as "reflective listening and guided response to help the writer" and typically provide a verbal summary at the end of the session (Hobson, 2001, p. 168). Whether in a classroom, a teacher conference, or the writing center, talking is considered a valuable partner in writing.

Writing as an element of multimodal literacy

The new digital technologies available for writing have changed composing processes, including collaborative processes, and the way we think about writing. In the past, writing most often meant writing by hand with pen or pencil, or with a typewriter. Writers today have access to a variety of text entry tools. Writers type texts using keyboards, swipe and pinch text on touchscreens, and orally dictate messages using voice recognition software. Revision is now facilitated by digital word processing tools and is more easily accomplished than with paper, pencil, or typewriters. Writers cut and paste and delete and search for synonyms and move blocks of text around with relative ease. The National Council of Teachers of English acknowledged the importance of multimodal writing in the 2005 position statement "Multimodal Literacies," which states,

"Creating images, sounds, designs, videos and other extra-alphanumeric texts is an aesthetic, self-originated, self-sponsored activity for many writers. Digital technologies have increasing capacity for individuals to adapt the tools for their own information and communication purposes" (para 10). For example, writers are now experimenting with crowdsourcing to help them, using different types of social media to connect with readers and get input. Writer and editor Jeff Elkins (2018) explains that he used crowdsourcing to decide what genre to pursue and how to focus his next series. Digital technologies also facilitate and transform procedures for collaborative writing. As we drafted this text, for instance, we were over 2,500 miles apart, but we had immediate access to each other's writing. Google docs, services like DropBox, and a phone can virtually put writers working at a distance into the same room, writing at the same time, even finishing each other's sentences.

Beyond their effects on composing processes and collaborative writing, digital technologies have redefined what it means to write and what is considered a written text. For example, Ivanic (2004) notes that " 'Text' can be viewed as multimodal, including visual . . . material as well as linguistic characteristics of written text" (p. 223). Similarly, Kress (1997, 2001) points out that communication has always been multisemiotic and that the ratio of art to print has changed over the years. Lotherington (2004) agrees, "Increasingly we are sending and receiving more information through imagery and less through print in our texts" (p. 307).

Multimodal composition assignments—such as blogs, podcasts, collages, PowerPoint slideshows, video or audio essays, comic strips, storyboards, documentaries, and movies—are now frequently part of the "writing" curriculum. In multimodal compositions, visual elements such as photographs, drawings, graphs, charts, and video, and audio elements such as speech, music, or other sound effects are used in combination with alphabetic writing to convey ideas, to express emotions, to inform, to persuade—in other words, to perform the many functions that writing once typically performed more or less on its own (e.g., Hawisher & Selfe, 1999; Palmeri, 2012; Shipka, 2011; Yancey, 2004b). As Cope and Kalantzis (2004) observe, the trend in the digital era "is a trend to multimodality, to the fabrication and distribution of texts which integrate linguistic, audio, and visual modes of meaning" (p. 200).

Writing is now understood to be a "a complex, multifaceted, and purposeful act of communication that is accomplished in a variety of environments, under various constraints of time, and with a variety of language resources and technological tools" (National Assessment Governing Board, 2017, p. 3). Many of our assessments lag far behind this definition, anchored as they are in outdated and inadequate theories about the nature of literacy. To design coherent educational assessment systems for the future, we will need to design assessments that reflect social perspectives on literacy and a complex and socially situated construct of writing.

Conceptions of learning: shifting toward the social

Like theories of writing, theories about learning have evolved over time, moving generally from a focus on the acquisition of knowledge and skill by the individual toward a conceptualization of learning as a social and participatory process. As new theories have emerged, the theoretical role of the social context in learning has evolved in significant ways, from being conceptualized as a source of stimulus for an individual's learning in the behaviorist paradigm to playing a significant role in the social process of literacy learning, "a complex of actions that take place inside a web of social relationships and social assumptions" (Resnick & Resnick, 1989, p. 192).

While cognitively oriented researchers focused on the acquisition of knowledge and skill by the individual, more socially oriented scholars emphasized the contextual and social nature of learning. For example, reflecting the work of Vygotsky (1978), social constructivism incorporates the role of others and of culture in learning and development. From this perspective, language and concepts transmitted through language are viewed as essentially social phenomena, and they involve interaction. In contrast to social constructivism, situated learning views learning as a *function* of the activity, context, and culture in which it occurs. Individuals, activities, and the world are seen as mutually constitutive; thus, social interaction is also a critical component of situated learning. But from this perspective, learning is conceptualized as increasing participation. As Lave and Wenger (1991) explain,

> In contrast with learning as internalization, learning as increasing participation in communities of practice concerns the whole person acting in the world. Conceiving of learning as participation focuses attention on ways in which it is an evolving, continuously renewed set of relations. . . . Further, given a relational understanding of person, world, and activity, participation . . . can be neither fully internalized as knowledge structures nor fully externalized as instrumental artifacts or overarching activity structures. Participation is always based on situated negotiation and renegotiation of meaning in the world.
>
> *(pp. 49–52)*

The social turn in learning highlights the need for "deep understanding" that moves beyond the focus on memorizing facts or isolated bits of information. Instead, students need to develop meaningful ways of "organizing information" (National Research Council, 2000, p. 42). By studying how experts use knowledge to solve problems and make meaning, researchers concluded that "novices might benefit from models of how experts approach problem solving—especially if they receive coaching in using similar strategies" (p. 42). Coaching, in the form of feedback, then is an effective practice as students develop deep understanding and competencies. Learners can transfer knowledge to use in new situations more readily when they develop deep understanding and can organize information in meaningful ways. One aspect of this kind of learning is what experts refer to as "conditionalized knowledge," which involves knowing the specific contexts in which knowledge is useful (National Research Council, 2000, p. 43). Conditionalizing requires situated learning and assessment practices that ascertain whether students can use their knowledge in context.

Learning of all kinds is facilitated, according to current theories and research, by providing activities and environments that help students build on what they already know and their previous experiences. In this approach, teachers attend to the "incomplete understanding, false beliefs, and naïve renditions of concepts that learners bring with them" (National Research Council, 2000, p. 10). In other words, teaching should begin with what students already know and then move students to more informed, deep understanding of the material. According to the Council, teachers should expand the role of assessment "beyond the traditional concept of testing" (p. 19). Using frequent "formative assessment helps make students' thinking visible to themselves, their peers, and their teacher" (p. 19).

Another important component of this approach to teaching and learning is its focus on metacognition, that is, encouraging learners to self-monitor their own performance and understanding. Fostering metacognitive strategies requires an expanded understanding of assessment to include activities such as goal setting, reflection, and self-assessment.

While these more recent understandings of how people learn are not specific to literacy, they inform our understanding of literacy learning and reinforce a contemporary construct of literacy. A strength of the "situative" perspective, according to Greeno et al. (1996), is its call for authentic literacy activities— "activities that have standing and motivation beyond the goal of sheer acquisition of knowledge and skill" (p. 76). Proposed as a model of instruction with implications for classroom practice, situated learning is designed to "enculturate students into authentic practices through activity and social interaction" (Brown et al., 1989, p. 37).

In highlighting these social perspectives on learning, we are not suggesting that we should ignore what we have learned from perspectives that focus on the individual or insist that all teaching practices align with social perspectives. Rather than view the individual, acquisition metaphor for learning and the social, participation metaphor for learning as "conflicting" or "mutually exclusive" metaphors, we agree with Sfard (1998) that they offer "mutually complementing outlooks" (p. 11). However, a critical component of this approach is that learning occurs at the intersection of the individual and the social. As the authors of *How People Learn* (2000) explain: "A scientific understanding of learning includes understanding about learning processes, learning environments, teaching, sociocultural processes, and the many other factors that contribute to learning" (National Research Council, 2000, p. 233). While they differ in some respects,

What teachers say about using formative assessment in instruction

- Formative assessment allows me to pin down more precisely the areas of instruction I need to focus on more intensively as opposed to those skills and concepts students have mastered or are on their way to master. (as cited in O'Neill, 2017, p. 4)
- Everything I do in class is a form of assessment: class discussions, small-group discussions, one-on-one conversations with students, informal writing assignments, formal essays. Students are constantly being assessed and I'm constantly updating my understanding of their progress. (as cited in NCTE, 2016, p. 3)
- Formative assessment revolutionized my classroom! I use it for assessing all my skills now in lieu of most paper tests! For example, when studying plot structure, I place my students into small groups; then my clipboard and I move throughout the class listening to the interaction in each group. The moment I knew this form of assessment was the answer I was looking for was when I heard two students, two underperforming, disinterested students, debating over which part of the story would best fit the criteria for the climax! Within a matter of minutes I could determine whether these students understood the elements of plot! No worksheet was necessary! (as cited in NCTE, 2016, p. 5)
- Formative assessments just make the most sense in a writing classroom. The point is to get better—and experienced writers know that most of that happens in revision. (as cited in NCTE, 2016, p. 4)
- I use all kinds of assessments . . . to drive my instruction, but my preference for literacy is observation, conferencing and running records. These assessments are immediate, personal, and targeted. . . . The child in question gets exactly what he needs in the moment he needs it. (as cited in NCTE, 2016, p. 6)
- Formative assessment is the piece of the teaching puzzle that allows us to quickly (and hopefully, accurately) gauge how well our students are understanding the material we've taught. From there, we make the important decisions about where our lesson will go next. Do we need to reteach, or are our students ready to progress? Do some students need additional practice? And which students need to be pushed to achieve the next level? (as cited in Mathis, 2021, para. 1).
- I assess learning in a writing class by reading students' writing in drafts, commenting on strengths and weaknesses, and then grading the final copy. When I read drafts, I can see what students understand and what they don't understand, and I help them learn through comments on drafts, consultations in my office, and comments and a grading sheet on a final paper. (as cited in NCTE, 2016, p. 5)
- Daily classroom feedback, from exit slips to quizzes or entry activities, helps me keep tabs on students and communicate with each individual frequently. (as cited in NCTE, 2016, p. 4)

the socio-constructivist view of learning and situated learning both emphasize interaction between and among individuals in varying contexts. In other words, both writing and learning are anchored in social interaction.

In addition to the social nature of learning, we've also learned that development, including development in writing, is variable, both because of individual differences but also because of life experiences and the "diverse social worlds people inhabit." Such differences "make no two students, no two writers, no two texts exactly the same" (Bazerman et al., 2018, p. 14). According to Vygotsky (1978),

> learning which is oriented toward developmental levels that have already been reached is ineffective from the viewpoint of a child's overall development. It does not aim for a new stage of the developmental process, but rather lags behind this process. The only good learning is that which is in advance of development.
>
> *(p. 82)*

Variability in development calls for formative approaches in assessment that provide information "that teachers can use to shape instruction to meet students' needs and that students can use to better understand and advance their learning" (Trumbull & Lash, 2013, p. 1). Formative assessment, which focuses on teaching and learning, can be part of performance assessments that are summative, such as portfolios that include student self-assessments or drafts in process. We discuss the link between formative and summative assessment, including accountability assessment, in the next section and in more detail in Chapter 4.

Implications of contemporary conceptions of writing and learning for the teaching of writing

In the remainder of this chapter, we focus on identifying and describing some of the most effective ways that writing—as a complex cognitive and social activity—can be and has been operationalized in classrooms to promote learning to write. We describe approaches and practices in teaching writing that reflect the social nature of writing as it happens in today's world—"in a variety of environments . . . and with a variety of language resources and technological tools" (National Assessment Governing Board, 2017, p. 3). These practices include having students write to real audiences for real purposes (other than just getting a grade); integrating writing with reading, speaking, and listening in instruction; incorporating multimodal technologies; and building genre knowledge to promote students' understanding of the ways writing varies across situations, discourse communities, and purposes for writing. While there are other practices that may reflect writing as a complex cognitive and social activity, we have focused attention on these because research has suggested they are particularly effective. These practices, of course, are not magic bullets. Teaching is the point where theoretical abstractions are transformed into concrete practices that support learning effectively or not. But they provide a starting point for thinking about how we might design assessments to be more closely aligned with a contemporary construct of writing and with social perspectives on learning.

Emphasizing writing for a purpose

A key finding in the Stanford Study of Writing, which began in September 2001 and included 189 students over a period of five years, was that students "do not do particularly well in writing papers just for the sake of writing papers. Rather, students value writing that 'makes something happen in the world'" (Davidson, 2017, p. 93). The *St. Martin's Handbook* (Lunsford, 2011) explains the issue this way:

> At some point during your college years or soon after, you are highly likely to create writing that is not just something that you turn in for a grade, but writing that you do because you want to make a difference. The writing that matters most to many students and citizens, then, is writing that has an effect in the world: writing that gets up off the page or screen, puts on its working boots, and marches out to get something done!
>
> *(p. 890)*

Using writing to accomplish a purpose in the social world outside of the classroom not only motivates students, but also it emphasizes that writing is more than just a demonstration of competence. The influence of this approach can be seen in teachers' efforts to create real communicative situations for students. One of the findings from the study conducted by Anderson et al. (2015), using data from the National Survey of Student Engagement, identified meaning-making activities, tasks that require integrative, critical, or original thinking, as a significant component of writing development: "First-year and senior students who reported that more of their writing assignments required meaning-making were especially likely to report greater participation in all three forms of Deep Approaches to Learning" (p. 226). Activities related to deep-learning focus on the underlying meaning of information, require integrating and synthesizing of information, and encourage seeing something from multiple perspectives (Anderson et al., 2015, p. 211).

Research has demonstrated that focusing on the purpose for writing helps students write more effectively. For example, setting specific goals based on the purpose for writing was found to be a very effective approach (effect size = .70) in the meta-analysis of teaching approaches conducted by Graham and Perin (2007). Given what we know about how writing varies in important ways across different cultures, contexts, and purposes for writing, it makes sense to figure out ways to help students acquire knowledge of a range of writing genres. As Ivanic (2004) explains, students "need to learn the linguistic characteristics of different text-types in order to be able to reproduce them appropriately to serve specific purposes in specific contexts" (p. 233). An example of teaching from this perspective at the elementary level can be seen in the work of Derewianka (1990), whose curricular recommendations are supported by the work of scholars such as Halliday and Martin (1993), Christie and Derewianka (2008), Christie and Martin (2007), and Kress (1997, 2001) on the development of functional linguistic and social semiotic approaches for use in schools. Derewianka (1990) describes units of work that focus on genres such as recounts, instructions, narratives, information reports, explanations, and arguments and the typical features of each. She uses sample texts in the genre chosen for study to help children become familiar with the genre's features, and for determining how well the children already can write the genre to inform further development of the unit, modeling, explicit discussion of the genre's features and their functions, joint construction of a text in the chosen genre and finally, independent construction of the genre, conferencing with the teacher, and revising. The activities are recursive, so that, for example, teachers might revisit discussion of model texts or genre features during conferences with the students.

Writing to real audiences in addition to the teacher

Research has suggested that students benefit from writing to real audiences beyond the teacher. Porter (2002), for example, reflects on what he learned as a writer in his journalism class for the high school newspaper:

> I learned how to write a lead, how to interview, how to develop an interesting or thought-provoking story line. . . . I learned that features needed to have a point, that writing could make people laugh, get them excited, or make them mad. . . . I learned that writing can have a political and social effect (not a lesson we learned in English classes). . . . I learned about the potential power of publishing.
>
> (p. 378)

Anchored in the situated "literacy as practice" perspective, the general idea behind emphasizing real audiences and purposes is that doing so will help students learn how to adapt their writing to different audiences, purposes, and situations. At the high school level, teaching strategies associated with this kind of literacy as practice view include, among other activities, having students interact with real audiences beyond the classroom teacher, for example, inviting community business leaders to review resumes and interview students (Burke, 2012); having students write public service announcements (Esposito, 2012); sending students into the community to interview Holocaust survivors and create a booklet (Berman et al.,

2014); or collaborating with a community organization to produce documents the group needed (Cox et al., 2009). College writing classrooms also encourage authentic engagement with audiences beyond the teacher through service learning and community-based projects with a wide-range of writing courses, including first-year writing, basic writing, technical communication, writing center, and other advanced composition and rhetoric courses (Adler-Kassner et al., 1997; Deans, 2000; Dubinsky & Carpenter, 2004; Parks & Goldblatt, 2000; Goldblatt, 2007; Rose & Weiser, 2010).

Literature on the impact of technology on composition also suggests that students can gain new insights about writing when they write to real audiences other than the teacher. Technology has significantly expanded students' access to audiences for their writing. At the same time, students' self-sponsored writing (e.g., blogs, texts, tweets, Facebook status updates, emails) has dramatically increased (Brandt, 2015; Grabill et al., 2010; Lenhart et al., 2008; Lenhart, 2012; Madden et al., 2013; Moore et al., 2016; Purcell et al., 2013; Stanford University, 2021; Yancey, 2009a, 2009b). While some scholars have expressed concern that these kinds of digital writing might lead to a decline in proficiency, others have speculated that self-sponsored writing could have a positive effect on student's writing. Lunsford (n.d.), for example, comments on the upside wrought by the digital revolution:

> If we look beyond the hand-wringing about young people and literacy today, beyond the view that paints them as either brain-damaged by technology or as cogs in the latest race to the top, we will see that the changes brought about by the digital revolution are just that: changes. These changes alter the very grounds of literacy as the definition, nature, and scope of writing are all shifting away from the consumption of discourse to its production across a wide range of genre and media, away from individual "authors" to participatory and collaborative partners-in-production; away from a single static standard of correctness to a situated understanding of audience and context and purpose for writing. Luckily, young people are changing as well, moving swiftly to join in this expanded culture of writing.
>
> *(n.d., para 10)*

Lunsford explains that while students in her longitudinal study of writing "were online a good part of every day" and "joined networking sites enthusiastically," these activities did not lead to illiteracy. Instead, these activities "seemed to help them develop a range or repertoire of writing styles, tones, and formats along with a range of abilities" (para 4). Evidence that this might be the case comes from a study of rhetorical understanding of effective writing conducted by Rosinski (2017), who reports that students "showed more rhetorical sensitivity (who to write, when, in what medium, how)" when talking about their self-sponsored digital writing than when talking about their academic writing (p. 266). The *Elon Statement on Writing Transfer* (2014) asserts that "Students' meta-awareness often plays a key role in transfer, and reflective writing promotes preparation for transfer and transfer-focused thinking" (p. 7). In the statement, practices "that foster the development of metacognitive awareness, including asking good questions about writing situations and developing heuristics for analyzing unfamiliar writing situations" are identified as activities that promote writing transfer (p. 8). Rosinski (2017) recommends that teachers engage students in "short, informal and low-stakes" activities in which they reflect on their own rhetorical knowledge and strategies and "the writerly decisions they make in their self-sponsored writing," to increase the likelihood they will transfer their knowledge to their academic writing (p. 267).

At the college level, instruction is focused more than ever on the need for students to know how to adapt their writing to the varied disciplines in college curricula and to the varied demands of writing in the workplace. The writing-across-the-curriculum movement is one example of the recognition that writing varies across disciplines, purposes, and situations, and some faculty advocate extending "teach-for-transfer" efforts to writing centers and first-year writing programs as well. Beaufort (2007), for example, proposes revamping writing programs so that students will become experts "at learning writing skills in multiple social contexts, rather than experts in a single context" (p. 8). To help the field move in this direction, she offers a conceptual model of writing expertise that will help students acquire "context-specific knowledge . . . heuristics, with which to organize knowledge and aid problem-solving," and knowledge they can "invoke for analyzing new writing situations" (p. 17). The domains of knowledge in her model include writing process knowledge, subject matter knowledge, rhetorical knowledge, genre knowledge, and discourse community knowledge.

Integrating the modes of literacy in instruction

Integrating writing with reading, speaking, and listening in instruction is also effective. For one thing, it more closely approaches what happens in the "real" world outside of school. In other words, an integrated approach is more authentic than approaches that separate the modes into different instructional units. Research has demonstrated that literate activities and cognitive abilities such as reading and writing are strongly integrated in the workplace and are not separated into separate aspects of workers' knowledge (e.g., Hull et al., 1996; Brandt, 2015). Approaches to teaching, such as using models or assigning tasks that include writing from sources, require students to read in order to write.

Given the assumption that social interaction supports students' cognitive development and learning, it also makes sense to interweave speaking and listening with reading and writing in teaching. Research has demonstrated that students gain insights into how communication works by being both readers and writers

(Nelson & Calfee, 1998), and there is an extensive body of research on shared knowledge in reading and writing (e.g., Nelson & Calfee, 1998; Reuter, 1993; Shanahan & Tierney, 1990; Stotsky, 1983; Tierney & Shanahan, 1991). Hillocks's (1984) meta-analysis of studies that compare strategies in writing instruction demonstrates the value of integrating the language arts in instruction. Many studies (e.g., King & Rentel, 1981; Clay, 1982) have also demonstrated that development of writing is anchored in oral language. At the elementary level, well-known case studies conducted by Graves (1983) and Calkins (1983) have demonstrated the energizing effect of oral interaction surrounding literacy events. Talk is the foundation for developing literacy, and in the best of worlds, students will have many opportunities in the classroom to engage in purposeful talk, in civil discourse, and to explore ideas. As Britton (1983) put it, "Reading and writing float on a sea of talk" (p. 11).

Building genre knowledge and rhetorical capacity

Like other areas of scholarship, genre studies have been influenced by the turn to the social. While early definitions of genre (and mode) focused on the features and structures of different types of text, more recent theory has focused on the idea of shared communicative purpose in recurring sociocultural contexts. Swales (1990) defines genre as "a class of communicative events" (p. 44) with "some set of shared communicative purposes" (p. 46). Like Swales, Martin (1985) and Miller (1984) emphasize shared purpose. Miller argues that "a rhetorically sound definition of genre must be centered not on the substance or the form of discourse but on the action it is used to accomplish" (1984, p. 151). Similarly, Martin (1985) emphasizes the task to be performed. From a "social" perspective, interest in genre theory is less in providing a taxonomic system that predicts or identifies types of text than in accounting for the way people communicate to get things done. "A key insight of genre theory is that language occurs in a social context and that it is structured according to the purposes it serves in a particular context and according to the social relations entailed by that activity" (Callaghan et al., 1993, p. 181). In fact, rather than defining genres as classes of texts or even as communicative events in which certain purposes are accomplished, some scholars define them as social processes that are patterned in predictable ways:

> Genres are the ways that we get particular things done through language—
> the ways we exchange information and knowledge and interact socially.
> Genres are a useful way of categorizing the social processes that are realized
> through the use of language.
>
> *(Callaghan et al., 1993, p. 192)*

Each of the three broad trends that we have sketched to this point has emphasized some aspects of writing—writer, text, or social context—to some degree at the expense of the others. But it could be argued that all three foci—text, writer, and social context—are equally important for students who are learning to write and for teachers who are attempting to teach them. It is true that conventional texts exhibit regularities that can be used to sort texts into formalist categories, but those same regularities facilitate communication. It is true that genres exercise a socially normative influence over individual acts of speaking and writing, but because genres are recognized socially, they are also effective tools that individual writers can use to accomplish individual purposes. Yes, writers create unique and creative pieces, but writers also use their knowledge of genre conventions to do so. The paradox, as Bawarshi (2003) contends, is that "Genres exist because writers produce them, but writers produce them because genres already exist" (p. 9). Seen in this light, genres are important resources for writers.

As a resource, genre models help students learn how to shape texts to accomplish particular purposes, to use and adapt appropriate patterns of organization, and to make appropriate language choices. Models can help students make, as Bawarshi (2003) says, "these sites of action visible to themselves in a way that allows them to participate more consciously and critically" (p. 48). He argues that an "explicit knowledge of genres can lead students to make more effective rhetorical decisions because they will have a better sense of what purposes their rhetorical choices are serving" (p. 164). Research confirms the value of using models in teaching writing. Among the 11 elements of effective adolescent writing instruction identified in the meta-analysis conducted by Graham and Perin (2007), the study of models, which "provides students with opportunities to read, analyze, and emulate models of good writing" (p. 4), resulted in effect sizes of 0.25. In an earlier meta-analysis conducted by Hillocks (1986), "the mean experimental/control effect size for studies focusing on models in the experimental groups but not in the control" was .22, a somewhat smaller but still meaningful effect (p. 216).

As an alternative to the use of models, which some scholars fear leads to a focus on text types as opposed to purposes or to formulaic approaches in responding to writing tasks, students can be engaged in inquiry about genres. For instance, Paltridge (2004) describes several ways that students can be involved in inquiry activities to gain knowledge of text structure components that would be of use to them in revising their own texts. Students can also be asked to examine differences across genres, or to determine how the same purpose can be met with different forms. And, students could be engaged in inquiry activities to gather information about the different ways a writer can execute one or more of the components of a genre (e.g., orientation of the reader to the context, character development, dialogue, etc.). The list of possible activities is long. But whatever the specifics of the activity are, the focus of an inquiry approach is on student discovery, and on the students' roles as researchers. As Johns (1997) explains, although teachers cannot predict and teach all of the genres their students might ultimately use, teachers can teach students "to ask questions of texts, of contexts, of experts—and of themselves" (p. 92). In this way, teachers can give students tools for inquiry to use when confronted with a new writing task or an unfamiliar text.

Incorporating multimodal technologies

With the increasing move to digital technologies, things have changed even more as Kinzer and Leu (2017) explain:

> Individuals no longer interact mainly with static print materials when reading and writing. Rather, they interact with moveable text, images, audio files, links, digital search engines, virtual keyboards, touch screens, motion-based and haptic interfaces, and other input and output devices as they communicate, create and consume information.
>
> *(pp. 1–2)*

A number of scholars have begun to recognize, as Anderson et al. (2006) explain, that "the bandwidth of literacy practices and values on which our profession has focused during the last century may be overly narrow" (p. 1). Scholars in the New London Group have argued that alphabetic writing is one modality among many and that we need to acknowledge that communication in today's digital world is much broader, taking advantage of a range of rhetorical and creative resources that include words, but also "still and moving images, sounds, music, animation—to create meaning" (Anderson et al., 2006, p. 1). Spanning elementary through college, the collection *Teaching the New Writing: Technology, Change, and Assessment in the 21st Century Classroom* (Herrington et al., 2009) shows us that students at all levels, from early elementary through college, are writing in multiple modalities, using a variety of digital technologies. In the last decade, there has been even a greater focus on the implications of new conceptualizations of literacy, in particular the idea that "meanings are made . . . through many representational and communicational resources, of which language is but one" (Jewitt, 2008, p. 246).

Evidence suggests that many postsecondary writing faculty now include some kind of instruction in multimodal texts in their curriculum. For example, in response to a survey investigating instructional approaches to teaching multimodal composition, 93% of respondents (n = 38) indicated "that they had students analyze and compose multimodal texts" (Anderson et al., 2006, p. 75). While there is little research available on the efficacy of particular strategies for teaching students how to create multimodal texts, it seems clear that teaching students how to navigate in this new digital world is an obligation we can't easily ignore. Scholars are in the process of developing effective frameworks for instruction in digital video composing (e.g., Miller, 2013), and the National Council of Teachers of English (NCTE) has supported multimodal approaches to literacy for decades as evidenced by resolutions in the early 1970s that advocated for including media literacy as part of the English Language Arts curriculum. In 1983, NCTE passed a resolution that it would "through its publications and professional meetings explore the effective use of computers in the teaching of English and language arts" (NCTE, 1983). Since then NCTE has published policy briefs, position statements, books, and journal articles and has offered webinars and professional development opportunities for teachers, all increasing interest in what NCTE labeled 21st century literacies.

Providing feedback on writing

In the literature on self-regulation in the field of psychology, feedback is viewed as an essential component within several self-regulation models (e.g., Butler & Winne, 1995; Bangert-Drowns et al., 1991; Nicol & Macfarlane-Dick, 2006; Pintrich, 2000; Zimmerman & Campillo, 2003). Response to drafts in progress has been a productive area of research and scholarship for decades, and a fairly broad range of approaches to providing response have been investigated, from various ways of marking papers to conferencing (e.g., Shaughnessy, 1977; Sommers, 1982; Haswell, 1983; Freedman et al., 1987; Sperling, 1990; Anson, 1989; Ashwell, 2000). As teaching has moved online and encompassed more multimodal options, writing researchers and teachers have also investigated how to continue to provide effective formative feedback via technology (Bless, 2017; Denton et al., 2008; Tuzi, 2004; van der Kleij & Adie, 2018).

In the field of writing, the practice of responding to drafts in progress, a form of formative assessment, has long been considered a best practice in teaching. Research supports this view. For example, Graham et al. (2011) found a large, weighted effect (0.77) on the quality of students' papers to be associated with verbal and written teacher and peer feedback. In a review of research on teacher response to student writing, Beach and Friedrich (2006) concluded that effective feedback can lead to substantive revision, help students understand the rhetorical demands of tasks, and develop skill in self-evaluation. In addition to response to writing drafts, formative assessment activities include strategies such as sharing success criteria with learners, classroom questioning, and peer and self-assessment (Wiliam, 2000, 2007; Black et al., 2003; Shute, 2008).

Peer review and feedback

While teachers' feedback based on formative assessment practices provides valuable support for student learning, another equally useful kind of assessment is the assessment that students do for each other. At the elementary and secondary levels, for example, research shows that process approaches to the teaching of writing that involve students in critiquing each other's work improve the quality of student writing (Sandmel & Graham, 2011; MacArthur et al., 1991; Cramer & Mason, 2015). According to MacArthur (2007), "Peer revising is most effective when it is combined with instruction based on evaluation criteria or revising strategies" (p. 146). Researchers have also found that peer feedback is meaningful and helpful when teachers provide explicit instruction on how to offer constructive feedback in an appropriate manner (Dahl & Farnan, 1998; Fitzgerald & Stamm, 1990; Patthey-Chavez & Ferris, 1997). Effective peer response groups help writers produce better work than they might have been able to on their own by providing insights into things the writer may have missed or clues about possible misinterpretations or unwanted reader reactions.

Teaching adolescents strategies for planning, revising, and editing their compositions is particularly effective—one of the two most effective interventions (effect size = .82) in the meta-analysis conducted by Graham and Perin (2006). Graham and Perin (2007) noted that this kind of intervention was "especially powerful with struggling writers (effect size = 1.02)" (p. 317). Research has consistently shown that collaborating with others is a big asset when it comes to learning. In their meta-analysis of research on writing instruction, Graham and Perin (2006) found that "collaborative arrangements in which students help each other with one or more aspects of their writing have a strong positive impact on quality" (p. 16). Similarly, in her analysis of a decade of studies on collaboration, Williams (2009) concluded that "students working in collaborative groups learn more than those in traditional classrooms" (p. 12). In a meta-analysis of 33 studies of the effects of self-and peer-grading, Sanchez and her colleagues (2017) reported that "both self-and peer-grading positively affected subsequent achievement performance" (p. 1059).

Among other benefits, according to Howard (1999), is that "scholars recommend the pedagogy of collaborative learning and writing . . . because it offers students practice in common forms of work-place writing" (p. 57). In the college composition community, socio-constructivist perspectives provide the foundation for collaborative pedagogy that informs peer review and other forms of peer interactions (Bruffee, 1973, 1984; Gere, 1987; Lunsford, 1991).

Self-assessment

Beyond teacher and peer review, developing writers benefit from self-assessment activities. While self-assessment may seem closer to an individualistic than a sociocultural approach, effective self-assessment promotes understanding of the sociocultural context and links previous knowledge with new knowledge. Several composition scholars have identified a number of purposes for engaging students in self-assessment. Some view self-assessment as a necessary evaluative activity in the revision process (e.g., Beach & Eaton, 1984). Some emphasize self-assessment and reflection as the basis for dialogue between student and teacher (e.g., Camp, 1998; Yancey, 1998a; Fox, 1998). Some see self-assessment as a way to encourage metacognitive thinking (e.g., Belanoff & Dickson, 1991; Camp & Levine, 1991; Mills-Court & Amiran, 1991). Others emphasize the opportunities self-assessments provide teachers for gaining insights into their students thinking (e.g., Evans, 2001; Beaven, 1977; Sommers, 1988; Fox, 1998). Yancey (1998b) calls self-assessment "reflection" and describes three stages:

reflection-in-action, which happens during the process of writing; constructive reflection, which happens between and among drafts or revisions; and reflection-in-presentation, a more formal kind of assessment, which happens when a task is complete.

Certainly, activities that engage students in evaluating their own work can have a powerful impact on learning. Several well-known composition scholars have demonstrated that self-assessment can influence the quality of a student's written work (e.g., Beach, 1976; Perl, 1979; Pianko, 1979; Flower & Hayes, 1980; Sommers, 1980). More recent research in the field of writing also suggests that teaching students how to assess their writing improves their performance. Ross (2006) explains that self-assessment training typically consists of systematic instruction that includes involving "students in defining assessment criteria," teaching "students how to apply the criteria . . . giving students feedback on their self-assessments," and helping "students use assessment data to develop action plans" (Ross, 2006, pp. 4–5). Using these approaches, Ross et al. (1999) found that students instructed in these approaches outperformed control students in grades 4–6 narrative writing. Andrade (2001) also recommends involving students in co-creating rubrics by critiquing examples.

Self-regulated strategy instruction also appears to support self-assessment. In a study to evaluate the effects of a curriculum for college developmental writing classes, MacArthur et al. (2015) reported that students "learned strategies for planning, drafting, and revising compositions with an emphasis on using knowledge of genre organization to guide planning and self-evaluation" (p. 855). When the writing of students in a "business-as-usual" control condition was compared to the writing of students who received self-regulated strategy instruction, "significant positive effects were found for overall quality of writing on a persuasive essay. . . . Significant positive effects were also found for self-efficacy and mastery motivation" (MacArthur et al., 2015, p. 855).

Research also suggests that providing students with rating scales to assess their work improves the quality of their writing (Hillocks, 1986). Other studies have shown a relation between writing scores and rubric-referenced student self-assessment (e.g., Andrade et al., 2008; Ross et al., 1999). Andrade et al. (2008) found that having students use model papers to generate criteria for a writing assignment and using a rubric to self-assess their first drafts was positively related to the quality of their subsequent writing. Andrade and Boulay (2003) found that teaching students how to use a rubric improved their writing performance, although the effects were limited to one of two writing genres and only to females. Goodrich (1997) found that rubric-referenced self-assessment had a positive effect on females' writing but not on males'.

As McDonald (2007) says,

> Clearly, we need a type of assessment that gives the learner a sense of belonging, achievement, autonomy, independence, empowerment, and

mastery over his or her own destiny, while simultaneously affording the learner a clear understanding of what is being learned.

(p. 25)

Self-assessment plays a key role in students' development of standards and criteria for meeting them and empowers student learners. And overall, although effects may in some instances be stronger for females than males, the evidence on self-assessment is quite positive.

Reflection

Reflection, which is sometimes considered a form of self-assessment, is in essence a mental and dialectical process, a consideration, and an exploration. It is multifaceted and linked to diverse disciplines and theoretical perspectives. Ryan (2011), for example, says that reflection stems from Dewey's work (1933) on reflective thinking in the field of psychology, but in more contemporary literature it has also been linked to critical social theories, such as those of Freire (1972) and Habermas (1974). Critical reflection is "underpinned by a commitment to social change by reading the world critically and imagining a better world that is less oppressive" (Ryan, 2011, p. 2). As Yancey (1998b) reminds us, "various constituencies within education have come to reflection as a means of doing something old better, or of doing something new" (p. 7). Some scholars observe that teachers employ reflection as a way to enhance their teaching or refine their curriculum (e.g., Applebee, 1996; Hillocks, 1995; Schon, 1983; Camp, 1998; Yancey, 1998b). Schon (1983) employed the term "reflective practitioner" and focused on improving educational practice through reflectivity and theory-in-use, as well as the ideas of "reflection-in-action" and "reflection-on-action." Camp (1998) argued that reflections provide a way to "make learning visible" (p. 11) to teachers. This "visible learning" provides the basis for "student–teacher dialogue" (p. 10). Similarly, Yancey (1998b) suggested that if we want to know how students are learning to write, what they are thinking, or how well they see their work measuring up to their standards, we should "*Try asking 'em*" (emphasis in original, p. 5). Scholars have also emphasized reflection as an important component of evaluation because it provides a link to curriculum (Camp, 1993; Moss, 1994; Murphy & Underwood, 2000; Yancey, 1998b). Leaders in education also see reflection as a way to reform education (Myers & Pearson, 1996).

In the field of writing, as Yancey (1998b) reminds us, the term *reflection* was first linked to composition in Pianko's (1979) article "Reflection: A Critical Component of the Composing Process." Pianko used the term to refer to a component of the composing process, "the act of reflection during composing—behaviorally manifested as pauses and rescannings" (pp. 277–278). Since then, the term has been used in various ways, as self-assessment, as goal setting, as analysis of learning, as a component of revising, and as baseline for measuring progress. Yancey's (1998b) own conception of reflection contains several dimensions:

> Reflection . . . is the dialectical process by which we develop and achieve, first, specific goals for learning; second, strategies for reaching those goals; and third, means of determining whether or not we have met those goals or other goals. Speaking generally, reflection includes the three processes of projection, retrospection (or review), and revision. For writing, it likewise includes three processes:
>
> 1. goal-setting, revisiting, and refining
> 2. text-revising in the light of retrospection
> 3. the articulating of what learning has taken place, as embodied in various texts as well as in the processes used by the writer
>
> *(p. 6)*

Drawing on these processes, Yancey (1998b) describes three kinds of reflection activities in the writing classroom:

> *reflection-in-action*, the process of reviewing and projecting and revising, which takes place within a composing event, and the associated texts
> *constructive reflection*, the process of developing a cumulative, multi-selved, multi-voiced identity, which takes place between and among composing events, and the associated texts
> *reflection-in-presentation*, the process of articulating the relationships between and among the multiple variables of writing and the writer in a specific context for a specific audience, and the associated texts
>
> *(pp. 13–14)*

According to Yancey, "Reflection makes possible a new kind of learning as well as a new kind of teaching." As they learn, students "witness their own learning: they show us how they learn" (1998b, p. 8). When reflections are articulated, they invite dialogue between teachers and students. As Fox (1998) says, students' reflections provide "an alternative to teaching in the dark" (p. 35). They provide information about what the students think they have done well, what they find to be least satisfying about their work, what they are interested in writing, what their criteria and standards for writing are, what processes work for them, what they understand about what they are learning, and how they measure their progress (Camp, 1998; Murphy, 1998).

The research reviewed in this chapter supports the success and value of socially oriented approaches in teaching, approaches in which students and teachers interact and build knowledge of the complexities of writing, including how writing

What students say when they reflect on their writing

- I like best that I used a lot of examples to prove my thesis. (as cited in Camp, 1998, p. 11)
- I think I use "overdone phrases" to transfer from topic to topic. It sounds stupid. (as cited in Camp, 1998, p. 11)
- The introduction and the conclusion are weak in comparison to the rest of the composition. I also have too many points thrown together in the paper without smooth transitions between them. (as cited in Camp, 1998, p. 12)
- I usta write hafe a page long for a hole story now I'm writing four to five pages long. (as cited in Murphy, 1998, p. 9)
- My best narrative piece would have to be the short story of a young ball player whose arm was ruined by the extensive greed of his coach, which was entitled "Greed." What I admire most about "Greed" are my use of setting, a sturdy plot, and ways where description wasn't told, but rather spoken through the voices of other characters. These all helped to develop the theme. (as cited in Murphy, 1998, p. 9)
- I am a multifaceted writer. I hope you can see that in my selections. I consider myself to be diverse in what I write. I chose these selections to send to show my diversity. . . . My editorial about gang violence should show that I can be fairly intimidating in my writing. (as cited in Black et al., 1994, p. 242)
- In the past, I put my ideas down on paper and called it good. I didn't think about how the words went on the page or what kind of words went on the page. A final draft was just a neater version of the rough one. Now, a final draft is a changed version of the rough one. It's revised, and sometimes the main idea or concept of the story is the only thing that remains. I focus on diction and vivid verbs. I try to make sure my sentence beginnings are varied. (as cited in Smith & Swain, 2017, p. 61)
- In the beginning of the year I wasn't really aware with my steps when I wrote. I remember doing a 1st draft-revision-final draft. But now my steps in writing have changed—Goals—Plans—prewrite—draft—revise—final draft. It is . . . longer. But I think it is better. That way I can make it exactly how I want it. The biggest changes in my steps are planning and prewrite. (as cited in Underwood, 1999, p. 181)
- Was that really me who wrote those papers?! I can't believe it! My writing style has changed so much within the last year or so. Back then I was so descriptive, with a little humor added to my work to liven things up! But now, I think I'm more serious about what I write and to read it is like a rainy, Sunday morning with no electricity at all while your friends are out. In other words, it's BORING. (as cited Bergamini, 1993, p. 149)
- I wish I could have the College Boards read some of this writing because I truly believe it reflects the true me, from my morals to my sense of humor. (as cited in Bergamini, 1993, pp. 149–150)

varies across subjects and situations and how to incorporate writing with other modes. These practices are rooted in social perspectives on learning and an understanding of the construct of writing as a complex, cognitive, communicative social activity, an understanding that is not aligned with the standardized, narrow, acontextual approach to writing that informs most large-scale writing assessments.

In the next chapter, we turn to a discussion of the need to align our assessment systems with best practices in teaching writing and with social perspectives on writing and learning. As contemporary researchers argue, to promote learning, classroom assessment needs to be more "learner-friendly" and formative, providing students with opportunities to revise and improve and teachers with the chance to identify the problems and areas to be remedied (National Research Council, 2000, pp. 24–25). Assessments also need to be grounded in a complex, socially situated construct of writing and provide meaningful information about student learning and how to support it. These principles, we argue in Chapter 4, should frame assessments so they provide useful feedback to teachers and students about learning and deep understanding.

References

Adler-Kassner, L., Crooks, R., & Watters, A. (Eds.). (1997). *Writing the community: Concepts and models for service learning in composition.* American Association for Higher Education with National Council of Teachers of English.

Adler-Kassner, L., & Wardle, E. (2015). *Naming what we know: Threshold concepts of writing studies.* University Press of Colorado.

Allen, N. J. (1993). Community, collaboration, and the rhetorical triangle. *Technical Communication Quarterly, 2*(1), 63–74.

Anderson, D., Atkins, A., Ball, C., Millar, K., Selfe, C., & Selfe, R. (2006). Integrating multimodality into composition curricula: Survey methodology and results from a CCCC research grant. *Composition Studies, 34*(2), 59–83.

Anderson, P., Anson, C. M., Gonyea, R. M., & Paine, C. (2015). The contributions of writing to learning and development: Results from a large-scale multi-institutional study. *Research in the Teaching of English, 50*(2), 199–235, A1–A3.

Andrade, H. G. (2001). The effects of instructional rubrics on learning to write. *Educational Theory and Practice Faculty Scholarship, 6.* https://scholarsarchive.library.albany.edu/etap_fac_scholar/6

Andrade, H. G., & Boulay, B. A. (2003). Role of rubric-referenced self-assessment in learning to write. *Journal of Educational Research, 97*(1), 21–34.

Andrade, H. G., Du, Y., & Wang, X. (2008). Putting rubrics to the test: The effect of a model, criteria generation, and rubric-referenced self-assessment on elementary school students' writing. *Educational Measurement: Issues and Practice, 27*(2), 3–13.

Anson, C. M. (Ed.). (1989). *Writing and response: Theory, practice and research.* National Council of Teachers of English.

Applebee, A. N. (1996). *Curriculum as conversation: Transforming traditions of teaching and learning.* University of Chicago.

Applebee, A. N. (2005). *NAEP 2011 writing assessment: Issues in developing a framework and specifications.* National Assessment Governing Board.

Ashwell, T. (2000). Patterns of teacher response to student writing in a multiple-draft composition classroom: Is content feedback followed by form feedback the best method? *Journal of Second Language Writing, 9*(3), 227–257.

Atwell, N. (1987). *In the middle: Writing, reading, and learning with adolescents.* Boynton/Cook.

Bain, A. (1866). *English composition and rhetoric: A manual.* Longmans Green and Co.

Baron, J. B. (1990). Performance assessment: Blurring the edges among assessment, curriculum, and instruction. In A. B. Champagne, B. E. Lovitts, & B. J. Calinger (Eds.), *Assessment in the service of instruction: Papers from the 1990 AAAS forum for school science* (pp. 128–147). American Association for the Advancement of Science. https://files.eric.ed.gov/fulltext/ED342652.pdf

Bawarshi, A. (2003). *Genre & the invention of the writer: Reconsidering the place of invention in composition.* Utah State University Press.

Bazerman, C. (2004a). Speech acts, genres, and activity systems: How texts organize activity and people. In C. Bazerman & P. Prior (Eds.), *What writing does and how it does it: An introduction to analyzing texts and textual practices.* Lawrence Erlbaum.

Bazerman, C. (2004b). Intertextuality: How texts rely on other texts. In C. Bazerman & P. Prior (Eds.), *What writing does and how it does it: An introduction to analyzing texts and textual practices.* Lawrence Erlbaum.

Bazerman, C., Applebee, A. N., Berninger, V. W., Brandt, D., Graham, S., Jeffery, J. V., Matsuda, P. K., Murphy, S., Rowe, D. W., Schleppegrell, M., & Wilcox, K. C. (2018). *The lifespan development of writing.* National Council of Teachers of English.

Bazerman, C., & Prior, P. (Eds.). (2004). *What writing does and how it does it: An introduction to analyzing texts and textual practices.* Lawrence Erlbaum.

Beach, R. (1976). Self-evaluation strategies of extensive revisers and nonrevisers. *College Composition and Communication, 27*(2), 160–164.

Beach, R., & Eaton, S. (1984). Factors influencing self-assessing and revision by college freshmen. In R. Beach & L. S. Bridwell (Eds.), *New directions in composition research* (pp. 149–170). Guilford Press.

Beach, R., & Friedrich, T. (2006). Response to writing. In C. A. MacArthur, S. Graham, & J. Fitzgerald (Eds.), *Handbook of writing research* (pp. 222–234). Guilford Press.

Beaufort, A. (2007). *College writing and beyond: A new framework for university writing instruction.* Utah State University Press.

Beaufort, A. (2008). Writing in the professions. In Charles Bazerman (Ed.), *Handbook of research on writing: History, society, school, individual, text* (pp. 221–235). Routledge.

Beaven, M. (1977). Individualized goal setting, self-evaluation, and peer evaluation. In C. R. Cooper & L. Odell (Eds.), *Evaluating writing: Describing, measuring, judging* (pp. 135–156). National Council of Teachers of English.

Belanoff, P., & Dickson, M. (Eds.). (1991). *Portfolios: Process and product.* Boynton/Cook.

Bangert-Drowns, R. L., Kulik, C. C., Kulik, J. A., & Morgan, M. (1991). The instructional effect of feedback in test-like events. *Review of Educational Research, 61*(2), 213–238.

Bergamini, J. (1993). An English department portfolio project. In M. A. Smith & M. Ylvisaker (Eds.), *Teachers' voices: Portfolios in the classroom* (pp. 145–159). National Writing Project.

Berman, M., Carroll, J., & Maloy, J. (2014). Rethinking critical service learning in developmental reading and writing courses at a two-year college. *Basic Writing e-Journal, 13*(1), 1–25.

Black, L., Daiker, D. A., Stygall, G., & Sommers, J. (Eds.). (1994). *New directions in portfolio assessment: Reflective practice, critical theory, and large-scale scoring.* Boynton/Cook.

Black, P., Harrison, C., Lee, C., Marshall, B., & Wiliam, D. (2003). *Assessment for learning: Putting it into practice.* Open University Press.

Bless, M. M. (2017). *Impact of audio feedback technology on writing instruction* [Walden Dissertations and Doctoral Studies 3282]. https://scholarworks.waldenu.edu/dissertations/3282

Bloome, D., & Katz, L. (1997). Literacy as social practice and classroom chronotopes. *Reading & Writing Quarterly: Overcoming Learning Difficulties, 13*(3), 205–225.

Brandt, D. (2015). *The rise of writing: Redefining mass literacy.* Cambridge University Press.

Breetvelt, I., Van den Bergh, H., & Rijlaarsdam, G. (1996). Rereading and generating and their relation to text quality: An application of multilevel analysis on writing process data. In G. Rijlaarsdam & E. Espéret (Series Eds.), G. Rijlaarsdam, H. Van den Bergh, & M. Couzijn (Vol. Eds.), *Studies in writing Vol. 1, theories, models and methodology in writing research* (pp. 1–20). Amsterdam University Press.

Britton, J. (1970). *Language and learning.* Penguin.

Britton, J. (1983). Writing and the story of the world. In B. M. Kroll & C. G. Wells (Eds.), *Explorations in the development of writing: Theory, research, and practice* (pp. 3–30). Wiley.

Britton, J., Burgess, T., Martin, M., McLeod, A., & Rosen, H. (1975). *The development of writing abilities.* Macmillan.

Broadfoot, P. (1996). *Education, assessment and society.* Open University Press.

Brown, J. S., Collins, A., & Duguid, P. (1989). Situated cognition and the culture of learning. *Educational Researcher, 18*(1), 32–42.

Bruffee, K. A. (1973). Collaborative learning: Some practical models. *College English, 34*(5), 634–643.

Bruffee, K. A. (1984). Collaborative learning and the conversation of mankind. *College English, 46*(7), 635–652.

Burke, J. (2012). Connecting the classroom, community, and curriculum. *English Journal, 101*(4), 17–28.

Butler, D., & Winne, P. (1995). Feedback and self-regulated learning: A theoretical syntheses. *Review of Educational Research, 65*(3), 245–281.

Calkins, L. (1983). *Lessons from a child: On the teaching and learning of writing.* Heineman.

Callaghan, M., Knapp, P., & Noble, G. (1993). Genre in practice. In B. Cope & M. Kalantzis (Eds.), *The powers of literacy* (pp. 179–202). University of Pittsburg Press.

Camp, R. (1993). The place of portfolios in our changing views of writing assessment. In R. E. Bennett & W. C. Ward (Eds.), *Construction versus choice in cognitive measurement: Issues in constructed response, performance testing, and portfolio assessment* (pp. 183–212). Lawrence Erlbaum.

Camp, R. (1998). Portfolio reflection: The basis for dialogue. *The Clearing House, 72*(1), 10–12.

Camp, R., & Levine, D. (1991). Portfolios evolving: Background and variations in sixth-through twelfth-grade classrooms. In P. Belanoff & M. Dickson (Eds.), *Portfolios: Process and product* (pp. 194–205). Boynton/Cook.

Carillo, E. C. (2015). *Securing a place for reading in composition: The importance of teaching for transfer.* Utah State University Press.

Christie, F., & Derewianka, B. (2008). *School discourse: Learning to write across the years of schooling.* Continuum.

Christie, F., & Martin, J. R. (Eds.). (2007). *Language, knowledge and pedagogy: Functional linguistic and sociological perspectives.* Continuum.

Clay, M. M. (1982). *Observing young readers: Selected papers.* Heinemann.

Cooper, M. (1986). The ecology of writing. *College English, 48*(4), 364–375.

Cope, B., & Kalantzis, M. (Eds.). (1993). *The powers of literacy: A genre approach to teaching writing.* University of Pittsburgh Press.

Cope, B., & Kalantzis, M. (2004). Text-made text. *E-learning, 1*(2), 198–282.

Cox, M., Ortmeier-Hooper, C., & Tirabassi, K. E. (2009). Teaching writing for the "real world": Community and workplace writing. *English Journal, 98*(5), 72–80.

Cramer, A. M., & Mason, L. H. (2015). Thank you for helping me write a better paper: Peer support in learning to write. In K. R. Harris & L. Meltzer (Eds.), *The power of peers in the classroom: Enhancing learning and social skills.* Guilford Press.

Cross, G. A. (1994). *Collaboration and conflict: A contextual exploration of group writing and positive emphasis.* Written Language Series. Hampton Press.

Crowley, S. (1990). *The methodical memory: Invention in current traditional rhetoric.* Southern Illinois University Press.

Dahl, K., & Farnan, N. (1998). *Children's writing: Perspectives from research.* International Reading Association.

D'Angelo, F. (1980). *Process and thought in composition.* Winthrop.

Davidson, C. (2017). *The new education: How to revolutionize the university to prepare students for a world in flux.* Basic Books.

Deane, P., Orendahl, N., Quinlan, T., Fowles, M., Welsh, C., & Bivens-Tatum, J. (2008). *Cognitive models of writing: Writing proficiency as a complex integrated skill.* Educational Testing Service. https://onlinelibrary.wiley.com/doi/abs/10.1002/j.2333-8504.2008.tb02141.x

Deans, T. (2000). *Writing partnerships: Service-learning in composition.* National Council of Teachers of English.

Denton, P., Madden, J., Roberts, M., & Rowe, P. (2008). Students' response to traditional and computer-assisted formative feedback: A comparative case study. *British Journal of Educational Technology, 39*(3), 486–500.

Derewianka, B. (1990). *Exploring how texts work.* Primary English Teaching Association.

Devitt, A. J. (1993). Generalizing about genre: New conceptions of an old concept. *College Composition and Communication, 44*(4), 573–586.

Dewey, J. (1933). *How we think.* Prometheus Books.

Dorff, D. L., & Duin, A. H. (1989). Applying a cognitive model to document cycling. *Technical Writing Teacher, 16*(3), 234–249.

Dubinsky, J. M., & Carpenter, J. H. (Eds.). (2004). *Civic engagement and technical communication.* Erlbaum.

Durst, R. K. (2015). British invasion: James Britton, composition studies, and anti-disciplinarity. *College Composition and Communication, 66*(3), 384–401.

Durst, R. K., & Newell, G. E. (1989). The uses of function: James Britton's category system and research on writing. *Review of Educational Research, 59*(4), 375–394.

Dyson, A. H. (1993). *The social worlds of children learning to write in an urban primary school.* Teachers College Press.

Elkins, J. (2018, December 28). Crowdsourcing for writers: The secret to connect with your readers and find your best ideas. *The Write Practice Blog.* https://thewritepractice.com/crowdsourcing-for-writers/

Elon University. (2014, May 22). *Elon statement on writing transfer.* Center for Engaged Learning. www.centerforengagedlearning.org/elon-statement-on-writing-transfer/

Esposito, L. (2012). Where to begin? Using place-based writing to connect students with their local communities. *English Journal, 101*(4), 70–76.

Evans, K. A. (2001). Rethinking self-assessment as a tool for response. *Teaching English in the Two-year College, 28*(3), 293–301.

Fitzgerald, J., & Stamm, C. (1990). Effects of group conferences on first graders' revision in writing. *Written Communication, 7*(1), 96–135.

Flower, L., & Hayes, J. R. (1980). Identifying the organization of writing processes. In L. W. Gregg & E. R. Steinberg (Eds.), *Cognitive processes in writing* (pp. 3–30). Lawrence Erlbaum.

Flower, L., & Hayes, J. R. (1981). A cognitive process theory of writing. *College Composition and Communication, 32*(4), 365–387.

Fox, P. (1998). Inviting dialogue: An alternative to teaching in the dark. *Clearing House, 72*(1), 35–38.

Freedman, S. W., Greenleaf, C., & Sperling, M. (1987). *Response to student writing.* National Council of Teachers of English.

Freire, P. (1972). *Pedagogy of the oppressed.* Penguin.

Gere, A. R. (1987). *Writing groups: History, theory, and implications.* Illinois University Press.

Gipps, C. (1999). Socio-cultural aspects of assessment. In P. D. Pearson & A. Iran-Nehad (Eds.), *Review of research in education* (Vol. 23, pp. 335–393). American Educational Research Association.

Glenn, C., & Goldthwaite, M. (2014). *The St. Martin's guide to teaching writing* (7th ed.). Bedford/St. Martin's.

Goldblatt, E. (2007). *Because we live here: Sponsoring literacy beyond the college curriculum.* Hampton Press.

Goodrich, H. (1997). Understanding rubrics. *Educational Leadership, 54*(4), 14–17.

Grabill, J., Hart-Davidson, W., Pigg, S., McLeod, M., Curran, P., Moore, J. L., Rosinski, P., Peeples, T., Rumsey, S., Courant-Rife, M., Tasaka, R., Lackey, D., & Brunk-Chavez, B. (2010). *Revisualizing composition: Mapping the writing lives of first-year college students.* Writing in Digital Environments Research Center [Whitepaper]. Reprinted in E. Wardle & D. Downs (Eds.). (2014). *Writing about writing: A college reader* (pp. 724–739). Bedford/St. Martin's.

Graham, S., Harris, K. R., & Hebert, M. (2011). *Informing writing: The benefits of formative assessment.* Report from the Carnegie Corporation of New York. Alliance for Excellent Education.

Graham, S., & Perin, D. (2006). *Writing next: Effective strategies to improve writing of adolescents in middle and high schools.* Report to Carnegie Corporation of New York. Alliance for Excellent Education.

Graham, S., & Perin, D. (2007). A meta-analysis of writing instruction for adolescent students. *Journal of Educational Psychology, 99*(3), 445–476.

Graves, D. (1983). *Writing: Teachers and children at work.* Heinemann.

Greeno, J. G., Pearson, P. D., & Schoenfeld, A. H. (1996, August). *Implications for NAEP of research on learning and cognition.* Report commissioned by the National Academy of Education Panel on the NAEP Trial State Assessment. Institute for Research on Learning. http://ldt.stanford.edu/~educ39107/hiroshis/project_documents_backup/partA/Perhaps2Use/Greeno_Pearson_Schoenfeld_1996.pdf

Habermas, J. (1974). *Theory and practice* (J. Viental, Trans.). Heinemann.

Halliday, M. A. K., & Martin, J. R. (1993). *Writing science: Literacy and discursive power.* University of Pittsburgh Press.

Haswell, R. H. (1983). Minimal marking. *College English, 45*(6), 600–604.

Hawisher, G. E., & Selfe, C. L. (Eds.). (1999). *Passions, pedagogies, and 21st century technologies.* Utah State University Press.

Hayes, J. R. (1996). A new framework for understanding cognition and affect in writing. In C. M. Levy & S. Ransdell (Eds.), *The science of writing: Theories, methods, individual differences, ad applications.* Lawrence Erlbaum Associates. www.researchgate.net/publication/271429714_A_new_framework_for_understanding_cognition_and_affect_in_writing

Herrington, A., Hodgson, K., & Moran, C. (Eds.). (2009). *Teaching the new writing: Technology, change, and the assessment in the 21st-century classroom*. Teachers College Press

Hillocks, G., Jr. (1984). What works in teaching composition: A meta-analysis of experimental treatment studies. *American Journal of Education, 93*(1), 133–170.

Hillocks, G., Jr. (1986). *Research on written composition: New directions for teaching*. National Council of Teachers of English.

Hillocks, G., Jr. (1995). *Teaching writing as reflective practice*. Teachers College Press.

Hobson, E. (2001). Writing center pedagogy. In G. Tate, A. Rupiper, & K. Schick (Eds.), *Guide to composition pedagogies* (pp. 165–182). Oxford University Press.

Howard, R. M. (1999). *Standing in the shadow of giants: Plagiarists, authors, and collaborators*. Ablex.

Hull, G., Jury, M., Ziv, O., & Katz, M. (1996). *Changing work, changing literacy? A study of skill requirements and development in a traditional and restructured workplace*. National Center for the Study of Writing.

Ivanic, R. (2004). Discourses of writing and learning to write. *Language and Education, 18*(3), 220–245.

Jewitt, C. (2008). Multimodality and literacy in school classrooms. *Review of Research in Education, 32*(1), 241–267.

Johns, A. M. (1997). *Text, role, and context: Developing academic literacies*. Cambridge University Press.

Kamberelis, G., & De La Luna, L. (2004). Children's writing: How textual forms, contextual forces, and textual politics co-emerge. In C. Bazerman & P. Prior (Eds.), *What writing does and how it does it: An introduction to analyzing texts and textual practices* (pp. 239–278). Lawrence Erlbaum Associates.

King, M. L., & Rentel, V. (1981). *How children learn to write: A longitudinal study*. Final Report. National Institute of Education. ED 203 369.

Kinzer, C. K., & Leu, D. J. (2017). New literacies and new literacies within changing digital environments. In M. A. Peters (Ed.), *Encyclopedia of educational philosophy and theory*. Springer.

Kress, G. (1997). Visual and verbal modes of representation in electronically mediated communication: The potentials of new forms of text. In I. Snyder (Ed.), *Page to screen: Taking literacy into the electronic era* (pp. 53–79). Allen & Unwin.

Kress, G. (2001, July). *Plenary address given at the eighth international literacy and education*. Research Network Conference on Learning, Spetses.

Lave, J., & Wenger, E. (1991). *Situated learning: Legitimate peripheral participation*. Cambridge University Press.

Law, J. (2007). Making a mess with method. In W. Outhwaite & S. P. Turner (Eds.), *The Sage handbook of social science methodology* (pp. 595–606). Sage.

Lea, M. R., & Street, B. V. (1998). Student writing in higher education: An academic literacies approach. *Studies in Higher Education, 23*(2), 157–161.

Lea, M. R., & Street, B. V. (2006). The "academic literacies" model: Theory and applications. *Theory into Practice, 45*(4), 368–377. https://doi.org/10.1207/s15430421tip4504_11

LeFevre, K. B. (1987). *Invention as a social act*. Southern Illinois University Press.

Lenhart, A. (2012). *Teens, smartphones & texting*. Pew Research Center. www.pewinternet.org/Reports/2012/Teens-and-smartphones.aspx?src=prc-headline

Lenhart, A., Arafeh, S., Smith, A., & Macgill, A. (2008). *Writing, technology and teens*. Pew Research Center. http://pewinternet.org/Reports/2008/Writing-Technology-and-Teens.aspx

Locker, K. O. (1992). What makes a collaborative writing team successful? A case study of lawyers and social workers in a state agency. In J. Forman (Ed.), *New visions of collaborative writing* (pp. 37–62). Heinemann.

Lotherington, H. (2004). Emergent metaliteracies: What the xbox has to offer the EQAO. *Linguistics and Education, 14*(3), 305–319. https://doi.org/10.1016/j.linged.2004.02.007

Lunsford, A. (1991). Collaboration, control, and the idea of a writing center. *Writing Center Journal, 12*(1), 3–10.

Lunsford, A. (2011). *St. Martin's handbook* (7th ed.). Bedford/St. Martin's.

Lunsford, A. (n.d.). *Our semi-literate youth? Not so fast.* https://ssw.stanford.edu/sites/g/files/sbiybj10266/f/OPED_Our_Semi-Literate_Youth.pdf

Lunsford, A., & Ede, L. (1994). Collaborative authorship and the teaching of writing. In M. Woodmansee & P. Jaszi (Eds.), *The construction of authorship: Textual appropriation in law and literature* (pp. 418–438). Duke University Press.

MacArthur, C. (2007). Best practices in teaching evaluation and revision. In S. Graham, C. A. Macarthur, & J. Fitzgerald (Eds.), *Best practices in writing instruction* (pp. 141–163). Guilford Press.

MacArthur, C. A., Philippakos, Z. A., & Ianetta, M. (2015). Self-regulated strategy instruction in college developmental writing. *Journal of Educational Psychology, 107*(3), 855–867. https://doi.org/10.1037/edu0000011

MacArthur, C. A., Schwartz, S. S., & Graham, S. (1991). Effects of a reciprocal peer revision strategy in special education classrooms. *Learning Disabilities Research and Practice, 6*(4), 201–210.

Madden, M., Lenhart, A., Duggan, M., Cortesi, S., & Gasser, U. (2013). *Teens and technology 2013.* Pew Research Center. www.pewinternet.org/2013/03/13/teens-and-technology-2013/

Mathis, M. (2021). *25 formative assessment options your students will actually enjoy.* Retrieved September 29, 2021, from www.weareteachers.com/25-formative-assessment-options/

Martin, J. R. (1985). *Factual writing: Exploring and challenging social reality.* Deakin University Press (reissued Oxford University Press, 1989).

Matsuhashi, A. (1981). Pausing and planning: The tempo of written discourse production. *Research in the Teaching of English, 15*(2), 113–134.

McDonald, B. (2007). Self assessment for understanding. *The Journal of Education, 188*(1), 25–40. http://csimmonds.pbworks.com/w/file/fetch/118283784/Self%20Assessment%20for%20Understanding.pdf

Messick, S. (1989). Validity. In R. L. Linn (Ed.), *Educational measurement* (3rd ed., pp. 13–103). Macmillan.

Miller, C. (1984). Genre as social action. *Quarterly Journal of Speech, 70*(2), 151–167.

Miller, S. M. (2013). A research meta-synthesis on digital video composing in classrooms: An evidence-based framework toward a pedagogy for embodied learning. *Journal of Literacy Research, 45*(4), 386–430.

Mills-Court, K., & Amiran, M. R. (1991). Metacognition and the use of portfolios. In P. Belanoff & M. Dickson (Eds.), *Portfolios: Process and product* (pp. 101–112). Boynton/Cook.

Moore, J. L., Rosinski, P., Peeples, T., Pigg, S. Rife, M. C., Chavez, B. B., Lackey, D., Rumsey, S. K., Tasaka, R., Curran, P., & Grabill, J. T. (2016). Revisualizing composition: How first-year writers use composing technologies. *Computers and Composition, 39*(1), 1–13.

Moss, P. A. (1994). Can there be validity without reliability? *Educational Researcher, 23*(2), 5–12. https://doi.org/10.3102/0013189X023002005

Murphy, S. (1998). Reflection—in portfolios and beyond. *The Clearing House, 72*(1), 7–9.

Murphy, S., & Underwood, T. (2000). *Portfolio practices: Lessons from schools, districts and states*. Christopher Gordon Publishers.

Murray, D. M. (1972). Teach writing as a process not product. *The Leaflet* (Reprinted in *Cross-Talk in Comp Theory*). https://mwover.files.wordpress.com/2018/05/murray-teach-writing-as-a-process-not-product.pdf

Myers, M., & Pearson, P. D. (1996). Performance assessment and the literacy unit of the new standards project. *Assessing Writing, 3*(1), 5–29. https://doi.org/10.1016/S1075-2935(96)90003-3

National Assessment Governing Board. (2017). *Writing framework for the 2017 national assessment of educational progress*. www.nagb.gov/naep-frameworks/writing/2017-writing-framework.html

National Council of Teachers of English. (1983). *Resolution on computers in English and language arts*. https://ncte.org/statement/computersinela/

National Council of Teachers of English. (2005). *Multimodal literacies*. https://ncte.org/statement/multimodalliteracies/

National Council of Teachers of English Assessment. (2016). *The assessment story project: What we learned from teachers sharing their experiences with literacy assessment*. https://cdn.ncte.org/nctefiles/assessmentstoryproject/2016assessmentstoryprojectreport.pdf

National Research Council (2000). *How people learn: Brain, mind, experience, and school* (Expanded Ed.). The National Academies Press. www.nap.edu/catalog/9853/how-people-learn-brain-mind-experience-and-school-expanded-edition

Nelson, N., & Calfee, R. C. (1998). The reading-writing connection viewed historically. In N. Nelson & R. C. Calfee (Eds.), *Ninety-seventh yearbook of the national society for the study of education* (Part II, pp. 1–52). National Society for the Study of Education.

Nicol, D. J., & Macfarlane-Dick, D. (2006). Formative assessment and self-regulated learning: A model and seven principles of good feedback practice. *Studies in Higher Education, 31*(2), 199–218.

Olsen, G. (1999). Toward a post-process composition: Abandoning the rhetoric of assertion. In T. Kent (Ed.), *Post-process theory: Beyond the writing process paradigm*. Southern Illinois University Press.

O'Neill, P. (2017, November 16–19). *Teachers as assessment leaders in literacy* [Conference session]. National Council of Teachers of English.

Palmeri, J. (2012). *Remixing composition: A history of multimodal writing pedagogy*. Southern Illinois University Press.

Paltridge, B. (2004). *Genre and the language learning classroom*. The University of Michigan Press.

Parks, S., & Goldblatt, E. (2000). Writing beyond the curriculum: Fostering new collaborations in literacy. *College English, 62*(95), 584–606.

Patthey-Chavez, G. G., & Ferris, D. (1997). Writing conferences and the weaving of multivoiced texts in college composition. *Research in the Teaching of English, 31*(1), 51–90.

Pelz, K. (1982). James Britton and the pedagogy of advanced composition. *Journal of Advanced Composition, 3*(1–2), 1–9. www.jaconlinejournal.com/archives/vol3/pelz-britton.pdf

Perl, S. (1979). The composing processes of skilled and unskilled college writers. *Research in the Teaching of English, 13*(4), 317–336.

Perl, S., & Egendorf, A. (1986). The process of creative discovery: Theory, research, and implications for teaching. In D. McQuade (Ed.), *The territory of language: Linguistics, stylistics, and the teaching of composition* (pp. 251–268). Southern Illinois University Press.

Perry, K. (2012). What is literacy?—A critical overview of sociocultural perspectives. *Journal of Language & Literacy Education, 8*(1), 50–71.

Pianko, S. (1979). Reflection: A critical component of the composing process. *College Composition and Communication, 30*(3), 275–278.

Pintrich, P. R. (2000). The role of goal-orientation in self-regulated learning. In M. Boekaerts, P. R. Pintrich, & M. Zeidner (Eds.), *Handbook of self-regulation* (pp. 451–502). Elsevier.

Porter, J. (2002). Why technology matters to writing: A cyberwriter's tale. *Computers and Composition, 20*(4), 375–394.

Prior, P. (2006). A sociocultural theory of writing. In C. A. MacArthur, S. Graham, & J. Fitzgerald (Eds.), *Handbook of writing research* (pp. 54–66). The Guilford Press.

Purcell, K., Buchanan, J., & Friedrich, L. (2013, July). *The impact of digital tools on student writing and how writing is taught in schools.* www.pewresearch.org/internet/2013/07/16/the-impact-of-digital-tools-on-student-writing-and-how-writing-is-taught-in-schools/

Reif, L. (1992). *Seeking diversity: Language arts with adolescents.* Heinemann.

Resnick, D. P., & Resnick, L. B. (1989). Varieties of literacy. In A. E. Barnes & P. N. Sterns (Eds.), *Social history and issues in human consciousness* (pp. 171–96). New York University.

Reuter, Y. (1993). *Les interactions lecture-écriture* [*The integration of reading- writing*]. Peter Lang.

Robinson, K. (2001). *Out of our minds: Learning to be creative.* Capstone Publishing.

Rose, S. K., & Weiser, I. (Eds.). (2010). *Going public: What writing programs learn from engagement.* Utah State University Press.

Rosenblatt, L. M. (1989). Writing and reading: The transactional theory. In J. M. Mason (Ed.), *Reading and writing connections.* Allyn and Bacon.

Rosinski, P. (2017). Students' perceptions of the transfer of rhetorical knowledge between digital self-sponsored writing and academic writing: The importance of authentic contexts and reflection. In C. M. Anson & J. L. Moore (Eds.), *Critical transitions: Writing and the question of transfer* (pp. 247–271). University Press of Colorado. https://doi.org/10.37514/PER-B.2016.0797.2.09

Ross, J. A. (2006). The reliability, validity, and utility of self-assessment. *Practical Assessment, Research and Evaluation, 11*(10), 1–13.

Ross, J. A., Rolheiser, C., & Hogaboam-Gray, A. (1999). Effect of self-evaluation on narrative writing. *Assessing Writing, 6*(1), 107–132.

Ryan, M. (2011). Improving reflective writing in higher education: A social semiotic perspective. *Teaching in Higher Education, 16*(1), 99–111. www.tandfonline.com/doi/full/10.1080/13562517.2010.507311

Sanchez, C., Atkinson, K., Koenka, A., Moshontz, H., & Cooper, H. (2017). Self-grading and peer-grading for formative and summative assessments in 3rd through 12th grade classrooms: A meta-analysis. *Journal of Educational Psychology, 109*(8), 1049–1066. https://doi.org/10.1037/edu0000190

Sandmel, K., & Graham, S. (2011). The process writing approach: A meta-analysis. *Journal of Educational Research, 104*(6), 396–407.

Schon, D. (1983). *The reflective practitioner.* Jossey-Bass.

Schumacher, G. M., Scott, B. T., Klare, G. R., Cronin, F. C., & Lambert, D. A. (1989). Cognitive processes in journalistic genres. *Written Communication, 6*(3), 390–407.

Sfard, A. (1998). On two metaphors for learning and the dangers of choosing just one. *Educational Researcher, 27*(2), 4–13.

Shanahan, T., & Tierney, R. J. (1990). Reading-writing relationships: Three perspectives. In J. Zutell & S. McCormick (Eds.), *Literacy theory and research: Analyses from multiple paradigms* (Thirty-ninth Yearbook of the National Reading Conference, pp. 13–34). National Reading Conference.

Shaughnessy, M. (1977). *Errors and expectations: A guide for the teacher of basic writing.* Oxford University.

Shipka, J. (2011). *Toward a composition made whole.* University of Pittsburgh Press.

Shute, V. J. (2008). Focus on formative feedback. *Review of Educational Research, 78*(1), 153–189.

Smith, M. A., & Swain, S. S. (2017). *Assessing writing, teaching writers: Putting the analytic writing Continuum to work in your classroom.* Teachers College Press.

Sommers, J. (1988). Behind the paper: Using the student-teacher memo. *College Composition and Communication, 39*(1), 77–80.

Sommers, N. (1980). Revision strategies of student writers and experienced adult writers. *College Composition and Communication, 31*(4), 378–388.

Sommers, N. (1982). Responding to student writing. *College Composition and Communication, 33*(2), 148–156.

Sperling, M. (1990). I want to talk to each of you: Collaboration and the teacher-student writing conference. *Research in the Teaching of English, 24*(3), 279–321.

Stanford University. (2021, August 27). *Stanford study of writing.* https://ssw.stanford.edu/.

Stotsky, S. (1983). Research on reading/writing relationships: A synthesis and suggested directions. *Language Arts, 60*(5), 627–643.

Street, B. (1995). *Social literacies: Critical approaches to literacy in development, ethnography and education.* Longman Group Limited.

Strickland, K., & Strickland, J. (1993). *Un-covering the curriculum: Whole language in secondary and postsecondary classrooms.* Boyton/Cook Publishers.

Strickland, K., & Strickland, J. (1996). I do whole language on Fridays. *The English Journal, 85*(2), 17–25.

Swales, J. (1990). *Genre analysis: English in academic and research settings.* Cambridge University Press.

Taylor, B. M., & Beach, R. W. (1984). The effects of text structure instruction on middle-grade students' comprehension and production of expository text. *Reading Research Quarterly, 18*, 134–146.

Tierney, R. J., & Leys, M. (1984). *What is the value of connecting reading and writing?* Reading Education Report No. 55. Bolt, Beranek & Newman & Center for the Study of Reading. https://files.eric.ed.gov/fulltext/ED251810.pdf

Tierney, R. J., & Shanahan, T. (1991). Research on the reading-writing relationship: Interactions, transactions, and outcomes. In R. Barr, M. L. Kamil, P. Mosenthal, & P. David Pearson (Eds.), *The handbook of reading research* (Vol. 2, pp. 246–280). Longman.

Trumbull, E., & Lash, A. (2013). Understanding formative assessment: Insights from learning theory and measurement theory. *WestEd.* www.wested.org/resources/understanding-formative-assessment-insights-from-learning-theory-and-measurement-theory/

Tuzi, F. (2004). The impact of e-feedback on the revisions of L2 writers in an academic writing course. *Computers and Composition, 21*(2), 217–235.

Underwood, T. (1999). *The portfolio project: A study of assessment, instruction, and middle school reform.* National Council of Teachers of English.

Van den Bergh, H., Rijlaarsdam, G., & Van Steendam, E. (2016). Writing process theory: A functional dynamic approach. In C. A. MacArthur, S. Graham, & J. Fitzgerald (Eds.), *Handbook of writing research* (pp. 57–71). Guilford Press.

Van der Kleij, F. S., & Adie, L. (2018). Formative assessment and feedback using information technology. In J. Voogt, G. Knezek, R. Christensen, & K. W. Lai (Eds.), *Second handbook of information technology in primary and secondary education* (pp. 601–615). Springer International Handbooks of Education. Springer. https://doi.org/10.1007/978-3-319-71054-9_38

Vygotsky, L. (1978). *Mind in society*. Harvard University Press.

Wendell, B. (1891). *English composition*. Scribners.

Wiliam, D. (2000). Formative assessment in mathematics part 3: The learner's role. *Equals: Mathematics and Special Educational Needs*, *6*(1), 19–22.

Wiliam, D. (2007). Keeping learning on track: Classroom assessment and the regulation of learning. In F. K. Lester Jr. (Ed.), *Second handbook of mathematics teaching and learning* (pp. 1053–1098). Information Age Publishing.

Williams, J. D. (2014). *Preparing to teach writing: Research, theory, and practice*. Routledge.

Williams, S. (2009). *The impact of collaborative, scaffolded learning in K-12 schools: A meta-analysis*. Cisco Systems/The Metiri Group. http://docshare01.docshare.tips/files/7943/79437698.pdf

Williamson, M. M. (1993). An introduction to holistic scoring: The social, historical and theoretical context for writing assessment. In M. Williamson & B. Huot (Eds.), *Validating holistic scoring for writing assessment: Theoretical and empirical foundations* (pp. 1–44). Hampton Press.

Winsor, D. A. (1996). *Writing like an engineer: A rhetorical education*. Routledge.

Witte, S., & Cherry, R. (1994). Think-aloud protocols, protocol analysis, and research design: An exploration of the influence of writing tasks on writing processes. In P. Smagorinsky (Ed.), *Speaking about writing: Reflections on research methodologies* (pp. 20–54). Sage.

Witte, S., & Haas, C. (2001). Writing as an embodied practice: The case of engineering standards. *Journal of Business and Technical Communication*, *15*(4), 431–457.

Yancey, K. B. (1998a). Getting beyond exhaustion: Reflection, self-assessment, and learning. *Clearing House*, *72*(1), 13–18.

Yancey, K. B. (1998b). *Reflection in the writing classroom*. University Press of Colorado, Utah State University Press.

Yancey, K. B. (1999). Looking back as we look forward: Historicizing writing assessment. *College Composition and Communication*, *50*(3), 483–503.

Yancey, K. B. (2004). Made not only in words: Composition in a new key. *College Composition and Communication*, *56*(2), 297–328.

Yancey, K. B. (2009a). 2008 NCTE presidential address: The impulse to compose in the age of composition. *Research in the Teaching of English*, *43*(3), 316–338.

Yancey, K. B. (2009b). *Writing in the 21st century: A report from the national council of teachers of English*. https://cdn.ncte.org/nctefiles/press/yancey_final.pdf

Zimmerman, B. J., & Campillo, M. (2003). Motivating self-regulated problem solvers. In J. E. Davidson & R. J. Sternberg (Eds.), *The psychology of problem solving* (pp. 233–262). Cambridge University Press.

4

REDESIGNING ASSESSMENTS TO SUPPORT LEARNING AND ALIGN WITH A COMPLEX COGNITIVE AND SOCIAL CONSTRUCT OF WRITING

As we have noted earlier, an effective remodel requires renovators to remove dysfunctional and outdated parts of a house, and to incorporate new technologies in remodeling. Renovators also need to make sure that a home remodel meets new building codes and supports requirements of contemporary life. Likewise, education reformers need to take stock of the basics of education with an eye toward making sure that reforms support teaching and learning and conform to professional standards. In this chapter, we explore some of the ways our assessment system might be redesigned to support learning and become more closely aligned with a complex cognitive and social construct of writing. For classroom-based assessment, we focus in particular on formative assessment, as well as ways to encourage metacognitive thinking, so that students can learn to evaluate, monitor, and guide their own learning (Darling-Hammond et al., 2008). For large-scale assessment, we explore ways to align assessment more closely with contemporary theories of writing and learning than it has been in the past, while minimizing some of the deleterious effects of the high-stakes accountability assessments that we discussed in Chapters 1 and 2.

Using assessment to promote learning

Scholars acknowledge the important role that assessment plays in learning. The National Research Council's Committee on Developments in the Science of Learning reviewed research on learning and concluded the following:

> The roles for assessment must be expanded beyond the traditional concept of testing. The use of frequent formative assessment helps make students' thinking visible to themselves, their peers, and their teacher. This provides

DOI: 10.4324/9781003296140-4

feedback that can guide modification and refinement in thinking. Given the goal of learning with understanding, assessments must tap understanding rather than merely the ability to repeat facts or perform isolated skills.

(2000, p. 19)

While we discussed formative assessment techniques as best practices in teaching writing in Chapter 3, here we address strategies such as feedback and reflection through an assessment lens. We are aware that there is some overlap, but we want to emphasize the critical role formative assessment plays in promoting effective teaching and in supporting learning to write. Furthermore, as we will show later in this chapter, this approach to assessment can also play a role in accountability assessments.

The current use of standardized tests represents a very narrow view of the role of assessment in education. As Black and Wiliam (1998), Shepard (2000), Graham et al. (2011), and many other researchers have observed, assessment, and in particular, formative assessment, is a key component of learning. Broadly speaking, formative assessment means taking stock of where students are and what they bring to the task of learning as a starting point for instruction. For example, the National Research Council (2000) recommends learner-centered environments that pay careful attention to what learners bring to educational settings, and promote "teaching practices that have been called 'culturally responsive,' 'culturally appropriate,' 'culturally compatible,' and 'culturally relevant'" (p. 134). Teachers in such environments "attempt to get a sense of what students know and can do as well as their interests and passions—what each student knows, cares about, is able to do, and wants to do" (p. 136). In other words, in addition to taking their students' backgrounds into account, they engage in various kinds of formative assessment.

Erickson (2007) describes formative assessment as "the continual 'taking stock' that teachers do by paying firsthand observational attention to students during the ongoing course of instruction—careful attention focused upon specific aspects of a student's developing understanding" (p. 187). In addition to observations, formative assessment refers to more formal kinds of assessment, including ongoing quizzes and the like. According to Black and Wiliam (1998), assessments are formative "when the evidence is actually used to adapt the teaching to meet student needs" (p. 2). Heritage (2010) notes that formative assessment is what enables teachers and students to work together in social and interactive processes that support learning. Vygotsky's notion of the zone of proximal development is particularly relevant here, Heritage (2010) argues, because it is "the area where learning takes place through a process of 'scaffolding'" (p. 8). Heritage elaborates on the teacher's role in formative assessment:

> Teachers are involved in a continuous process of evidence gathering and interpretation so as to structure learning that builds on "maturing functions" (Vygotsky, 1978). Teachers need to lead learning, not retrospectively

react to it. Only by keeping a very close eye on emerging learning through formative assessment can teachers be prospective, determining what is within the students' reach, and providing them experiences to support and extend learning.

(p. 8)

Similarly, Black and Wiliam (2009), drawing on the work of Ramaprasad (1983), describe three key processes for teaching that involve formative assessment:

- Establishing where the learners are in their learning
- Establishing where they are going
- Establishing what needs to be done to get them there

(p. 4)

According to Darling-Hammond et al. (2008), studies consistently show that highly effective teachers use assessment, among other things, to support the process of meaningful learning by:

- Diagnosing student understanding in order to scaffold the learning process step by step
- Assessing student learning continuously and adapting teaching to student needs
- Providing clear standards, constant feedback, and opportunities for work

(p. 5)

Evidence in the research literature confirms the value of formative assessment. In a comprehensive review of studies across groups "from 5-year-olds to university undergraduates, across several school subjects, and over several countries," Black and Wiliam (1998) found that "innovations that include strengthening the practice of formative assessment produce significant and often substantial learning gains. . . . Typical effect sizes of the formative assessment experiments were between 0.4 and 0.7" (p. 3). In their meta-analysis of the effects of formative assessment on disabled children in 21 studies, Fuchs and Fuchs (1986) found an average weighted effect size of .70. A more recent meta-analysis of studies on the impact of formative assessment resulted in more modest results (a mean of .20), but the effects were generally positive (Kingston & Nash, 2011). And in yet another review conducted by Wiliam et al. (2004), the average effect size was .30. Another study of a computer-based formative assessment system of writing resulted in an effect size of .28 (Rich et al., 2008). These studies document the effectiveness of formative assessment in general, and in the case of the last study, of its use in writing instruction in particular. Heritage (2010) notes that the student learning gains "triggered by formative assessment are a powerful argument" for teachers to engage in it (p. 2). Rather than use assessments as a prod for teachers to get better, it makes sense to emphasize formative assessment. In the hands of thoughtful teachers, formative assessment is a particularly robust way to promote learning.

Students, along with teachers, can engage actively in formative assessment. Black and Wiliam (2009), for example, include strategies in their framework for formative assessment in the classroom that put students in active and authoritative roles: (1) "activating students as instructional resources for one another"; and (2) "activating students as the owners of their own learning" (p. 5). According to Black and Wiliam (2009), the idea that students can be instructional resources for each other is linked to research on reciprocal teaching (Brown & Campione, 1996) and collaborative learning (Slavin et al., 2003).

As Andrade and Valtcheva (2009) note, "Self-assessment is a key element in formative assessment because it involves students in thinking about the quality of their own work, rather than relying on their teacher as the sole source of evaluative judgments" (p. 13). At the same time, students' reflections on their processes and work provide teachers with information that would otherwise be unavailable for formative assessment purposes. In social–cognitive theory, self-assessment is closely interconnected with the concepts of self-efficacy and self-regulation. Bandura (1994) defines self-efficacy as the beliefs people have about their capabilities to produce designated levels of performance. According to Bandura (1997), students who see themselves as having been successful on a task, and who interpret their performance as evidence of having mastered the task, are more likely to believe they will achieve success in the future. While there is evidence that repeated negative self-assessments can lead students to make excuses for their performance, make little effort, and adopt unrealistic personal goals (e.g., Ross et al., 2002; Stipek et al., 1992), positive self-assessments appear to promote self-efficacy and an upward learning cycle (Ross, 2006): "Students with greater confidence in their ability to accomplish the target task are more likely to visualize success than failure. They set higher standards of performance for themselves. . . . Confident students persist" (Ross, 2006, p. 6).

While self-assessment involves evaluating one's work or performance, self-regulation involves monitoring and controlling one's thinking, actions, and affective behaviors (Keane & Griffin, 2015; Kaunhoven & Dorjee, 2017). Self-regulators set goals, self-monitor, and self-reinforce (Harris & Graham, 1999). In the literature on self-regulation in the field of psychology, feedback is viewed as an essential component within several self-regulation models (e.g., Butler & Winne, 1995; Bangert-Drowns et al., 1991; Nicol & Macfarlane-Dick, 2006; Pintrich, 2000; Zimmerman & Campillo, 2003). According to Keane and Griffin (2015), some evidence "suggests that children's self-assessments must be accurate relative to actual performance in order to evoke self-regulatory processes (e.g.,

Nicol, 2009)" (p. 39), while other research points to the influence of developmental stage, prior academic attainment, and gender differences in the accuracy of self-assessments (Keane & Griffin, 2015). Research evidence also indicates that self-regulation influences children's academic achievement (McClelland et al., 2006; Zimmerman & Schunk, 2001). Andrade and Valtcheva (2009) explain:

> Students who set goals, make flexible plans to meet them, and monitor their progress tend to learn more and do better in school than students who do not. Self-assessment is a core element of self-regulation because it involves awareness of the goals of a task and checking one's progress toward them. As a result of self- assessment, both self-regulation and achievement can increase.
>
> *(p. 13)*

According to Zimmerman and Schunk (2008), self-regulation is also linked to motivation. Self-regulated students are motivated and active. They set goals. They analyze task requirements and devise strategies to achieve their objectives. When learning is self-regulated, learners are "aware of *what* strategies are available to help them; they understand *how* they should be applied; and they understand *why* they are necessary" (Paris & Ayres, 1994, p. 30). Further, when learners "are provided choice, challenge, control, and collaboration in their classrooms, they are motivated intrinsically to learn" (p. 28). According to Paris and Ayres, self-regulated learners need choices because "self-selected goals are governed by curiosity and intrinsic motivation to display one's competence" (p. 27). Self-regulated learners set goals for themselves that are challenging but within reach, and they "have *control* of their own learning" (p. 28). That is, they know how to use the resources available to them, when to use them, and why, and they use them intentionally. They also collaborate, reaping the benefit of strategic help when necessary. In the literature on portfolios, many authors have noted that in the process of creating portfolios, learners exercise judgment about their own work, monitor their own progress, set goals for themselves, and present themselves and their work to others (Camp, 1992a, 1992b; Murphy & Smith, 1991; Reif, 1990; Tierneyet al., 1991; Wolf, 1989; Yancey, 1998a, 1998b).

Evidence in the fields of psychology and education indicates that self-assessments can contribute to the development of skills for learning and self-regulation (Brookhart et al., 2004; Paris & Paris, 2001; Ross, 2006). Researchers also view self-assessment as a way to encourage meta-cognition (e.g., Andrade & Valtcheva, 2009; Graham et al., 2011). And evidence supports the claim that self-assessment contributes to student achievement (Hughes et al., 1985; Schunk, 1996), particularly when teachers provide direct instruction in how to self-assess (e.g., Ross et al., 1999, 2002; Ross & Starling, 2005; Andrade et al., 2008).

While formative assessment has shown positive results in research, it has not always been implemented effectively in our schools. Black and Wiliam (1998) point to several obstacles with which we are all too familiar, including the negative impact of our testing culture:

- The giving of marks and the grading function are overemphasized, while the giving of useful advice and the learning function are under emphasized.
- Approaches are used in which pupils are compared with one another, the prime purpose of which seems to them to be competition rather than personal improvement; in consequence, assessment feedback teaches low-achieving pupils that they lack "ability," causing them to come to believe that they are not able to learn.

(p. 5)

The picture in the United States is eerily similar to the picture in the United Kingdom. In both countries, high-stakes external tests dominate teaching and assessment. Black and Wiliam (1998) contend that such tests may give "teachers poor models for formative assessment because of their limited function of providing overall summaries of achievement rather than helpful diagnosis" (p. 5).

State departments of education have assessed individual students annually in English language arts since implementation of No Child Left Behind, but these achievement tests were not designed to help teachers identify an individual student's learning needs or to provide information that could be used to revise subsequent curriculum. While they may provide information relevant for accountability, such as identifying how many students meet grade-level standards, they are not tied closely enough to classroom curriculum and instruction to identify what skills students are missing, or to help teachers plan appropriate instruction or revise curriculum. And as we pointed out in Chapters 1 and 2, the consequences of these assessment systems may actually undermine deep learning and best practices in teaching.

A number of educators have called for more balanced and coherent assessment systems, systems that would support learning as well as provide information for accountability purposes (Darling-Hammond & Pecheone, 2010; Pellegrino, 2006; Wilson & Draney, 2004; Pellegrino et al., 2001). Darling-Hammond (2017) explains what such a system might entail:

A comprehensive assessment . . . is designed to provide the opportunities for high-quality teaching, student learning, and evaluation in a carefully integrated system that artfully blends state and local components to provide reliable information about learning while minimizing unnecessary testing and maximizing the benefits of assessment for learning. As in many jurisdictions abroad, periodic statewide standardized measures are used to validate local assessment results, while classroom embedded performance assessments are used to inform instruction, provide feedback to students and teachers, and enable diagnostic decisions, as well as to provide evidence of ambitious student learning. Collections of evidence that allow students to evaluate their own progress and revise and present their work to meet a standard can also play a role in giving students ownership and agency in the process of developing evidence of their readiness for college and careers.

(p. 38)

Formative assessment plays a critical role in such a system. Like Heritage (2010) and others, we view the formative assessment process as the gathering of information about how student learning is progressing so that instruction can be tailored to enhance student learning. We also believe that formative assessment in terms of feedback during the writing process is critical for student writing development. Formative assessment should work from students' emerging understandings, should support learning through instructional scaffolding, including feedback on students writing, and students should have opportunities to monitor their own ongoing progress (Council of Chief State School Officers, 2018). We are not advocating for more frequent assessments, as in the creation of new series of mini-assessments or interim benchmarking assessments. Enough time is routinely taken away from instruction as it is. Rather, we want to emphasize instead the development of systems that would support and promote learning in the classroom. As Bambrick-Santoyo says, ideally, "assessments are not the end of the teaching-learning process; they're the starting point" (2010, p. 7).

Cizek (2010) has identified the important features of formative assessment, features that could easily promote new thinking about assessment design:

Formative assessment:

1. Requires students to take responsibility for their own learning.
2. Communicates clear, specific learning goals.
3. Focuses on goals that represent valuable educational outcomes with applicability beyond the learning context.
4. Identifies the student's current knowledge/skills and the necessary steps for reaching the desired goals.
5. Requires development of plans for attaining the desired goals.
6. Encourages students to self-monitor progress toward the learning goals.
7. Provides examples of learning goals, including, when relevant, the specific grading criteria or rubrics that will be used to evaluate the student's work.
8. Provides frequent assessment, including peer and student self-assessment and assessment embedded within learning activities.
9. Includes feedback that is non-evaluative, specific, timely, and related to the learning goals, and that provides opportunities for the student to revise and improve work products and deepen understandings.
10. Promotes metacognition and reflection by students on their work.

(Cizek, 2010, p. 8)

While formative assessment is typically associated with classroom-based assessment that promotes learning, it can also play a role in large-scale assessments. For example, as we discuss later in the chapter, teachers can provide formative assessments in the classroom as students work on developing the contents of their portfolios. The completed portfolio can then be used successfully in summative and large-scale assessments.

A particularly promising approach in the teaching of writing is the use of rubrics for formative assessment. A formative assessment approach is much different than simply using the mandated assessment rubric to score students' writing, which some teachers are required to include in the classroom as a form of test-prep or to do as part of instructional feedback. Summative scoring rubrics often describe several different attributes of writing under each of the score point headings (see, e.g., the AWPE scoring guide in Figure 4.1). The Analytical Writing Placement Exam (AWPE), formerly called the "Subject A," was the writing placement exam used by several of the campuses at the University of California as an alternative for satisfying the Entry Level Requirement, a policy regulated by the System-wide Academic Senate (Briggs, 2018). The AWPE has a strong record of reliability in scoring. However, it is not designed for formative assessments. Grouping the attributes under a single score point heading makes it difficult for students and teachers to trace a student's progress on a single attribute across score points over time.

Score

6   **A paper with a score of 6 may:**
- Command attention because of its insightful development and mature style
- Present a cogent response to the text, elaborating with well-chosen examples and persuasive reasoning
- Show that its writer can choose words aptly, use sophisticated sentences effectively, and observe the conventions of written English

5   **A paper with a score of 5 may:**
- Clearly demonstrate competence
- Present a thoughtful response to the text, elaborating with appropriate examples and sensible reasoning
- Have less fluent and complex style than a 6, but shows its writer can usually choose words accurately, vary sentences effectively, and observe the conventions of written English

FIGURE 4.1   The University of California Analytical Writing Placement Exam Scoring Guide. Used with permission by the University of California.

Credit Line: University of California. "About the Exam." Entry Level Writing Requirement. https://admission.universityofcalifornia.edu/elwr/about-the-exam/

Score

4   **A paper with a score of 4 may:**
- Be satisfactory
- Present an adequate response to the text, elaborating with sufficient examples and acceptable reasoning
- Have less developed examples and reasoning than those in a 5 paper
- Have less effective style than a 5 paper
- Show that its writer can usually choose words of sufficient precision, control sentences of reasonable variety, and observe the conventions of written English

3   **A paper with a score of 3 may:**
- Be unsatisfactory in one or more of the following ways:
  - Responds to the text illogically
  - Lacks coherent structure and/or elaboration with examples
  - Reflects an incomplete understanding of the text or the topic
- Use prose characterized by at least one of the following:
  - Frequently imprecise word choice
  - Little sentence variety
  - Occasional major errors in grammar and usage, or frequent minor errors

2   **A paper with a score of 2 may:**
- Show serious weaknesses
- Present a simplistic, inappropriate, or incoherent response to the text, one that may suggest some significant misunderstanding of the text or the topic
- Use prose characterized by at least one of the following:
  - Simplistic or inaccurate word choice
  - Monotonous or fragmented sentence structure
  - Many repeated errors in grammar and usage

1   **A paper with a score of 1 may:**
- Suggest severe difficulties in reading and writing conventional English
- Disregard the topic's demands, or lacks any appropriate pattern of structure or development
- Be inappropriately brief
- Reveal a pervasive pattern of errors in word choice, sentence structure, grammar, and usage

FIGURE 4.1 (Continued)

For readers who may not be familiar with rubrics used for formative assessment in teaching, we provide brief descriptions here of two kinds, the Analytic Writing Continuum (AWC) developed by the National Writing Project (2010) and the genre-based rubrics published by New Standards (see Figures 4.2 and 4.3).

Ideally, we would provide the complete rubrics, but while most summative assessment rubrics are short, and can be presented in a page or two, rubrics useful for teaching are long and include many specific details. In its entirety,

Content (including quality and clarity of ideas and meaning)—The content category describes how effectively the writing establishes and maintains a focus, selects and integrates ideas related to content (i.e., information, events, emotions, opinions, and perspectives), and includes evidence, details, reasons, anecdotes, examples, descriptions, and characteristics to support, develop, and/or illustrate ideas.

Structure—The structure category describes how effectively the writing establishes logical arrangement, coherence, and unity within the elements of the work and throughout the work as a whole.

Stance—The stance category describes how effectively the writing communicates a perspective through an appropriate level of formality, elements of style, and tone appropriate for the audience and purpose.

Sentence Fluency—The sentence fluency category describes how effectively the sentences are crafted to serve the intent of the writing, in terms of rhetorical purpose, rhythm, and flow.

Diction (Language)—The diction category describes the precision and appropriateness of the words and expressions for the writing task and how effectively they create imagery, provide mental pictures, or convey feelings and ideas.

Conventions—The conventions category describes how effectively the writing demonstrates age-appropriate control of usage, punctuation, spelling, capitalization, and paragraphing.

(Marlink & Wahleithner, 2011, pp. 16–17)

FIGURE 4.2   The attributes of writing described in the National Writing Project's Analytic Writing Continuum. Used with permission.

Credit Line: Marlink, J., & Wahleithner, J. (2011). *Improving students' academic writing: Building a bridge to success*. Final Report for the National Writing Project Local Sites Research Initiative. California Writing Project. https://archive.nwp.org/cs/public/download/nwp_file/15419/ISAW_LSRI_final_report.pdf?x-r=pcfile_d

the AWC covers several pages of text, and the genre-specific rubrics published by New Standards and the International Reading Association (now the International Literacy Association) are presented in several individual grade-level books. For an in-depth look at the language in the AWC, see Smith and Swain (2017, pp. 15–20). For an in-depth look at genre-specific rubrics, see the series of books titled *Using Rubrics to Improve Student Writing* (Hampton et al., 2009).

A rubric that is useful for teaching writing requires language that helps teachers focus students' attention on a particular element of their writing, such as organization, or structure, or transitions. For example, at first glance, the

AWC might seem like a standard scoring rubric, but the descriptions of levels are more detailed, and the attributes are described under separate headings, making it easy to trace an attribute from high to low across score points. The language in the AWC describes six attributes of writing across six levels of performance (6 high, 1 low). For example, Level 5 of the structure category contains the following descriptors:

- Presents an organization that reinforces the central idea or theme
- Includes an order and structure that are maintained with a consistent flow of ideas
- Includes a strong and purposeful opening and a closure that reinforces unity and provides a clear sense of resolution
- Includes transitions that are effective and clearly connect events, ideas, and/or details

(Smith & Swain, 2017, p. 16)

Because the language in the AWC attributes is not genre-specific, "anchor papers" (examples of responses at different score points) are used along with the Continuum to illustrate performance in different kinds of writing. When papers are scored, examples of each of the levels of performance along the continuum are provided so that scorers (or students) can see what the descriptors mean in actual sample papers. In other words, as Swain and Le Mahieu (2012) explain, the AWC has "the flexibility to accommodate multiple prompts, multiple genres, multiple grade levels, and varied conditions for writing—from first draft on-demand writing to fully revised pieces from student portfolios" (p. 47). The AWC is thus useful as an assessment system that can address a variety of local and large-scale inquiry questions and assessment needs.

While the language of the AWC is fairly generic, other rubrics are more closely linked to expectations for particular genres and employ genre-specific language. For example, instead of a generic term like "structure," New Standard's genre-specific rubrics use "Plot development and organization for a narrative rubric" (see Figure 4.3). Each of the four rubrics addresses one of four genres of writing: narrative, report of information, instructions, and response to literature. Using genre-specific language, they characterize performance across five levels at each grade level: exceeds standard (5), meets standard (4), needs revision (3), needs instruction (2), and needs substantial support (1).

Rubrics like the AWC can be adapted to different kinds of writing via the writing samples used to illustrate aspects of the rubric. Genre-based rubrics, on the other hand, provide specific information about expectations for particular genres. As illustrated by the levels, both kinds of rubric can result in a single score.

Orientation and Context—The writer "orients and engages the reader" (e.g., sets the time, indicates the location where the story takes place, introduces character(s), or enters immediately into the story line).

Plot Development and Organization—The writer "creates a series of events or incidents, develops the complicating action (focal event), paces [the] narrative to highlight the significance of events or incidents, to create drama or suspense, etc.," and "omits irrelevant events or incidents."

Character/Narrator Development—The writer "describes actions and emotions of the main characters" and "develops characters (e.g., by providing motivation for action).

Closure—The writer "provides a sense of closure to the writing," and "if writing an autobiographical narrative, may provide reflective comments."

Detail—The writer "builds characters through the selective use of detail" and "includes details to develop plot and character."

Dialogue—"Dialogue, if present, advances the action or develops character."

Other—"Uses literary language" and "uses temporal words, phrases, and clauses to indicate shifts in time."

(Hampton et al., 2009, pp. 12–13)

FIGURE 4.3   Attributes of Score Point 4 in the New Standards Narrative Rubric. Used with permission of the National Center on Education and the Economy.

Credit Line: Hampton, S., Murphy, S., & Lowery, M. (2009). *Using rubrics to improve students writing (Grades 1–5).* New Standards and International Reading Association.

But single scores provide limited information for teaching since writing is multidimensional. Winner (1993), her teacher colleagues and administrators from the Pittsburg Public School System, and researchers at Harvard Project Zero and the Educational Testing Service explain the limitations:

> One of the misconceptions supported by traditional models of assessment is that learning is unidimensional and can thus be evaluated by a single score. . . . Tests and classroom grading practices reflect this view when students are assigned a single grade or score. . . . In many instances, student learning does not fit such a model very well at all. A student may perform at a low level in one verbal area (reading comprehension), at an average level in another verbal area (organizing a paper), and at a superior level in yet a third area (writing dialogue). Thus a global summary of performance (e.g., You are a c-level writing student) provides

limited information to students, to parents, to administrators, or to next year's teacher. The C must be "opened up" so that teachers and students understand what the student has done well and what the student needs to work on.

(Winner, 1993, pp. 14–15)

While generic and genre-specific rubrics can be designed to provide a single score, they can also be designed to give teachers and students language for analyzing and talking about student writing. For example, teacher Julie Sherman "encourages her students to use the language of the [AWC] continuum during conferencing" (Smith & Swain, 2017, p. 51). Using the language of the attributes herself, she highlights where the student's text fits on the continuum of a particular attribute of the rubric and asks students to set goals in relation to that attribute for their next draft. When used in this way, rubrics can help students self-assess and take charge of their growth as writers.

Teacher Kay Faile credits the AWC for initiating a breakthrough in her teaching practice. She showed her students that they might perform poorly on one attribute and they could build on that. They might also find another attribute on which they do better, and could build on that as well:

So I now meet my students where they are, and the rubric is first and foremost. . . . It hit me one night like a lightning bolt. I used to bleed all over the papers, all over. So when that hit me you can't do that anymore. You have got to get rid of all of that. This is their writing. It's a personal thing; you must make it personal. And the Analytic Writing Continuum can help you do that. You can make this personal because if you teach them how to use that instrument, they will begin to be able to look and see where they are on their own and want to pull themselves up.

(quoted in a personal communication in Smith & Swain, 2017, p. 65)

While Faile's students were able to use the AWC successfully, notwithstanding its somewhat complex language, not all teachers will choose to use rubrics straight out of the box. Other teachers have found they need to simplify and adapt the language of rubrics like the AWC, especially for younger children. For example, Smith and Swain (2017) quote Jolene Hetherington who explained how she adapted the Continuum and invited her fourth graders to tell her what words confused them: "students didn't know what the words *relevant, thoroughly,* and *exceptionally* meant. They turned those words into kidlish. So *relevant* became *has to do with the topic, thoroughly* changed to *totally,* and *exceptionally* evolved into *all* or *perfectly*" (p. 63, emphasis in original).

Teachers and researchers can also adapt generic rubrics like the AWC for specific purposes. For example, following the initial development of the AWC, the National Writing Project developed several AWC-based variants. One variant, the Civically Engaged Writing Analysis Continuum (CEWAC), focuses specifically on the analysis of civic writing. The rubric includes attributes such as "employs a public voice," "advocates civic engagement or action," "argues a position based on reasoning and evidence," and "employs a structure to support a position" (National Writing Project, 2018). Another variant, the Analytic Writing Continuum for Source-Based Argument, uses the attributes of the original AWC (content, structure, stance, and conventions) but focuses in particular on developing "argument through the selection and use of evidence from source material" (National Writing Project, 2020, p. 1).

Any of the different kinds of rubrics described here might also be the starting point for creating other, more task-specific rubrics. Writing Project leader Rebekah Caplan points out that students learn from the process of building a rubric: "I believe students should have a hand in developing rubrics along with the teacher. As students read models of work in a genre, they should be building the 'features' as they read more and more examples" (as cited in Smith & Swain, 2017, p. 97). Hampton et al. argue that "Ideally, [rubrics] should grow out of the work of the classroom. . . . Students and teachers need formative rubrics that emerge from the teaching in a classroom and that specify work yet to be done" (Hampton et al., 2009, pp. 2–3). Teacher Andrew Miller advises teachers to embed a rubric in instruction.

> You have to use the rubric with the students. It means nothing to them if you don't. We've all had that time when we gave students the rubric and they threw it away, or the papers lay like snow at the end of class. In order for students to keep a rubric, and more importantly to find it useful in terms of their learning, they must see a reason for using it.
>
> *(Miller, A., January 18, 2012, para 4)*

When teachers and students work together to construct rubrics, Smith and Swain (2017) also caution that they should check rubric revisions against actual samples of student writing: "One of the cardinal rules of creating or tweaking rubrics is to be sure they mirror what is actually in the writing" (p. 96). In other words, rubrics need to be grounded in writing and grow out of writing. To emphasize the improvement perspective of rubrics created collaboratively in class, Hampton et al. (2019) also suggest "Growing a rubric," that is, adding levels as students' writing develops, and deleting levels that no longer apply.

While most teachers think of rubrics as a table, chart, or list, Broad (2003) encourages writing teachers to identify "what we really value" in student texts and then use that information to create a heuristic—what he calls a dynamic criteria map (DCM)—to articulate evaluation criteria. Broad advocates for a

What teachers say about using rubrics for teaching

- Simply stated, I refuse to have my intuition about the quality of students' writing limited by an arbitrary set of subcategories with an equally arbitrarily assigned weighted value. One cannot communicate what encompasses good writing with a chart. (Machera, 2019, para. 14)
- I have found that whether they [rubrics] are good, bad, or even ugly depends on how they are created and how they are used. (Andrade, 2005, p. 27)
- I was no stranger to rubrics. In fact, I had become quite skeptical of them. In the beginning of my teaching career, I used rubrics as summative assessments for the majority of my assignments. Rubrics seemed to be a la mode—everyone was using them. . . . Finally out of frustration I stopped using them because my students would not read my long extensive comments on the rubric I used for that assignment. When I gave the final assignments back to them, they only looked at the grade. (as cited in Smith & Swain, 2017, p. 45)
- The AWC was changing my thinking about how rubrics can be used and made me realize how important formative assessment is with writing as opposed to summative assessment. . . . One of the wonderful aspects I love about the AWC is it is a fluid continuum that doesn't put writing pieces in nice tidy boxes or "coffins" if you will. It is not the end all. It is a guide for navigating writing. (as cited in Smith & Swain, 2017, p. 48)
- I build a grading rubric collaboratively with the students. We begin in peer review, by noting each other's strengths as writers. We arrange the strengths into categories (intro, evidence, organization, context, audience, etc.). Gradually, we build that list of strengths over several assignments, until near mid-semester, we put the categories of strengths into description. That description becomes how we as a community define "good writing." . . . All along, we use our sense of strengths in peer review and other forms of feedback. Once we have the rubric, students have robust descriptors of standards, and they use that in self-assessment and peer review. . . . I then use it to grade their portfolios. This engages students in a more active process of learning how to improve their writing. (as cited in O'Neill, 2017, p. 3)
- A rubric is worth little if it is not accompanied by the following activities: analysis of writing samples; practice using rubrics to evaluate those samples; sharing and discussion of examples of the writing assignment at hand; peer sharing and review; revision; and written and verbal feedback from the teacher. All of these activities add richness, complexity, context, and definition to the simplistic, vague language of the rubric. (as cited in Gallagher & Turley, 2012, p. 20)

communal writing assessment—much like the AWC project we discussed earlier. Several college writing programs have developed maps and used them in their programs for assessment. For example, Alford (2009) explained how his writing program used the maps to create rubrics that "reflect what the faculty identified as measurable standards" (p. 46). Detwiler and McBride (2009) explained that their program's mapping project led to a "nine-pointed star" for evaluating writing portfolios (see Figure 4.4). The star design involved a circle formation with nine lines radiating from a center point (the zero point), each identified with

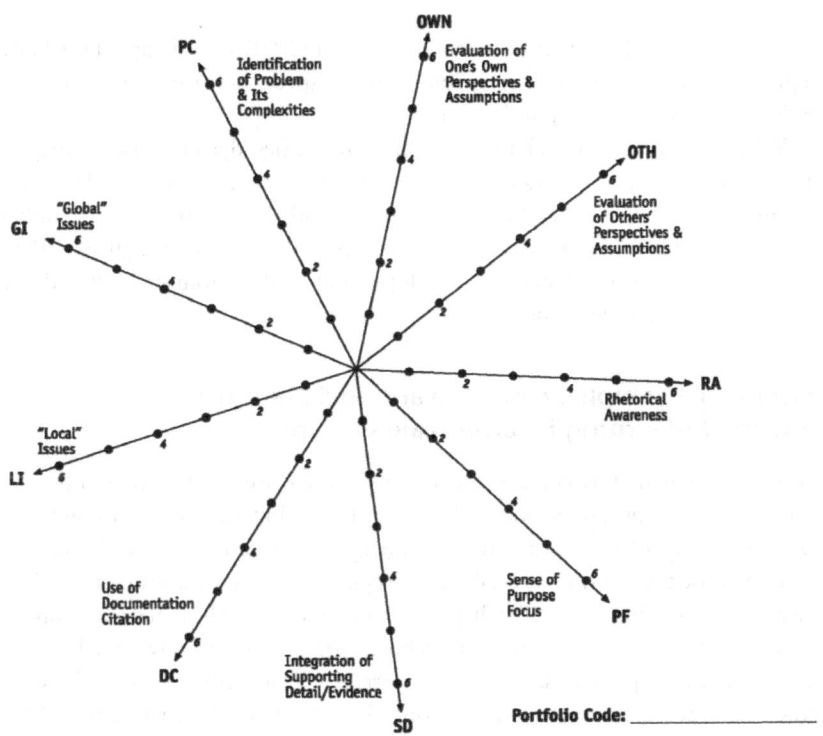

FIGURE 4.4   The Nine-Pointed Star Portfolio Rubric developed through dynamic criteria mapping by the writing program at University of Nevada Reno. Used with permission of Utah State University Press.

Credit Line: Detwiler, J., & McBride, M. (2009). Designs on assessment at UNR: University of Nevada, Reno. In Broad, B., Adler-Kassner, L., Alford, B., & Detweiler, J. (2009). *Organic writing assessment: Dynamic criteria mapping in action* (pp. 52–72). Utah State University Press. https://digital commons.usu.edu/usupress_pubs/165 an attribute of writing and divided into six points on the line. The star-shape, explained Detweiler and McBride,

> reflected our community's sense that all of the aspects of writing we were describing were integrally linked, inseparable, flowing, together. . . . When a portfolio was scored using the chart, and lines drawn to connect the hatchmarks on each of the rays, we would have a visual representation suggesting a shape of the whole (higher scores all around would make a "fuller" circle around the star; an area of lower scores would appear as a divot or flattening of the circle).
>
> *(2009, pp. 61–62)*

The star-shaped chart, explained Detweiler and McBride, disrupted the linear approach that could be seen to privilege some aspects of writing over others as evaluators moved from top to bottom.

Whatever you want to call them—rubrics, heuristics, dynamic criteria maps— these tools can help teachers identify the features of a writing or a collection of writing and articulate that for themselves and other constituencies, including students and other educators. The important thread that runs through all of these examples is the way the rubrics are developed and used to promote teacher development and student learning.

Assessing a complex cognitive and socially situated construct of writing in large-scale systems

Beyond employing formative assessment techniques, we need to assess a broader range of genres, purposes, and audiences within a broader range of conditions for writing to move toward better alignment with a complex, socially situated writing construct. This is especially important for large-scale assessments, which have a profound impact on what happens in classrooms and how writing is operationalized. Increasingly composition scholars are arguing that we need to take steps that will help students see, as Beaufort says, that writing is not a "generic skill that, once learned, becomes a 'one size fits all intellectual garb'" (2007, p. 10). We need to put students, she says, "on a course of life-long learning so that they know *how to learn* to become better and better writers in a variety of social contexts" (emphasis in original, Beaufort, 2007, p. 7). We need to teach and assess the kinds of knowledge domains writers "would need to invoke for analyzing new writing tasks in new discourse communities," that is, "situated knowledge entailed in acts of writing: discourse community knowledge, subject matter knowledge, genre knowledge, rhetorical knowledge, and writing process knowledge" (Beaufort, 2007, pp. 17–18).

While social perspectives on writing have spotlighted the varying contexts in which writing occurs, including the social situations that lead to different purposeful acts of communication, our large-scale assessment systems have typically worked against the idea that writing varies in significant ways across audiences, purposes, and situations, casting writing ability instead as a generic set of skills that can be measured with multiple-choice items or with one or two samples of writing. Traditional, standardized writing assessments haven't been designed to show the extent to which students can manage the complex, multifaceted domain of writing. Instead, they have typically been used to make generalizations about students' overall writing ability—a truly questionable practice, given what we know about the extent to which writing performance varies across tasks, time frames, genres, and tools for writing. And as we explained in Chapter 2, multiple samples are required to reach an acceptable level of generalizability in order to draw conclusions about writing proficiency.

When we standardize tests by writing type, narrowing the sample taken to a single genre, as many states and districts have done, we forgo the opportunity to obtain evidence about students' abilities to shape their writing for other situations, for other audiences and purposes—abilities that are now clearly emphasized in two of the Common Core Standards for writing:

4. Produce clear and coherent writing in which the development, organization, and style are appropriate to task, purpose, and audience.
10. Write routinely over extended time frames (time for research, reflection, and revision) and shorter time frames (a single sitting of a day or two) for a range of tasks, purposes, and audiences.

(National Governors Association et al., 2010, p. 41)

At a minimum, measuring a complex construct of writing would require assessing a range of performance tasks in a range of conditions for writing, not just one or two. Contemporary large-scale assessment systems omit important aspects of a complex view of writing, and in particular, those associated with literacy as social practice. Traditional writing assessments have not been designed, for example, to tell us whether students can adapt their writing and rhetorical strategies to the demands of different genres, tasks, and situations for writing. Assessing a range of genres could provide this kind of information and, at the same time, make it more likely that students would be taught a range of genres in the curriculum. Although the desire for individual student scores makes it impossible to achieve this with any single test, if we consider the assessment system broadly, from the individual classroom to the large-scale stage of district, state, and national policies, there are ways the current system can be restructured, so to speak, to better align our assessments with what we know about the complex nature of writing. To return to the metaphor with which we began this book, we could remodel our assessment system by redesigning and renovating it. To this end, we need to broaden the range of our assessments.

Broadening the range of situations and conditions for writing

Broadening the range means we will need to promote performance assessments at various levels of the system so that we can encourage breadth in the writing curriculum and, at the same time, assess higher order skills. These changes aren't something that can be done, of course, all at once. It is an effort that will require reshaping policies and practices at several levels of our current educational system.

As noted earlier, the current K–12 curriculum standards already address the need to broaden the scope of student writing explicitly with their emphasis on giving students experience with "a range of tasks, purposes and audiences" (National Governors Association et al., 2010). At the college level, the WPA Outcomes Statement indicates that students "develop rhetorical knowledge by negotiating purpose, audience, context, and conventions as they compose a variety of texts for different situations." Students "gain experience," by "reading and composing in several genres to understand how genre conventions shape and are shaped by readers' and writers' practices and purposes" (Council of Writing Program Administrators, 2014, para 3). Similarly, *The Framework for Success in Postsecondary Writing*, which aims to articulate the habits of mind and experiences students need to be successful in college writing, notes that teachers help students develop rhetorical knowledge when they provide them with opportunities to "learn and practice key rhetorical concepts such as audience, purpose, context, and genre through writing and analysis of a variety of types of texts (nonfiction, informational, imaginative, printed, visual, spatial, auditory, and otherwise)" (Council of Writing Program Administrators et al., 2011, p. 6). The *Framework* also states the need for a broad range of writing: "Standardized writing curricula or assessment instruments that emphasize formulaic writing for unidentified or non-authentic audiences will not reinforce the habits of mind and the experiences necessary for success as students encounter the writing demands of postsecondary education" (p. 3).

While few, if any standardized tests reflect the principles outlined in these documents, we do have some large-scale assessment models in K–12 and college to which policy makers can turn to expand the range of writing and the conditions in which it is produced. Frequently, the models we describe do both. For example, in the Advanced Placement (AP) Seminar, students complete various in-class tasks—an individual research report, a team multimedia presentation and defense, an individual written argument, an individual multimedia presentation, and an oral defense. In the end-of-course exam, students answer short questions that require them to analyze an argument, and they write an evidence-based argument essay (College Board, 2022). Scores for the performance tasks are combined with scores from the end-of-course summative exam to create a summative score. Students write in more than one genre, and they do their writing within various conditions, some of which combine reading and writing (e.g., the evidence-based argument essay), some of which integrate writing with other modalities (e.g., the multimedia presentation), and some of which involve collaboration (e.g., the team multimedia presentation). Similarly, to earn an International Baccalaureate Diploma, students complete a variety of embedded tasks, such as presentations, essays, and extended research-based essays, as well as exams: "In most subjects, students also complete in-school assessment tasks. These are either externally assessed or marked by teachers and then moderated by the IB" (International Baccalaureate Organization, 2022, para 3). The AP and IB models are not without problems, of course, but certainly are useful as places to start.

Writing portfolios also broaden—and offer opportunities to assess—a range of different kinds of writing done for different purposes and audiences, and they typically include writing produced in different conditions. When created in the classroom, portfolios give students opportunities to write in different genres, and they give teachers ways to help students see how writing varies for different purposes and across situations, to communicate progress to parents, to see evidence of both finished work and writing processes, and to encourage students' ownership of their writing.

Portfolios are not limited, of course, to classroom use. They have also been used in large-scale assessments. For example, Kentucky and Vermont used writing portfolios in their statewide assessment systems for several years. According to Darling-Hammond (2017), "Both states experienced increases in their students' achievement on NAEP during these years" (p. 31). There are many benefits to adopting portfolios in large-scale assessments as reported by Darling-Hammond (2017):

> The benefits of a portfolio process include the fact that common standards and high-quality tasks can guide classroom practice throughout the school year; students experience similar kinds of high-quality instruction across classrooms and schools; and students learn how to revise work toward high standards.
>
> *(p. 31)*

In college writing programs, portfolios have been used for decades for large-scale placement and proficiency assessments. For example, Elbow and Belanoff (1986), with their colleagues, created a portfolio assessment to replace the composition exit exam at their university. Washington State University has long had a rising junior portfolio that all students must submit before they can graduate (Haswell, 2001). The portfolio contents include papers written and graded in courses across the disciplines as well as a timed impromptu essay and a self-reflection. Many programs have used portfolios for placement into first year writing. The University of Louisville ran a portfolio option for several years that allowed students to challenge the standard placement process, which used ACT scores and an impromptu essay, for those who scored below a cut off (Lowe & Huot, 1997; Hester et al.,

What teachers say about portfolios

- These [portfolios] allow them to see both finished products and processes; they connect them to one another; they provide a visual and written connection across assignments and they allow the students to reflect and self-assess. (as cited in O'Neill, 2017)
- We were writers and we were thinkers. Through portfolio development and assessment we [students and teacher] had changed, we knew we had changed, and we knew how we had changed. (Deen, 1993, p. 59)
- For me, portfolios provide a strong link between home and school, and they help me involve parents in recognizing and respecting their child's growth. (Brandts, 1993, p. 117)
- The portfolio assessment we used in our fifth grade became a valuable teaching and learning tool for all of us. I think this is assessment at its best, teacher and student evaluating so that each can improve. (Green, 1993, p. 79)
- After all, a test score is only one number; the portfolio, a collection of information and thoughtful rumination, can be the life jacket that holds them [students] afloat in the testing tsunami. (Piazza, 2001, p. 78)
- Portfolios help to pull together lots of pieces. I wanted students to produce a record that would demonstrate that they were thinking like scientists. I wanted them to connect the work of science with the skill of writing. I wanted them to be free to present what they had learned in a form compatible with their talents and I wanted them to reflect, select, and take responsibility for their own work. (Dorroh, 2001, p. 69)
- Portfolio assessment helps me most, because the students take ownership and care about their progress. I give them immediate feedback through conferencing and the students give each other feedback through peer editing. (as cited in Filkins, 2015)
- I think portfolios of written work collected throughout the year is the best way to assess the students' progress. That would be a real standards based assessment. It should be clear on the assignment . . . the standards being addressed and how well students met them. (as cited in Filkins, 2015)
- In the tenth week of the quarter we began our portfolio norming. . . . We as a group, are negotiating standards together; we are trying to square those with some sense of "programmatic" or "departmental" standards, and we are negotiating with our students, trying to engage them in the process of framing acceptance of the standards that inform our community. (Durst et al., 1994, pp. 291–292)
- K–12 portfolios with student work would truly represent the best of each young person. If a portfolio moved with the student each year, his/her history and best work would always be available. This could be done digitally or on paper. (as cited in Filkins, 2015)
- To the extent that the tasks included in the portfolio are narrowly set and standardized, to reduce the "messiness" of the data and make performance more comparable from student to student, the portfolio will, like other external tests before it, dictate rather than reflect curriculum. And to the extent that the pieces collected are written "for the test" rather than for the learners and their audiences, the opportunities for students to engage in purposeful task definition, reflection, and self-evaluation will be truncated. (as cited in M. A. Smith, 1993, p. 2)

2007). The portfolio was originally compiled in the senior year of high school as part of the state-mandated testing and included a variety of pieces—a letter to the reviewer; a personal narrative or essay; a short story, poem, or play; and three expository pieces, two of which were from non–English-content areas. For the project, the portfolio was sent to the university and evaluated by first-year writing instructors to determine the student's placement into first-year writing. (This program also allowed for more cross-pollination between Kentucky high schools and the university writing program.) All of these portfolio programs, which are just a handful of the many reported in the composition literature, used a range of writing to evaluate individual students for assessments beyond the classroom, and they all incorporated work done within the context of the classroom.

In the K–12 arena, a different approach to assessing multiple purposes or genres of writing in large-scale assessment was employed for a number of years in California. The California Assessment Program (CAP) employed a matrix sampling design. Individual students in a class were randomly assigned different kinds of writing. Results for each of the different kinds of writing were collated and reported at the school level for the particular grades assessed. In addition to recognizing the importance of conventions, correct syntax, accurate spelling, and effective diction, the CAP approach focused on the "most important characteristics necessary to a particular type of writing, rather than those that are common to all types" (Peckham, 1987, p. 31). Another advantage of the CAP approach was that teachers got timely information about how students in the grade level performed across different kinds of writing—information that was potentially useful in long-term curriculum planning. An additional benefit was that teachers were employed to develop the assessment and score the student writing—not the writing of their own students, of course, but of other students in California. Exemplary writing teachers wrote prompts, guides for writing each type assessed, and guides for scoring the writing. The training sessions for teachers who learned how to score the essays "functioned as in-service workshops, giving teachers an opportunity to talk about what criteria are important in a specific type of writing" (Peckham, 1987, p. 32). The test was thus intentionally designed to improve instruction in writing, not by threatening individual teachers and students with "play or punish" policies, but by supporting teachers to use best practices with low stakes for students. Test materials and sample prompts for the different types of writing were available to all, and teachers benefited from the assessment training and from instructional ideas shared at the scoring sessions. Mary Ann Smith, Director of the California Writing Project during the CAP years, said:

> The enlightened, enthusiastic folk in testing and accountability at the California Department of Education remarked more than once "We should fly a plane over the state and drop the prompts everywhere." That was how eager they were for the assessment to make a difference in the daily lives of teachers and students.
>
> *(M. A. Smith, personal communication, July 2, 2022)*

The National Assessment of Educational Progress (NAEP) also assesses a range of writing by employing a matrix design, and there are no stakes attached for individuals, either teachers or students, or for schools. NAEP acknowledges the inherently social nature of writing in its definition: "Writing is a complex, multifaceted and purposeful act of communication that is accomplished in a variety of environments, under various constraints of time, and with a variety of language resources and technological tools" (National Assessment Governing Board, 2017, p. 3). NAEP's 2017 Writing Framework explains that "writing . . . can be thought of as a relationship or negotiation between the writer and reader to satisfy the aims of both parties." The focus of the framework is "writing for communicative purposes and on the relationship of the writer to his or her intended audience" (p. 3).

Students who took the most recent NAEP exam wrote for two different purposes, but across the sample, data were collected for three purposes: to persuade, to explain, and to convey experience. The broad purpose categories allowed for a wide range of tasks. The scores from student responses to NAEP's assessment items were translated into scale scores and then percentages of students attaining particular achievement levels: basic, proficient, or advanced. Average scores were reported for selected student and school characteristics, such as race/ethnicity, gender, and school location (National Center for Education Statistics (2011, p. 2). NAEP's purpose-based design could be adapted for assessments at a state or district level, and the results used for curriculum planning.

These examples all illustrate existing ways to assess more than one kind of genre or purpose for writing on a large scale. Of course, the models have drawbacks of one kind or another. For example, neither CAP nor NAEP were designed to provide individual scores, a problem given the current federal policy requirement that all students receive them. Of the examples provided here, portfolios seem to offer the most promise in this regard because they can be used to assess multiple types of writing and at the same time provide scores for individual students, as was done in the past in Kentucky and Vermont. Early concerns about portfolio reliability have been effectively addressed. While attaining reliability has been a challenge in portfolio assessment in the past, several programs at the K–12 level have done so successfully (e.g., LeMahieu et al., 1995; Murphy & Underwood, 2000). At the state level, reliability of scores for the Vermont portfolios were low in 1992, but as Koretz et al. (1992) explain, the scoring system was complex, and "the so-called 'pilot' implementation . . . was less a true pilot of a developed program than an integral part of the development effort" (p. 6). Moreover, the analysis showed that "there was no sizable systematic bias in teachers' ratings of their own students" (p. 9). Reliability of scoring Kentucky's writing portfolios increased substantially over several years, and an independent review conducted by the National Center for Fair and Open Testing (n.d.) provided evidence that portfolios "can be used for accountability, provided that scores are not the sole basis for high-stakes decisions for individuals or schools and provided that there is sufficient professional development" (para 4). At the college level, reliability of portfolio assessments has been studied in various ways as we discussed in Chapter 2. Researchers have demonstrated that scoring can produce reliable scores for both eportfolios and traditional print-based portfolios (e.g., Elliot et al., 2007; Hamp-Lyons & Condon, 2000; Haswell, 2001; Hester et al., 2007; Kelly-Riley et al., 2016).

As we noted previously, social perspectives have illuminated contexts for writing—the social situations that lead to different purposes for writing and different genres. They have also shed light on impact of context in another sense: the variety of conditions in which writing occurs and the variety of time frames, processes, integrations, and combinations with other modes that can result. The Washington State portfolio example described earlier, in which students wrote in different time frames, is just one example of the many different conditions in which writing could be (and has been) assessed. In addition to varying time constraints in assessment, in some cases assessment designers have integrated writing with reading as part of the assessment process. In other cases they have provided supportive speaking, listening, and discussion activities. In still other cases, they have introduced digital technology and have assessed multimodal productions, that is, productions in which writing is combined with other modes for making meaning such as visuals or sound.

Integrating reading and writing

While writing has been treated as a stand-alone performance in most large-scale state writing assessments, we do have some assessment models that purposefully integrate reading and writing at the program level. Some assessment designs explicitly require students to write *about* something they are asked to read. For example, believing that "reading and writing should be seen as complex, interactive processes, not as an accumulation of discrete skills," faculty at Pace University turned to an integrated reading/writing exam as an alternative to standardized tests of writing alone. They designed a test that asked students to respond to an author's ideas. Responses were scored via a point system for both reading (e.g., "Reader clearly states the author's significant ideas.") and writing ("Writer has a focus and a logical plan of organization."). Most of the scorers were faculty who would be teaching the reading/writing classes in which students would be placed. The value of this approach, according to the faculty, was that "we were able to see firsthand what strengths and weaknesses our students were bringing with them to class" (De Fina et al., 1991, p. 356).

In postsecondary contexts, writing assessors have created a variety of alternative placement assessments that broaden the range of conditions for the assessment. For example, at the University of Pittsburgh, students were given a reading and then a series of questions to respond to before writing an essay. W. L. Smith (1993) explained that

> because our composition program was based on the interrelation of reading and writing, the students are given a passage to read and a series of questions designed to focus their response. These prompts, then, closely resemble the assignments given students in courses.
>
> *(p. 146)*

W. L. Smith (1993) found that this practice helped the faculty separate students into different groups: (1) those who struggled with the reading, (2) those who seemed to have a clear grasp on the reading but struggled with written expression, (3) those who performed both reading and writing at the level required for the standard first-year course, and (4) those students deemed exempt because their performance exceeded the expectations of the standard course. The first two groups were placed into the appropriate course to meet their needs, and the third into a standard course.

As was the case at the University of Pittsburgh, placement exams typically require students to create a single sample on demand in one sitting in testing conditions, but there have been attempts to improve this model by extending the time and test-taking context while also integrating reading and other activities. For example, SUNY Stonybrook, a large state university, had students produce a writing sample in a classroom-style session. Robertson (1994) explained that students were divided into groups of 25 during orientation and met in classrooms with writing instructors. Students

> for an hour participated in activities that encapsulated the teaching that occurs daily in our composition classes. . . . In brief the new design encompassed all the aspects of writing our program emphasized: students in each class freewrote, shared and responded to the writings and then talked in small groups about topics generated within the class before putting pen to blue book and actually composing an individual essay.
>
> *(p. 57)*

In this case, the students read and responded to others' freewrites in small groups before they wrote their placement essay. In a placement program used at Louisiana State, students could challenge their placement into composition that had been determined through their SAT or ACT scores by writing an essay after reading a collection of articles (Peckham, 2009). The process, which was administered online when students were not on campus, extended the placement exam across several days with students receiving eight to ten articles to read about a topic and then having three days to complete a writing task related to the articles (Peckham, 2009). This assessment task mimicked the type of reading and writing students were expected to do in the composition course, and it was facilitated through an online system that tracked their time spent writing and other components of the test administration (Peckham, 2009).

In some K–12 assessments, the reading/writing task has been integrated with talk and other supportive instructional activities. For example, in one California test students were engaged in reading, discussion, and prewriting activities before writing to a genre-specific prompt. An iteration of this kind of exam was adopted as the New Standards Reference Examination. On day one, students wrote to a genre-specific writing prompt. On day two, students responded to a reading passage and prompts with three short answers and one longer text-based essay. On day three, students responded to three reading passages and two editing passages followed by multiple-choice items (Wiley & Resnick, 1997). The Maryland School Performance Assessment Program (MSPAP), which was implemented in the early 1990s, used innovative performance assessments, administered across five or six days in one or one-and-a-half hour sessions led by teachers that included interactive components, such as whole-class discussion or sharing with a partner (Yen & Ferrara, 1997). Reading and writing were linked, and the MSPAP specifically addressed different purposes for writing (to inform, to persuade, and to express personal ideas) as well as various steps in the writing process. The readings were drawn from literature, science, and social studies, and students wrote both brief and extended responses (Yen & Ferrara, 1997, pp. 65–66). Like the CAP, the MSPAP used sampling so not all students did all tasks. The results provided information about the curriculum, schools, and districts with no direct stake attached to individual students.

Large-scale assessments linked to the Common Core Standards also integrate writing and reading. For example, both the Smarter Balanced Assessment Consortium (SBAC) and the Partnership for Assessment of Readiness for College and Careers (PARCC) consortium have designed assessments that integrate writing and reading. PARCC emphasizes text analysis. The writing tasks include analysis of an informational topic presented "through several texts or multimedia stimuli" (PARCC Guide to ELA/Literacy Released Items, n.d., p. 2), analysis of a literary text, and a narrative response to a prompt based on a literary text. The range of different kinds of writing is thus somewhat narrowly limited to writing about reading texts. SBAC (2014) includes writing about reading tasks but assesses a somewhat broader range of different kinds of writing, including narrative, informational, and argumentative writing. However, only one type of writing is assessed with a "full write" performance task each year. As a result, the assessment provides less information about how students perform across different types of writing than it would if multiple samples were assessed. Both of these examples illustrate that it is difficult for a single test to adequately represent such a complex construct as writing in a single exam. Factors such as time and cost invariably get in the way.

Collecting impromptu and classroom-based writing samples

As explained earlier, at the college level, writing programs have long used collections of tasks in both classroom-based and large-scale performance assessment because they allow for multiple samples, written for various purposes and audiences, in multiple genres (e.g., Belanoff & Dickson, 1991; Black et al., 1994; Yancey & Weiser, 1997). But in addition to assessing multiple genres, some programs have also assessed writing produced under varying conditions, such as different time frames or different courses. For example, as we mentioned earlier, Haswell (2001) and his colleagues at Washington State University developed a rising junior writing portfolio in the early 1990s. The current version of the University Writing Portfolio is designed as a "mid-career diagnostic used to determine if students' writing abilities demonstrate readiness for the writing demands of advanced level courses in their academic program" (Washington State University Writing Program, 2022). Students submit "two academic essays or papers . . . written for college-level courses" that the student thinks demonstrate their best writing (p. 2). Students also submit answers to reflection questions within the submission site to "articulate what the texts show about their capabilities as college writers." Group work may be submitted as long as the portion the student wrote is highlighted and the student's answers to the reflection questions are "thorough and clearly related" to the sections the student indicated as their own (see FAQ link). The portfolios are evaluated by instructors from across the campus who are trained by the writing program in norming sessions.

College faculty have used collections of classroom-based samples to demonstrate learning to regional accreditors through direct assessment of students. For example, Choseed (2016) explained that the programmatic approach to assessment developed at his community college, part of the State University of New York (SUNY) system, involved collecting random writing samples from both Composition I and Composition II. The samples are evaluated with rubrics based on the general education requirement in basic communication and the humanities. At the University of California Santa Barbara, faculty collected samples of student work from a variety of different disciplinary courses as part of the general education assessment and used locally designed rubrics to evaluate the samples (Adler-Kassner & Gonzalez, 2016). At a rural North Carolina community college, faculty created a comprehensive writing program that included a writing center, an online writing lab, and a writing-across-the-curriculum program in response to the accreditation demand for a quality enhancement project, and then built an assessment of the program that scored student writing samples as part of the evaluation of the new program (Elmore & Van Sickle, 2016).

These examples of postsecondary writing assessments highlight the role that classroom instructors can play in designing low-stakes, embedded assessments that are implemented and reported by local faculty to external evaluators. These kinds of assessment can support instruction while ensuring that educational institutions are meeting the needs of students and providing appropriate opportunities to learn. While the demands for writing assessment in the postsecondary context are quite different than the requirements faced by K–12 institutions, the methods and approaches used in colleges showcase how mandated assessments can serve students and learning, as well as accountability needs, and could perhaps be adapted for the K–12 context.

Incorporating digital technology

Introducing digital technology is another way to broaden the range of genres assessed as well as the conditions for writing. Evidence in the research literature suggests a need for this expansion. For example, Lotherington (2004) investigated "how children are learning to access and enact digital literacies" (p. 306), and whether the standardized literacy testing in the province of Ontario addressed them. Her research revealed, "The concept of literacy tested in gate-keeping . . . assessment does not include the sophisticated digital literacies children are developing in peer-mediated, screen-based, pop culture interactive media, though such media are increasingly influencing classroom materials and practices" (p. 305). Lotherington points out that children in the schools she investigated learn sophisticated digital literacy skills. They "can operate computer hardware, and navigate sophisticated software. As students progress through elementary school, they learn to locate useful and current information through focused digital searches, and create educational websites and multimedia presentations" (p. 313). Lotherington argues that the nature of reading and writing is changing and that electronic literacies should be considered an important part of school curriculum. She notes that while "these are extremely useful contemporary literacy practices . . . they are currently unrecognized as literacy" by the Canadian assessment system (p. 313).

While few assessment systems have directly tackled the issue of multimodal assessment, some have incorporated digital technology in the assessment of writing. For example, NAEP introduced computer technology after the National Assessment Governing Board commissioned the development of a new framework for writing in 2011. The new writing assessment was designed to "measure the ability of students to write using word processing software with commonly available tools" (National Assessment Governing Board, 2011, p. 2). In prior assessments, students had composed with paper and pencil. NAEP also used videos and sound in prompts for writing, but students did not produce multimodal texts. While multimodal productions are now fairly common in composition classes at the college level, and to some degree at the K–12 level, the development of *ways to assess* multimodal text produced by students—especially in high-stakes, large-scale assessments—is still very much in its infancy.

For many reasons, large-scale assessment of multimodal texts is difficult. One challenge is the inherent diversity of multimodal texts; mechanisms are constantly changing. Another is the tension between design-based criteria such as the principles of graphic design or video production and existing criteria for writing. A third challenge is that multimodal technologies change rapidly in unpredictable ways. Another is that much of the students' work on multimodal projects in school is collaborative, so that it can be difficult to single out an individual's contribution. And still another challenge is uneven access to digital tools and teachers prepared to teach and evaluate multimodal projects. All of these challenges, of course, overlap and interact, creating a variety of issues. For example, the National Center for Education Statistics (NCES, 2017) reports that access to digital learning resources varies in relation to income, locale (suburban versus rural areas), and ethnicity. And as for teachers, NCES reports that conclusions from relevant literature reviews

> suggest that at the individual level, teachers are less likely to use technology in the classroom if they lack the confidence, skills, and pedagogical training to do so; if they do not perceive a benefit of using a new technology over current instructional approaches; or if they anticipate the new approach will be difficult or time-intensive to adopt.
>
> *(para 21)*

Fulwiler and Middleton (2012) argue that we are "caught up in a whirlwind of change as old and new media renegotiate their functions" (p. 39). This whirlwind is about more than the actual technological tools and gets at the very act of composing itself. Multimodal texts, their uses, and the tools used to create them, in other words, are very much in flux. Without a doubt, multimodal or digital literacy is an important aspect of literacy, but it is clear that it involves more than just translating traditional print texts to an online environment (Jewitt, 2008). Audience, purpose, genre, and context are all still important, but how they are enacted and created varies quite a bit, which makes it even more difficult for assessment, especially standardized assessments, which by their very nature tend not to be flexible and adaptable.

In postsecondary contexts, programs and institutions are using eportfolios across the campus or a variety of evaluation needs, including for individual courses, programs, and accreditation (e.g., Cambridge et al., 2009; Campbell, 1996; Dunn et al., 2013; Whithaus, 2002a, 2002b; Wills & Rice, 2013; Yancey,

2019). Yancey (2004a) explains that "web sensible" eportfolios are more than just transferring print texts to an online environment. They are multimodal. An eportfolio can include

> text boxes, hyperlinking, visuals, audio texts, and design elements [that] not only inhabits the digital space and is distributed electronically but also exploits the medium . . . this model may include print texts, but it will include as well images and visuals, internal links from one text to another, external links that provide multiple contexts, and commentary and connections to the world outside the immediate portfolio.
>
> *(Yancey, 2004a, pp. 745–746)*

Yancey continued:

> Depth of thought is created and demonstrated through multiple contexts: evoked verbally, evoked visually, evoked through internal links, evoked through external links. The arrangement of this portfolio, modeled on the gallery, thus provides for the invention of a different particular kind of student: one who can make multiple connections and who creates depth through multiplicity and elaboration, who can work in visual and verbal and aural modalities, who can offer a reader multiple narratives extending ever outward.
>
> *(pp. 750–751)*

Assessing this type of multimodal portfolio demands a different approach to evaluation than is found in a print-based portfolio assessment or essay exams. Gallagher (2014) offers a theory that acknowledges the importance and complexity of context with multimodal texts. He suggests that we can account for context "in meaningful ways in writing assessment situations" that are performance-based and "position texts and contexts as mutually constitutive" (2014, p. 11). Drawing on a variety of theories, Gallagher explains that writing is not merely surrounded by context but helps create the context in which it exists. For multimodal texts, the interface used is part of what creates the context. Multimodal texts are not static, as a printed text is, but the interface is dynamic, often participatory. The dynamic act of reading multimodal texts changes how we approach them as assessment artifacts. Burnett et al. (2014) explain how they developed and used a program-wide rubric that is specifically designed for multimodal assessment. The rubric is designed to provide consistency in evaluation across the program yet allow faculty flexibility in using it in classes.

In making a case to move beyond traditional rubrics for multimodal assessments, Sills (2016) argues that a traditional rubric-based approach to assessment doesn't work with multimodal texts. In other words, because most rubrics have not been designed to accommodate multimodal texts, instructors find them difficult to use. As an alternative to the traditional, print-based rubric approach and to idiosyncratic assignment-specific criteria, Sills (2016) proposed using a "sensemaking" framework for multimodal assessments. According to Sills, "assessment as sensemaking allows greater attention to the contextual processes informing the construction of the assessed text, and by extension, the opportunity to generate new assessment values attuned to these contexts" (para 17). Instead of using rubrics to "manufacture consensus," "sensemaking" employs "plastic, scalable assessment categories that can be adapted to local contexts" (para 4).

For example, the National Writing Project (NWP) sponsored the Multimodal Assessment Project (MAP) to develop guidelines for the assessment of multimodal artifacts, processes, and habits of mind. The goal was to provide tools for formative assessment to support students as they were developing their skills. Using an "iterative process to consult relevant literature, review student-composed multimodal composition, and solicit comments from other NWP colleagues," the MAP research team found six broad dimensions to be "critical to multimodal composing: artifact, rhetorical skills [attention to context], substance, process management, technical skills, and habits of mind" (Wahleithner, 2014, p. 8). Eidman-Aadahl, Director of National Programs and Site Development for NWP, explained that the "critical shift" in the development of the MAP framework was the shift from "a narrow sense of assessment as developing the tools to array artifacts on a scale" toward a developmental perspective that focused on "the things that a young composer—well any composer—can get better at" (as cited in Wahleithner, 2014, p. 82). In other words, the shift from evaluating artifacts as end products to evaluating what students can get better at is a move that puts learning in the spotlight. Further, as Sills (2016) explains, these dimensions operate at both macro and micro levels. They resonate with the guidelines and outcomes developed by national organizations (Conference on College Composition and Communication, 2014; National Council of Teachers of English, 2013a; Council of Writing Program Administrators et al., 2011), and they "emerged from an effort to *align* the sensemaking of teachers and students, composers and audience, and 'scale up' these alignments" (Sills, 2016, p. 6). Sense-making frameworks such as those developed in the MAP project offer flexible but scalable categories that can be deployed and refined in context-specific ways in individual classrooms and programs.

Although assessment of multimodal literacy is challenging, there is no doubt that it is an important literacy to promote and to assess. Scholars such as those in the New London Group, recognizing the growing importance of multimodal communication in our students' lives and the need to prepare them for the future, call for a pedagogy of multiliteracies, "one in which language and other modes of meaning are dynamic representational resources, constantly being remade by their users as they work to achieve their various cultural purposes" (Cazden et al., 1996). As the NCTE *Framework for 21st Century Curriculum and Assessment* (2013a) indicates, and Baldwin (2016) notes, "writing teachers at all educational levels face the challenges that come with incorporating multimodal writing— texts composed using a combination of sound, images, video, etc.—into the classroom" (p. 1). Baldwin's research on what leading teacher-scholars value in students' multimodal writing suggests that assessment ought to include not just evaluation of the product, but also "the situated composing practices of writers" and highlight the "goal of developing writer's metacognitive awareness and sense of agency" (p. 1).

Assessing collaborative writing tasks

In addition to multimodal composing, broadening the conditions for writing assessment means addressing collaboration. After all, writing has long been considered a social activity, not a lone endeavor done by an individual. There are good reasons for integrating collaboration in the writing classroom, including built-in occasions for peer review and the opportunities students will have to learn from each other. There are good reasons for including collaboration in assessment as well: collaborative tasks are expected in professional writing assignments that aim to replicate real world conditions for writing (Kiefer et al., 2000–2018). Kiefer et al. note that there is increasing emphasis on digital technologies to enhance collaboration, such as wikis and other web tools. In addition, surveys of employers commissioned by the American Association of Colleges and Universities identify the ability to work in teams as one of the learning priorities that employers value highly (Watson & McConnell, 2018).

While collaboration is common in both classrooms and workplaces, it hasn't been common in assessment contexts, especially the high-stakes variety. Typically, the accountability agenda focuses on assessment of individuals and individually created products. But if collaboration is considered part of the construct of writing, then it needs to be addressed in some way in the assessment of writing at some level of the overall assessment system. For example, collaboration could be incorporated in writing assessment by allowing students to work with peers as they do during regular class sessions, sharing their ideas for writing and getting responses to their freewrites during a stage in the assessment process, as was done in the composition placement test at SUNY Stonybrook described by Robertson (1994) that we mentioned earlier. Alternatively, students might be required to produce a product working as a team, as is the case in the Advanced Placement Seminar performance assessment. Still another option might be to assess students' ability to manage collaborative processes successfully, a skill that has become increasingly important in today's collaborative and technological world.

Several resources for assessing collaboration can now be found on the Internet, including checklists for students to assess the development their own skills.

See, for example, the Guidelines for Assessing Collaborative Learning in the Classroom published by Collaborative Education Lab (Valente, 2018) or the Guide to Assessing Teamwork and Collaboration produced by the Galileo Educational Network in 2008. While these resources are not focused on writing per se, they highlight the increased need to consider collaboration more explicitly in our assessment of writing. Many writing experts have provided guidance for assessing group or collaborative writing, and there is a rich area of literature published on the topic since the 1980s (see, e.g., the influential 1987 article authored by Morgan et al. on collaborative writing in the classroom). More recently, issues related to assessing collaboration via technology are becoming prevalent. For example, Tharp (2010) describes her approach to evaluating a wiki-based collaborative writing project in her article "Wiki, Wiki, Wiki—WHAT." She reviewed challenges in assessment and grading related specifically to online digital work, for example, the lack of resources to help teachers design rubrics and criteria.

Culminating projects, whether collaborative or individual, also offer a structured way of gathering assessment information while expanding the conditions for assessment. Darling-Hammond (2017) describes several that require "weeks or even months as students demonstrate a comprehensive set of skills within or across fields" (p. 26). Projects of this kind are designed to "gauge student knowledge and skill cumulatively . . . [and] evaluate deep understanding of an area of study. . . . In Singapore, the culminating project must also be collaborative, integrating another key skill" (p. 26). Curriculum-embedded assessment of this kind is only one of an array of performance assessment options for renovating and redesigning assessment systems that broaden the conditions in which the assessment of writing occurs.

Designing performance assessments and portfolios to support learning

When NCLB ended and the Every Student Success Act (ESSA) became the law, states were given new flexibility in designing and building their own assessment systems. According to Darling-Hammond, the law "explicitly allows the use of multiple assessments including 'portfolios, projects or extended-performance tasks' as part of state systems" (2017, p. 1). In short, Darling-Hammond is telling us that we have come a long way from NCLB:

> Rather than trying to have one test address all needs, different methods can be combined in a system of assessments that strategically uses different types of information for different purposes. Performance assessments can be designed to provide formative and/or summative information, to gauge

student growth on learning progressions, to support proficiency determinations, or to be combined in a student profile or portfolio.

(2017, p. 7)

As of January 2018, 17 states had enacted policies that support performance assessments, including policies making performance assessment experiences part of graduation requirements, policies providing support for the development of performance assessments, and policies allowing performance assessments to be used as waivers of state exams for selected schools (Guha et al., 2018, p. 1).

> Performance assessments offer several benefits. One is that the assessment does not need to be secret in order to be a useful test . . . Rather than relying on secrecy around what facts must be memorized, a robust performance assessment evaluates the way knowledge and skills are mastered, combined, and used in practice.
>
> *(Guha et al., 2018, p. 4)*

Another benefit is that "rigorous, validated, high-quality performance assessments" can "drive improvements in teaching and learning" along with "rigorous curriculum and high-quality instruction" (Guha et al., 2018, p. 1). Yet another is that performance assessments can be used to assess the complex "higher order" sets of skills so needed in today's world (Darling-Hammond, 2017). As Darling-Hammond explains:

> current tests in the U.S. . . . do not provide incentives for teaching the more complex skills students increasingly need to succeed in the rapidly evolving U.S. society and economy . . . well-developed thinking skills, problem solving abilities, design strategies, and communication capabilities.
>
> *(2017, p. 2)*

While well-designed multiple-choice tests may be useful in the classroom for some diagnostic purposes or for gauging the impact of certain instructional units, they are not useful by themselves for making claims about higher-order skills or writing competence. As we demonstrated in Chapter 3, writing is a complex, meaning-making, socially situated activity, and effective writers need to know much more than what can be determined by multiple-choice questions about language, grammar, and rhetoric. Including high-quality performance assessments in statewide systems would incentivize the teaching of higher-order skills such as writing.

Darling-Hammond (2017) explains that many different kinds of performance-based components can be and are used in assessments. They include performance tasks on tests such as essays and open-ended questions used to examine students' reasoning and knowledge, problem-solution tasks that require showing one's work and explaining one's thinking, and computer-based simulations and research tasks that require students to investigate questions and use and evaluate evidence. They also include curriculum-embedded performance tasks and portfolios. These performance-based components can be integrated into assessment systems in several ways, "all of which have been used successfully at scale in states and nations around the world" (p. 1). Performance items or tasks can be included as part of "traditional 'sit-down' tests"; "curriculum-embedded tasks" conducted in the classroom can be "stand alone or be combined with tests results to produce a summative score"; "multiple tasks can be aggregated" into portfolios to "display a broad set of competencies in multiple domains or genres"; and "traditional sit-down tests, curriculum-embedded tasks, and a portfolio leading to a student defense . . . each serving complimentary purposes" can be combined into comprehensive assessment systems (Darling-Hammond, 2017, p. 1).

As a means for ensuring that students encounter and learn to write for a variety of different purposes and audiences, portfolios offer an especially useful assessment approach, especially if they contain curriculum-embedded tasks and a variety of different types of writing. As we explained in Chapter 3, research has shown that an individual's performance can vary across purposes and topics for writing. Several scholars have heightened our awareness that the skills and strategies needed in writing for one mode or purpose are not necessarily those needed in writing for another (Greenberg & Witte, 1988; Freedman & Pringle, 1980; Pringle & Freedman, 1985; Scardamalia & Bereiter, 1985). Teaching a range of writing gives students opportunities to learn how writing varies across contexts, and including several different kinds of tasks in portfolios provides a stronger and potentially more valid representation of a student's overall writing competence.

Portfolios have long been considered more valid than other kinds of assessment for other reasons as well. They typically include writing samples collected under more authentic and natural conditions, for example, with attention to the writing process and over a period of time. They have been widely used as a stable form of documentation of performance skills in writing, providing students and teachers with a way to display and judge evidence of proficiency with a range of samples. Portfolios can also reflect and support worthwhile and effective teaching practices such as self-assessment, revision, and reflection. However, while portfolios offer great promise as an alternative to less representative and less authentic forms of writing assessment, some portfolio designs may support reflection and self-assessment better than others. For example, the Kentucky Writing Portfolio Assessment System required students to submit writings not just from their English classes, but from other subject areas as well. One of the requirements was a piece of reflective writing focusing on the student's growth as a writer—a kind of self-assessment. The design of the portfolio thus required self-assessment, but it was required only at the end of the portfolio collection process, not throughout.

In contrast, other portfolio programs may ask students to reflect on their processes and products routinely throughout a semester or year. Like the Kentucky portfolio system, the Arts PROPEL project was designed to assess a range of genres and audiences. According to Wolf (1989), the range was "deliberately diverse." A student might include "pieces as diverse as journal entries, letters, poems or essays from social studies classes" (p. 37). But the Arts PROPEL project added a new layer and integrated a new overall purpose for the project as a whole—reflection in support of learning. Instead of asking students to reflect on a collection of their best or most representative works when the portfolio was due, the Arts PROPEL teachers asked students *periodically* to evaluate and reflect on their work. They also asked students to provide evidence of and to reflect on the process of creating their works. For example, a student writer might include "the notes, diagrams, drafts, and final version of a poem" (Wolf, 1989, p. 7) along with a written reflection on the process of its creation. As Wolf explains, the teachers asked "students to read their own progress in the 'footprints' of their works" (p. 37). The portfolios were used to help teachers keep a close eye on their students' emerging learning so that they could provide feedback and experiences to support and extend it. Gardner (1992) explained that the Arts PROPEL "process-folios" were "instruments of learning rather than showpieces of final accomplishment" (p. 103). Portfolios that enhance learning include documentation and evidence, but they also promote reflection and collaborative mentoring.

Reflection on the work and the processes employed in making the work in portfolios benefits both students and teachers. As Bereiter and Scardamalia (1987) explain, reflection helps student writers "themselves, and not just the teacher, have a sense of where development is heading—where the growing edge of their competence is and what possibilities lie ahead" (p. 336).

Portfolios are not the only way to promote self-assessment and formative assessment more generally. Regional School District No.15 in Connecticut took up the idea of self-assessment and reflection as the focus of its educational reform efforts in the '90s to a new level. The goal of the system was to develop self-regulated learners at all levels of the system, including students, teachers, and administrators. Teachers engaged students in generative and interactive activities based on the self-assessment concept. For example, some teachers asked students to brainstorm criteria in small groups that were then shared with other groups in the class and sometimes synthesized by the teacher and students together into a master list. Teachers also developed performance tasks that "were engaging to students and well connected to content knowledge, process skills, and work habits" promoted in the curriculum. They embedded the performance tasks in instruction. They created assessment lists of criteria, "tailored to student needs and instructional objectives," and they provided models of excellent work for students to examine and discuss (Hibbard et al., 1996, p. 47, as cited in Murphy & Underwood, 2000, p. 148). The teachers also selected particularly engaging "anchor" tasks that were required of all students.

At the college level, faculty have often used portfolios to support learning in several different ways. Since the early 1990s, when Haswell (2001) was developing the WSU portfolio, the use of portfolios has continued to grow with the popularity of eportfolios (Cambridge, 2001; Cambridge et al., 2009; Wills & Rice, 2013). At Arizona State University the focus is on the creation of an eportfolio that supports metacognition, collaboration, and self-directed learning (Struckey et al., 2018). The Kalamazoo College eportfolio, according to Whithaus (2002a), requires students to write a "Foundation Essay" when they start, and then a Senior Reflection that looks back at the essay and other materials in the portfolio. Whithaus explains that "the Kalamazoo College Portfolio was designed to give students, faculty, and administrators a sense of a student's development over time" (Whithaus, 2002a, para 3). As a graduation requirement, the K-portfolios perform particular institutional functions within Kalamazoo College. "They monitor but also encourage student learning; they act as 'gate-keepers' for graduation but unlike exit exams, K-portfolios show a series of authentic student performances" (Whithaus, 2002a, para 3).

At the University of Georgia, faculty replaced the three-hour exit exam from first-year composition with eportfolios, then used a sample of the eportfolios to assess general education outcomes (Desmet et al., 2008). Building on the work of Desmet et al. (2008), Whithaus (2013) and his colleagues at University of California Davis used eportfolios to develop a "system that would allow us to assess how students' knowledge about the writing skills stressed in their lower division writing courses transfer to their upper division writing experiences" (p. 213). These uses of portfolios, whether electronic or print-based, demonstrate how writing programs use performance-based assessment to obtain information useful for program evaluation and for designing curriculum to support learning; at the same time, they promote a socially situated construct of writing in which students produce a variety of genres.

Portfolio programs are more likely to support learning to write than more traditional approaches to assessment. For example, Whithaus (2002a) describes the contrast between a more traditional approach to assessment and the Alverno College digital portfolio:

> [T]he Alverno Digital Portfolios work on an institutional level and represent communication skills writ large as well as writing skills. Their design demonstrates their agenda of targeting the long-term develop [sic] of student abilities rather than a micro-level examination of a particular skill set at a given moment in time.
>
> *(2002a, para 5)*

The explicit goal of the Alverno Diagnostic Digital Portfolio (DDP) is to assist student learning. Created in 1999, it was designed to enable students to follow and reflect on their learning progress throughout their years of study at the college. "Student Assessment-as-Learning" is described as "A multidimensional process, integral to learning, that involves observing performances on an individual learning in action and judging them on the basis of public developmental criteria, with resulting feedback to the learner" (Alverno College Faculty, 1994, p. 4). Ehley (2006) describes the portfolio design:

> The learning artifacts stored in the DDP are snapshots of student performances rather than the institution's official record of abilities demonstrated within courses. Also woven into the DDP's design was the concept of creating specific and identifiable times in a student's curriculum where she would be asked to reflect on her development . . . and create learning goals. . . . The DDP was designed to assist in the reflection process by providing an accessible place for students to review some of their past performances, self assessments, and feedback in order to analyze their patterns of learning.
>
> *(p. 65)*

Research conducted by Ehley (2006) indicates that "undergraduates students and faculty WERE logging onto the DDP and they perceived the DDP as an easy to use, useful tool. . . . Student and faculty use of the DDP has continued to increase since it was implemented in 1999" (p. ii).

Portfolios conceptualized as more than just collections of student work, as in these examples, encourage the pursuit of personal cognitive learning goals, the kind of learning that Bereiter and Scardamalia (1989) call "intentional." When portfolios are treated as "instruments of learning," they prompt students to look back, to digest and debrief, and to set new goals and determine next steps (Camp, 1992a; Johnston, 1983; Zessoules & Gardner, 1991). In short, they provide students with opportunities to engage in both reflection and formative self-evaluation. Bandura (1991) explains in his treatise on the social cognitive theory of self-regulation that human functioning is "regulated by an interplay of self-generated and external sources of influence" (p. 249). Many teachers and researchers see students' participation in reflecting on, and in making decisions about, the contents of their portfolios as critical for learning to write. As LeMahieu et al. (1995) put it, "the ability to reflect on and evaluate one's own writing is seen as a critical component of one's development as a writer" (p. 23). More recently, Yancey (2019) explained how eportfolio literacy supports student learning through reflective practices and activities such as

> collecting potential artifacts; engaging in processes of selecting appropriate artifacts for a given purpose and audience; contextualizing and curating artifacts; using design as an intentional feature of ePortfolio curation,

navigation and aesthetics; revising a full ePortfolio or parts of it; remixing parts . . . reflecting on artifacts and experiences; and sharing the ePortfolio locally and globally.

(p. 3)

According to Darling-Hammond (2017), assessment strategies can be characterized as existing along a continuum:

At one end are the multiple-choice and close-ended items found in today's traditional tests. These items measure recall and recognition, but cannot measure higher level thinking skills or the ability to apply them . . . at the other end are assessments that require substantial student initiation of designs, ideas, and performances, tapping the planning and work management skills especially needed for college and careers . . . at each step along the continuum, tasks become more complex, measuring progressively larger and more integrated sets of knowledge and skill, more cognitively complex aspects of learning, and more robust applications of knowledge to new problems and situations.

(p. 6)

Along the continuum are embedded performance assessments that extend over several days or weeks and that more closely approach the "expectations for performance found in colleges and careers" (Darling-Hammond, 2017, p. 15). Further along are projects of longer duration such as culminating projects and exhibitions that put more responsibility on the student for choosing and refining the topic, organizing the project, and finding the necessary information for completing it.

At the far end of the continuum are portfolios, "collections of evidence" about students' learning. Often collections of other performance tasks, portfolios can be focused on a single-subject, such as history or writing, or they can be used to assess multiple subjects, as portfolios are sometimes used as requirements for graduation. For example, in all of the schools in the New York Performance Standards Consortium, students include at least four entries in their portfolios:

- An analytic essay (often a literary analysis)
- An applied mathematics product (involving mathematical modeling)
- A science investigation
- A research paper (often a social science paper)

(Darling-Hammond, 2017, p. 34)

Students in the Consortium schools also engage in a portfolio defense that includes a formal presentation plus questions and answers about the work. The portfolio entries and defenses are evaluated using common scoring rubrics that reflect critical skills in each discipline. Teachers are trained within schools and departments to calibrate their scoring, and they periodically "engage in cross-school moderation sessions to calibrate the scoring across the consortium as a whole" (Darling-Hammond, 2017, p. 35). We share this multiple subject example to show that portfolios can be scaled up, and support systems can be provided to ensure reliability of scoring. Districts and schools can form consortia to support portfolio development. For our purposes, however, we prefer focusing on a single subject—writing. Adequate assessment of a complex, socially situated construct of writing requires several samples of writing collected under a variety of conditions—a goal that is possible if performance assessments that involve writing are introduced across a system as a whole.

What we are suggesting here is similar to the system used in Queensland, Australia, described by Darling-Hammond (2017). Programs, schools, and districts could develop and combine a system of performance assessments, including writing portfolios, with external tests that incorporate performance components providing additional information on occasion, not as accountability measures, but to serve as checks on external validity. According to Darling-Hammond (2017), "Portfolio scoring is moderated by panels that include teachers from other schools and professors from the higher education system" (p. 35). She describes the particular benefits that portfolios offer, including their potential for "developing self-directed learners":

> The process develops students' metacognitive skills and gives them opportunities for reflection and revision. As students see their own progress over time and reflect on how they have improved and can improve further, they develop a growth mindset. Not incidentally, these processes also support student learning by deepening teachers' learning about what constitutes high-quality work and how to support it, both individually and collectively as a staff. Furthermore, through the use of rubrics and public presentations, students can receive feedback that is specific and detailed, providing them a much better idea of how to improve than would an item analysis from a standardized test.
>
> (Darling-Hammond, 2017, pp. 35–36)

Across grade levels and educational settings, writing teachers and scholars have embraced portfolios as a means of providing a richer, fuller representation of writing competence that draws from different contexts of writing and includes a broad range of writing genres. Portfolios also provide opportunities for formative assessment. While large-scale assessments typically don't provide formative information for either teachers or students because of the time delay in getting results, classroom portfolios offer that opportunity. The models we detailed all included feedback on student writing, by peers and/or teachers, before the final assessment occurs. In fact, the use of a portfolio system emphasizes the role of formative assessment in learning to write when the teaching associated with the portfolio includes ongoing, low-stakes feedback; review and reflection; collection of work; and selection of work for inclusion. Portfolios also support a social perspective on learning and literacy because they typically are collaborative, interactive, and embedded in the context. Portfolio assessment, however, is uncommon in large-scale, mandated assessments.

Taking social perspectives on learning, accountability, and assessment

As we explained in Chapter 3, literacy scholars agree on the significance of a social perspective on literacy and learning. However, this approach to literacy has received less attention in the field of assessment, a field that has been dominated by psychometricians, professionals who practice the science of measurement. For instance, Shepard (1991) contends that psychometricians are highly influenced by behaviorist theory and a learning model of instruction that "requires sequential mastery of constituent skills and explicit testing of each learning step" and assumes that component skills can be mastered out of context (p. 2). Although some very important work has been done to accommodate emerging social perspectives (e.g., Camp, 1993; Fredericksen et al., 1993; Fredericksen & Collins, 1989; Linn et al., 1990; Messick, 1989, 1994), relatively few test development experts in the United States reflect learner-oriented or social perspectives. It may not be surprising then, that relatively little attention has been paid to social perspectives on learning in the assessment field in general or in the corridors of policy.

The National Council of Teachers of English (2018) statement *Literacy Assessment: Definitions, Principles, and Practices* makes learning the focus of assessment. Two of the principles of literacy assessment they propose have particular relevance here:

> Literacy assessment is meaningful to the learner,
> Literacy assessments are valid only to the extent that they help students learn.

Our focus in this chapter has been on ways we can redesign the assessment system to better support learning by turning it inside out. That is, by giving teachers and students more agency in assessments. Turning the standard approach to writing assessment inside out also means that what we know about language and learning should be the driving force in determining assessment practices, not the psychometric theories and practices that currently dominate large-scale assessments. A traditional psychometric approach seeks to standardize, to control variability, and to isolate writing from the social factors that are at the heart of identifying effective writing—audience, purpose, genre, context. To put writing, students, and teachers at the heart of assessment, we need to collect multiple samples of different genres written within different conditions in order to obtain representative samples of student proficiency and to broaden the writing curriculum. Students need these wide-ranging experiences to acquire the rhetorical knowledge for handling new situations.

We have argued that we need to design performance and portfolio assessments to support intentional learning, goal setting, and self-assessment, and that we need to promote formative assessment, the kind of ongoing assessment that improves teaching and individual student learning, as well as the kind that informs curriculum development and program improvement. These kinds of assessments are in tension with assessments designed for accountability at the K–12 level where the focus is on individual scores from standardized exams, such as the high school exit exams required by several of the states. Across K–16 educational venues, standardized exams continue to play a disrupting role in the experience of many students and their teachers. With the "rise of writing" in terms of literacy and its link to the knowledge economy (Brandt, 2015), assessment of writing and written communication will continue to be part of the accountability and assessment mandates. This makes attention to the social dimensions of literacy and the redesign of our assessment systems all the more critical.

The changes we are suggesting—discarding high stakes based on standardized tests, encouraging breadth in the writing curriculum and the assessment of writing, promoting performance and portfolio assessments so that assessment serves learning, putting students at center-stage in the system through self and formative assessments—can't be made all at once, or at a single level of the system. The current ESSA legislation allows for the possibility of some of these changes, but it will take time. And there is another consideration on which all of these changes hinge. In order to move in this direction, we need to rethink the way teachers are currently positioned in assessment and educational decision making more generally, a topic we take up in the next chapter. As the NCTE Joint Task Force on Assessment says, teachers are "the primary agents, not passive consumers, of assessment information. It is their ongoing formative assessments that primarily influence students' learning" (NCTE, 2013b, p. 3). What we suggest calls for turning the assessment system inside out—so teachers, students, and classrooms drive the system, not testing organizations. To put teaching and learning front and center—to rebuild our educational accountability system to support what we know about teaching, learning, and writing—means valuing teachers' voices and enhancing the professional development of teachers, because teachers are the ones who transform policies and mandates into classroom learning.

References

Adler-Kassner, L., & Gonzalez, L. (2016). "Everybody writes": Accreditation-based assessment as professional development at a research-intensive university. In W. Sharer, T. Morse, M. F. Eble, & W. P. Bank (Eds.), *Reclaiming accountability: Improving writing programs through accreditation and large-scale assessments* (pp. 242–262). Utah State University Press.

Alford, B. (2009). DCM as the assessment program: Mid Michigan community college. In B. Broad, L. Adler-Kassner, B. Alford, & J. Detweiler (2009). *Organic writing assessment: Dynamic criteria mapping in action* (pp. 37–50). Utah State University Press. https://digitalcommons.usu.edu/usupress_pubs/165

Alverno College Faculty. (1994). *Student assessment-as-learning at Alverno College.* Alverno College Institute.

Andrade, H. G. (2005). Teaching with rubrics: The good, the bad, and the ugly. *College Teaching, 53*(1), 27–30.

Andrade, H. G., Du, Y., & Wang, X. (2008). Putting rubrics to the test: The effect of a model, criteria generation, and rubric-referenced self-assessment on elementary school students' writing. *Educational Measurement: Issues and Practice, 27*(2), 3–13.

Andrade, H. G., & Valtcheva, A. (2009, Winter). Promoting learning and achievement through self-assessment. *Theory into Practice, 48*(1), 12–19.

Baldwin, K. M. (2016). *Multimodal assessment in action: What we really value in new media texts* [Doctoral Dissertation, University of Massachusetts]. https://scholarworks.umass.edu/cgi/viewcontent.cgi?article=1778&context=dissertations_2

Bambrick-Santoyo, P. (2010). *Driven by data: A practical guide to improve instruction.* Jossey-Bass.

Bandura, A. (1991). Social cognitive theory of self-regulation. *Organizational Behavior and Human Decision Processes, 50*(2), 248–287.

Bandura, A. (1994). Self-efficacy. In L. W. Levy, K. L. Karst, & A. Winkler (Eds.), *Encyclopedia of human behavior* (Vol. 4, pp. 71–81). Academic Press.

Bandura, A. (1997). *Self-efficacy: The exercise of control.* Freeman.

Bangert-Drowns, R. L., Kulik, C. C., Kulik, J. A., & Morgan, M. (1991). The instructional effect of feedback in test-like events. *Review of Educational Research, 61*(2), 213–238.

Beaufort, A. (2007). *College writing and beyond: A new framework for university writing instruction.* Utah State University Press.

Belanoff, P., & Dickson, M. (Eds.). (1991). *Portfolios: Process and product.* Boynton/Cook.

Bereiter, C., & Scardamalia, M. (1987). *The psychology of written composition.* Lawrence Erlbaum.

Bereiter, C., & Scardamalia, M. (1989). Intentional learning as a goal of instruction. In L. B. Resnick (Ed.), *Knowing, learning, and instruction: Essays in honor of Robert Glaser* (pp. 361–392). Lawrence Erlbaum.

Black, L., Daiker, D. A., Stygall, G., & Sommers, J. (Eds.). (1994). *New directions in portfolio assessment: Reflective practice, critical theory, and large-scale scoring.* Boynton/Cook.

Black, P., & Wiliam, D. (1998). Inside the black box: Raising standards through classroom assessment. *Phi Delta Kappa.* https://kappanonline.org/inside-the-black-box-raising-standards-through-classroom-assessment/

Black, P., & Wiliam, D. (2009). Developing the theory of formative assessment. *Educational Assessment, Evaluation and Accountability (formerly the Journal of Personnel Evaluation in Education), 21*(1), 5–31.

Brandt, D. (2015). *The rise of writing: Redefining mass literacy.* Cambridge University Press.

Brandts, L. (1993). A first grade perspective. In M. A. Smith & M. Ylvisaker (Eds.), *Teachers' voices: Portfolios in the classroom* (pp. 107–117). National Writing Project.

Briggs, J. (2018). The folly of weakening the analytical writing placement examination and promoting directed self-placement. *Berkeley Writing: College Writing Programs.* https://writing.berkeley.edu/article/folly-weakening-analytical-writing-placement-examination-and-promoting-directed-self

Broad, B. (2003). *What we really value: Beyond rubrics in teaching and assessing writing.* Utah State University Press.

Broad, B., Adler-Kassner, L., Alford, B., & Detweiler, J. (2009). *Organic writing assessment: Dynamic criteria mapping in action.* Utah State University Press. https://digitalcommons. usu.edu/usupress_pubs/165

Brookhart, S., Andolina, M., Zuza, M., & Furman, R. (2004). Minute math: An action research study of student self-assessment. *Educational Studies in Mathematics, 57*(2), 213–227.

Brown, A., & Campione, J. (1996). Psychological theory and the design of innovative learning environments: On procedures, principles, and systems. In L. Schauble & R. Glaser (Eds.), *Innovations in learning: New environments for education* (pp. 291–292). Lawrence Erlbaum.

Burnett, R. E., Frazee, A., Hanggi, K., & Madden, A. (2014). A programmatic ecology of assessment: Using a common rubric to evaluate multimodal processes and artifacts. *Computers and Composition, 31*(Special Issue: Multimodal Assessment), 53–66. https:// doi.org/10.1016/j.compcom.2013.12.005

Butler, D., & Winne, P. (1995). Feedback and self-regulated learning: A theoretical synthe-ses. *Review of Educational Research, 65*(3), 245–281.

Cambridge, B. (Ed.). (2001). *Electronic portfolios: Emerging practices in student, faculty, and institutional learning.* American Association of Higher Education.

Cambridge, D., Cambridge, B., & Yancey, K. (Eds.). (2009). *Electronic portfolios 2.0: Emergent research on implementation and impact.* Stylus.

Camp, R. (1992a). Portfolio reflections in middle and secondary school classrooms. In K. B. Yancey (Ed.), *Portfolios in the writing classroom* (pp. 61–79). National Council of Teachers of English.

Camp, R. (1992b). Assessment in the context of schools and school change. In H. Marshall (Ed.), *Redefining student learning: Roots of educational change* (pp. 241–263). Ablex.

Camp, R. (1993). The place of portfolios in our changing views of writing assessment. In R. E. Bennett & W. C. Ward (Eds.), *Construction versus choice in cognitive measurement: Issues in constructed response, performance testing, and portfolio assessment* (pp. 183–212). Lawrence Erlbaum.

Campbell, J. (1996). Electronic portfolios: A five-year history. *Computers and Composition, 13*(2), 185–194.

Cazden, C., Cope, B., Fairclough, N., Gee, J. et al. (1996). A pedagogy of multiliteracies: Designing social futures. *Harvard Educational Review, 66*(1), 60–92. http://newarcpro ject.pbworks.com/f/Pedagogy+of+Multiliteracies_New+London+Group.pdf

Choseed, M. (2016). A tool for program building: Programmatic assessment and the English department at Onondaga community college. In W. Sharer, T. A. Morse, M. Eble, & W. Banks (Eds.), *Reclaiming accountability: Improving writing programs through accreditation and large-scale assessments* (pp. 129–144). Utah State University Press.

Cizek, G. J. (2010). An introduction to formative assessment: History, characteristics, and challenges. In H. Andrade & G. Cizek (Eds.), *Handbook of formative assessment* (pp. 3–17). Routledge.

College Board. (2022). *AP seminar: The exam.* https://apcentral.collegeboard.org/courses/ ap-seminar/exam

Conference on College Composition and Communication. (2014). *Writing assessment* [Position statement]. https://cccc.ncte.org/cccc/resources/positions/writingassessment

Council of Chief State School Officers. (2018). *Revising the definition of formative assessment.* https://ccsso.org/sites/default/files/2018-06/Revising%20the%20Definition%20of%20Formative%20Assessment.pdf

Council of Writing Program Administrators. (2014, July 7). *WPA outcomes statement for first-year composition (3.0)* [Position Statement]. http://wpacouncil.org/positions/outcomes.html

Council of Writing Program Administrators, National Council of Teachers of English and the National Writing Project. (2011). *Framework for success in postsecondary writing.* http://wpacouncil.org/aws/CWPA/asset_manager/get_file/350201?ver=7548

Darling-Hammond, L. (2017). *Developing and measuring higher order skills: Models for state performance assessment systems.* Learning Policy Institute Report, Council of Chief State School Officers. https://learningpolicyinstitute.org/sites/default/files/product-files/Models_State_Performance_Assessment_Systems_REPORT.pdf

Darling-Hammond, L., Barron, B., Pearson, P. D., Schoenfeld, A. H., Stage, E. K., Zimmerman, T. D., Cervetti, G. N., & Tilson, J. L. (2008). *Powerful learning: What we know about teaching for understanding.* Jossey-Bass.

Darling-Hammond, L., & Pecheone, R. (2010). *Developing an internationally comparable balanced assessment system that supports high quality learning.* Educational Testing Service. www.ets.org/Media/Research/pdf/Darling HammondPechoneSystemModel.pdf

Deen, M. K. (1993). Portfolios as discovery. In M. A. Smith & M. Ylvisaker (Eds.), *Teachers' voices: Portfolios in the classroom* (pp. 49–59). National Writing Project.

De Fina, A. A., Anstendic, L. L., & De Lawther, K. (1991). Alternative integrated reading/writing assessment and curriculum design. *Journal of Reading, 34*(5), 354–359.

Desmet, C., Miller, D., Griffin, J., Balthazor, R., & Cummins, R. (2008). Reflection, revision, and assessment in first-year composition eportfolios. *The Journal of General Education, 57*(1), 15–30. https://reader.zlibcdn.com/articles/fd0bd07dffdc44ae5946d-950c3ccefa7/1.jpg

Detwiler, J., & McBride, M. (2009). Designs on assessment at UNR: University of Nevada, Reno. In B. Broad, L. Adler-Kassner, B. Alford, & J. Detweiler (2009). *Organic writing assessment: Dynamic criteria mapping in action* (pp. 52–72). Utah State University Press https://digitalcommons.usu.edu/usupress_pubs/165

Dorroh, J. (2001). The evolution of a biology teacher. In M. A. Smith & J. Juska (Eds.), *The whole story: Teachers talk about portfolios* (pp. 59–69). National Writing Project.

Dunn, J. S., Luke, C., & Nassar, D. (2013). Valuing the resources of infrastructure: Beyond from-scratch and off-the-shelf technology options for electronic portfolio assessment in first-year writing. *Computers and Composition, 30*(1, Special Issue: Writing on the Frontlines), 61–73. https://doi.org/10.1016/j.compcom.2012.12.001

Durst, R. K., Roemer, M., & Schultz, L. M. (1994). Portfolio negotiations: Acts in speech. In L. Black, D. A. Daiker, J. Sommers, & G. Stygall (Eds.), *New directions in portfolio assessment: Reflective practice, critical theory; and large-scale scoring* (pp. 286–300). Boynton/Cook.

Ehley, L. (2006). *Digital portfolios: A study of undergraduate student and faculty use and perceptions of Alverno college's diagnostic digital portfolio* [Unpublished doctoral dissertation]. Cardinal Stritch University.

Elbow, P., & Belanoff, P. (1986). Staffroom interchange: Portfolios as a substitute for proficiency examinations. *College Composition and Communication, 37*(3), 336–339.

Elliot, N., Briller, V., & Joshi, K. (2007). Quantification and community. *Journal of Writing Assessment, 3*(1), 5–29. www.journalofwritingassessment.org/archives/3-1.2.pdf

Elmore, J., & Van Sickle, T. (2016). Going all in: Creating a community college writing program through the QEP and the reaccreditation process. In W. Sharer, T. A. Morse, M. F. Eble, & W. Banks (Eds.), *Reclaiming accountability: Improving writing programs through accreditation and large-scale assessments* (pp. 67–86). Utah State University Press.

Erickson, F. (2007). Some thoughts on "proximal" formative assessment of student learning. In P. A. Moss (Ed.), *Evidence and decision-making: Yearbook of the national society for the study of education* (Vol. 106, pp. 186–216). Blackwell Publishing.

Filkins, S. (2015, November 19–22). *NCTE assessment story project: What we have learned.* Annual Convention, National Council of Teachers of English.

Fredericksen, N., Mislevy, R. J., & Bejar, I. I. (Eds.). (1993). *Test theory for a new generation of tests.* Erlbaum.

Fredericksen, J. R., & Collins, A. (1989). A systems approach to educational testing. *Educational Researcher, 18*(9), 27–32.

Freedman, A., & Pringle, I. (1980). *The writing abilities of a representative sample of grade 5, 8, and 12 students: The Carleton writing project (Part 2. Final report).* Carleton Board of Education. https://eric.ed.gov/?id=ED217413

Fuchs, L., & Fuchs, D. (1986). Effects of systematic formative evaluation: A meta-analysis. *Exceptional Children, 53*(3), 199–208.

Fulwiler, M., & Middleton, K. (2012). After digital storytelling: Video composing in the new media age. *Computers and Composition, 29*(1), 39–50. https://doi.org/10.1016/j.compcom.2012.01.002

Galileo Educational Network. (2008). *Guide to assessing teamwork and collaboration.* www.galileo.org/tips/rubrics/t-c_rubric.pdf

Gallagher, C. (2014). Staging encounters: Assessing the performance of context in students' multimodal writing. *Computers and Composition, 3*(1), 1–12.

Gallagher, C., & Turley, E. (2012). *Our better judgment: Teacher leadership for writing assessment.* National Council of Teachers of English.

Gardner, H. (1992). Assessment in context: The alternative to standardized testing. In B. Gifford & M. C. O'Connor (Eds.), *Changing assessments: Alternative views of aptitude, achievement, and instruction.* Kluwer Academic Publishers.

Graham, S., Harris, K. R., & Hebert, M. (2011). *Informing writing: The benefits of formative assessment.* Report from the Carnegie Corporation of New York. Alliance for Excellent Education.

Green, N. (1993). Portfolios in a fifth grade classroom. In M. A. Smith & M. Ylvisaker (Eds.), *Teachers' voices: Portfolios in the classroom* (pp. 73–79). National Writing Project.

Greenberg, K., & Witte, S. (1988). Validity issues in direct writing assessment. *Notes from the National Testing Network in Writing, 8*, 13–14.

Guha, R., Wagner, T., Darling-Hammond, L., Taylor, T., & Curtis, D. (2018, January). *The promise of performance assessments: Innovations in high school learning and college admission.* Learning Policy Institute. https://learningpolicyinstitute.org/product/promise-performance-assessments

Hamp-Lyons, L., & Condon, W. (2000). *Assessing the portfolio: Principles for practice, theory, and research.* Hampton Press.

Hampton, S., Murphy, S., & Lowery, M. (2009). *Using rubrics to improve students writing (grades 1–5).* New Standards and International Reading Association.

Harris, K. R., & Graham, S. (1999). Programmatic intervention research: Illustrations from the evolution of self-regulated strategy development. *Learning Disability Quarterly*, *22*(4), 251–262.

Haswell, R. H. (Ed.). (2001). *Beyond outcomes: Assessment and instruction within a university writing program*. Ablex.

Heritage, M. (2010). *Formative assessment and next-generation assessment systems: Are we losing an opportunity*. Council of Chief State School Officers.

Hester, V., O'Neill, P., Neal, M., Edgington, A., & Huot, B. (2007). Adding portfolios to the placement process: A longitudinal perspective. In P. O'Neill (Ed.), *Blurring boundaries: Developing writers, researchers and teachers: A tribute to William L. Smith* (pp. 61–90). Hampton Press.

Hilbbard, K. M., Van Wagenen, L., Lewbel, S., Waterbury-Wyatt, S., Shaw, S., Pelletier, K., Larkins, B., Dooling, J., Elia, E., Palma, S., Maier, J., Johnson, D. Honan, M., Nelson, D., & Wislocki, J. (1996). *A teacher's guide to performance-based learning and assessment*. Association for Supervision and Curriculum Development.

Hughes, B., Sullivan, H., & Mosley, M. (1985). External evaluation, task difficulty, and continuing motivation. *Journal of Educational Research*, *78*(4), 210–215.

International Baccalaureate Organization. (2022). *Understanding DP assessment*. https://ibo.org/programmes/diploma-programme/assessment-and-exams/understanding-ib-assessment/

Jewitt, C. (2008). Multimodality and literacy in school classrooms. *Review of Research in Education*, *32*(1), 241–267.

Johnston, B. (1983). *Assessing English: Helping students to reflect on their work*. Open Court Press.

Kaunhoven, R., & Dorjee, D. (2017). How does mindfulness modulate self-regulation in pre-adolescent children? An integrative neurocognitive review. *Neuroscience & Biobehavioral Reviews*, *74*(Pt. A), 163–184.

Kelly-Riley, D., Norbert, E., & Rudniy, A. (2016). An empirical framework for eportfolio assessment. *International Journal of ePortfolio*, *6*, 95–116.

Kiefer, K., Palmquist, M., Carbone, N., Cox, M., & Melzer, D. (2000–2018). *An introduction to writing across the curriculum*. The WAC Clearinghouse. https://wac.colostate.edu/resources/wac/intro

Kingston, N., & Nash, B. (2011). Formative assessment: A meta-analysis and a call for research. *Educational Measurement Issues and Practice*, *30*(4), 28–37.

Keane, L., & Griffin, C. (2015). Testing the limits of self-assessment: A critical examination of the developmental trajectories of self-assessment processes. *Irish Teacher's Journal*, *3*(1), 37–51.

Koretz, D., McCaffrey, D., Klein, S. P., Bell, R. M., Stecher, B. M. (1992). *The reliability of scores from the 1992 Vermont portfolio assessment program: Interim report*. Rand. www.rand.org/pubs/drafts/DRU159.html

LeMahieu, P. G., Gitomer, D. H., & Eresh, J. T. (1995). Portfolios in large-scale assessment: Difficult but not impossible. *Educational Measurement: Issues and Practice*, *14*(3), 11–28.

Linn, R. L., Baker, E., & Dunbar, S. B. (1990). Complex, performance-based assessment: Expectations and validation criteria. *Educational Researcher*, *20*(8), 15–21.

Lotherington, H. (2004). Emergent metaliteracies: What the xbox has to offer the EQAO. *Linguistics and Education*, *14*(3), 305–319. https://doi.org/10.1016/j.linged.2004.02.007

Lowe, T. J., & Huot, B. (1997). Using KIRIS writing portfolios to place students in first year composition at the University of Louisville. *Kentucky English Bulletin*, *20*, 47–64.

Machera, P. (2019). I am an English teacher: Rubrics are no way to teach writing. *Education Week*, para 14. www.edweek.org/teaching-learning/opinion-i-am-an-english-teacher-rubrics-are-no-way-to-teach-writing/2019/12

Marlink, J., & Wahleithner, J. (2011). *Improving students' academic writing: Building a bridge to success*. Final Report for the National Writing Project Local Sites Research Initiative. California Writing Project. https://archive.nwp.org/cs/public/download/nwp_file/15419/ISAW_LSRI_final_report.pdf?x-r=pcfile_d

McClelland, M. M., Acock, A. C., & Morrison, F. J. (2006). The impact of kindergarten learning-related skills on academic trajectories at the end of elementary school. *Early Childhood Research Quarterly, 21*(4), 471–490.

Messick, S. (1989). Meaning and values in test validation: The science and ethics of assessment. *Educational Researcher, 18*(2), 5–11.

Messick, S. (1994). The interplay of evidence and consequences in the validation of performance assessments. *Educational Researcher, 23*(2), 13–23.

Miller, A. (2012). *Tame the beast: Tips for designing and using rubrics: Clarifying "what" and "how" for your students*. www.edutopia.org/blog/designing-using-rubrics-andrew-miller

Morgan, M., Allen, N., Moore, T., Atkinson, D., & Snow, C. (1987). Collaborative writing in the classroom. *Business Communication Quarterly, 50*(3), 20–26.

Murphy, S., & Smith, M. A. (1991). *Writing portfolios: A bridge from teaching to assessment*. Pippin Publishing Limited.

Murphy, S., & Underwood, T. (2000). *Portfolio practices: Lessons from schools, districts and states*. Christopher Gordon Publishers.

National Assessment Governing Board. (2011). *Writing framework for the 2011 national assessment of educational progress*. www.nagb.gov/content/nagb/assets/documents/publications/frameworks/writing/2011-writing-framework.pdf

National Assessment Governing Board. (2017). *Writing framework for the 2017 national assessment of educational progress*. www.nagb.gov/naep-frameworks/writing/2017-writing-framework.html

National Center for Education Statistics, U.S. Department of Education (2011). *The nation's report card: Writing 2011: National assessment of educational progress at grades 8 and 12*. https://nces.ed.gov/nationsreportcard/pdf/main2011/2012470.pdf

National Center for Education Statistics, U.S. Department of Education. (2017). *Student access to digital learning resources outside of the classroom*. https://nces.ed.gov/pubs2017/2017098/index.asp

National Center for Fair and Open Testing. (n.d.). *Kentucky portfolio scoring improves*. http://fairtest.org/kentucky-portfolio-scoring-improves

National Council of Teachers of English. (2013a). *NCTE framework for 21st century curriculum and assessment*. https://cdn.ncte.org/nctefiles/resources/positions/framework_21stcent_curr_assessment.pdf

National Council of Teachers of English. (2013b). *Formative assessment that truly informs instruction*. http://www2.ncte.org/statement/formative-assessment/

National Council of Teachers of English. (2018). *Literacy assessment: Definitions, principles, and practices*. https://ncte.org/statement/assessmentframingst/

National Governors Association Center for Best Practices and Council of Chief State School Offices. (2010). *Common core state standards for English language arts and literacy in history/social studies, science, and technical subjects*. www.corestandards.org/assets/CCSSI_ELA%20Standards.pdf

National Research Council. (2000). *How people learn: Brain, mind, experience, and school* (Expanded Ed.). The National Academies Press. www.nap.edu/catalog/9853/how-people-learn-brain-mind-experience-and-school-expanded-edition

National Writing Project. (2010). *Analytic writing Continuum.* Continuum. https://archive.nwp.org/cs/public/download/nwp_file/21466/NWP_Analytic_Writing_Continuum.pdf?x-r=pcfile_d

National Writing Project. (2018). *Civically engaged writing analysis Continuum.* https://cewac.nwp.org/what-are-the-attributes-of-civic-writing/

National Writing Project. (2020). *Analytic writing continuum for source-based argument.* https://sites.google.com/nwp.org/2021-nwp-c3wp-scoring-exchange/awc-sba/awc-sba

Nicol, D. J., & Macfarlane-Dick, D. (2006). Formative assessment and self-regulated learning: A model and seven principles of good feedback practice. *Studies in Higher Education, 31*(2), 199–218.

O'Neill, P. (2017, November 16–19). *Preparing students for first-year college assessments. Teachers as assessment leaders in literacy: Roundtable discussions* [Conference session]. NCTE Annual Convention.

PARCC (Partnership for Assessment of Readiness for College and Careers). (n.d.). *Guide to English language arts/literacy released items: Understanding scoring.* https://files.eric.ed.gov/fulltext/ED573563.pdf

Paris, S. G., & Ayres, L. R. (1994). *Becoming reflective students and teachers with portfolios and authentic assessment.* American Psychological Association.

Paris, S. G., & Paris, A. H. (2001). Classroom applications of research on self-regulated learning. *Educational Psychologist, 36*(2), 89–101.

Peckham, I. (1987). Statewide direct writing assessment. *English Journal, 76*(8), 30–33.

Peckham, I. (2009). Online placement in first-year writing. *College Composition and Communication, 60*(3), 517–540.

Pellegrino, J. W. (2006, November). *Rethinking and redesigning curriculum, instruction, and assessment: What contemporary research and theory suggests.* National Center on Education and the Economy.

Pellegrino, J. W., Chudowsky, N., & Glaser, R. (2001). *Knowing what students know: The science and design of educational assessment.* National Academy Press.

Piazza, L. (2001). Throw me a life jacket: The portfolio as an instrument of school survival. In M. A. Smith & J. Juska (Eds.), *The whole story: Teachers talk about portfolios* (p. 78). National Writing Project.

Pintrich, P. R. (2000). The role of goal-orientation in self-regulated learning. In M. Boekaerts, P. R. Pintrich, & M. Zeidner (Eds.), *Handbook of self-regulation* (pp. 451–502). Elsevier.

Pringle, I., & Freedman, A. (1985). *A comparative study of writing abilities in two modes at the grade 5, 8, and 12 levels.* Ministry of Education. https://eric.ed.gov/?id=ED258202

Ramaprasad, A. (1983). On the definition of feedback. *Behavioral Science, 28*(1), 4–13. https://doi.org/10.1002/bs.3830280103

Reif, L. (1990). Finding the value in evaluation: Self-assessment in a middle school classroom. *Educational Leadership, 47*(6), 24–29.

Rich, C. S., Harrington, H., Kim, J., & West, B. (2008, March). *Automated essay scoring in state formative and summative writing assessment* [Paper presentation]. American Educational Research Association 2008 Convention.

Robertson, A. (1994). Teach, not test: A look at a new writing placement procedure. *Writing Program Administration, 18*(1–2), 56–63.

Ross, J. A. (2006). The reliability, validity, and utility of self-assessment. *Practical Assessment, Research and Evaluation, 11*(10), 1–13.

Ross, J. A., Hogaboam-Gray, A., & Rolheiser, C. (2002). Self-evaluation in grade 11 mathematics: Effects on achievements and student beliefs about ability. In D. McDougall (Ed.), *OISE papers on mathematical education*. University of Toronto.

Ross, J. A., Rolheiser, C., & Hogaboam-Gray, A. (1999). Effect of self-evaluation on narrative writing. *Assessing Writing, 6*(1), 107–132.

Ross, J. A., & Starling, M. (2005, April). *Effects of self-evaluation training on achievement and self-efficacy in a computer-supported learning environment* [Paper presentation]. American Educational Research Association Convention. https://legacy.oise.utoronto.ca/research/field-centres/ross/Ross-Starling AERA 05.pdf

Scardamalia, M., & Bereiter, C. (1985). Research on written composition. In M. Wittrock (Ed.), *Handbook of research on teaching* (3rd ed., pp. 708–803). Macmillan.

Schunk, D. H. (1996). Goal and self-evaluative influences during children's cognitive skill learning. *American Educational Research Journal, 33*(2), 359–382.

Shepard, L. A. (1991). Psychometricians' beliefs about learning. *Educational Researcher, 20*(7), 2–16.

Shepard, L. A. (2000). The role of assessment in a learning culture. *Educational Researcher, 29*(7), 4–14.

Sills, E. (2016). Multimodal assessment as disciplinary sense-making: Beyond rubrics to frameworks. *The Journal of Writing Assessment, 9*(2), 1–7. https://escholarship.org/uc/item/06g1d5b5

Slavin, R. E., Hurley, E. A., & Chamberlain, A. M. (2003). Cooperative learning and achievement. In W. M. Reynolds & G. J. Miller (Eds.), *Handbook of psychology: Vol. 7, educational psychology* (pp. 177–198). Wiley.

Smarter Balanced Assessment Consortium. (2014). *Smarter balanced scoring guide for grades 3, 6, and 11 English/language arts performance task full-write baseline sets*. https://portal.smarterbalanced.org/library/en/scoring-guide-for-ela-full-writes.pdf

Smith, M. A. (1993). Introduction: Portfolio classrooms. In M. A. Smith & M. Ylvisaker (Eds.), *Teachers' voices: Portfolios in the classroom* (p. 2). National Writing Project.

Smith, M. A., & Swain, S. S. (2017). *Assessing writing, teaching writers: Putting the analytic writing Continuum to work in your classroom*. Teachers College Press.

Smith, W. L. (1993). Assessing the reliability and adequacy of using holistic scoring of essays as a college composition placement technique. In M. Williamson & B. Huot (Eds.), *Validating holistic scoring for writing assessment: Theoretical and empirical foundations* (pp. 142–205). Hampton Press.

Stipek, D., Recchia, S., & McClintic, S. (1992). Self-evaluation in young children. *Monographs of the Society for Research in Child Development, 57*(1), i–vi, 1–95. https://doi.org/10.2307/1166190

Struckey, M., Waggoner, Z., & Erdem, E. (2018). Writing and reflecting for transfer: Using high impact ePortfolios in online first-year composition. In B. Eynon & L. Gambino (Eds.), *Catalysts in action: Case studies of high-impact eportfolio practice* (pp. 113–124). Stylus.

Swain, S., & LeMahieu, P. (2012). Assessment in a culture of inquiry: The story of the national writing project's analytic writing Continuum. In N. Elliot & L. Perlman (Eds.),

Writing assessment in the 21st century: Essays in honor of Edward M. White (pp. 45–66). Hampton Press.

Tharp, T. (2010). Wiki, wiki, wiki—what? Assessing online collaborative writing. *The English Journal, 99*(5), 40–46. www.jstor.org/stable/27807190

Tierney, R. J., Carter, M., & Desai, L. (1991). *Portfolio assessment in the reading writing classroom.* Christopher Gordon Publishers, Inc.

University of California. About the exam. *Entry Level Writing Requirement.* https://admission.universityofcalifornia.edu/elwr/about-the-exam/

Valente, L. (2018). *CO-LAB guidelines for assessing collaborative learning in the classroom.* Collaborative Education Lab. http://colab.eun.org/c/document_library/get_file?uuid=6481260d-0e05-41a0-ac8f-535e4b5c5536&groupId=5897016

Vygotsky, L. (1978). *Mind in society.* Harvard University Press.

Wahleithner, J. M. (2014). The national writing project's multimodal assessment project: Development of a framework for thinking about multimodal composing. *Computers and Composition, 31*, 79–86. https://doi.org/10.1016/j.compcom.2013.12.004

Washington State University Writing Program. (2022). *The university writing portfolio.* https://writingprogram.wsu.edu/jwpsubmission/

Watson, C., & McConnell, K. (2018). What really matters for employment? *Liberal Education, 104*(4), para 4. www.aacu.org/liberaleducation/2018/fall/watson_mcconnell

Whithaus, C. (2002a). *Green squiggly lines: Self assessment, reflection, and a wider audience.* https://wac.colostate.edu/aw/articles/whithaus2002/

Whithaus, C. (2002b). Electronic portfolios: Emerging practices for students, faculty, and institutions [review essay]. *Kairos: A Journal of Rhetoric, Technology, and Pedagogy, 7*(1). https://kairos.technorhetoric.net/7.1/reviews/whithaus/implicit.htm

Whithaus, C. (2013). ePortfolios as tools for facilitating and assessing knowledge transfer from lower division, general education courses to upper division, discipline-specific courses. In K. V. Wills & R. Rice (Eds.), *ePortfolio performance support systems: Constructing, presenting, and assessing portfolios* (pp. 205–220). WAC Clearinghouse; Parlor Press. https://doi.org/10.37514/PER-B.2013.0490.2.11

Wiley, D. E., & Resnick, L. (1997). *The new standards reference examination standards-referenced scoring system* (CSE Report 470). National Center for Research on Evaluation, Standards, and Student Testing. http://cresst.org/publications/cresst-publication-2842/

Wiliam, D., Lee, C., Harrison, C., & Black, P. (2004). Teachers developing assessment for learning: Impact on student achievement. *Assessment in Education: Principles, Policy and Practice, 11*(1), 48–65.

Wills, K. V., & Rice, R. (Eds.). (2013). *ePortfolio performance support systems: Constructing, presenting, and assessing portfolios.* The WAC Clearinghouse; Parlor Press. https://doi.org/10.37514/PER-B.2013.0490

Wilson, M., & Draney, K. (2004). *Some links between large-scale and classroom assessments: The case of the BEAR assessment system* (pp. 132–154). Yearbook of the National Society for the Study of Education.

Winner, E. (Ed.). (1993). *Arts propel: An introductory handbook.* Educational Testing Service and the President and Fellows of Harvard College (on behalf of Project Zero, Harvard Graduate School of Education). www.pz.harvard.edu/sites/default/files/Arts%20Propel%20-%20A%20Handbook%20for%20Imaginative%20Writing.pdf

Wolf, D. (1989). Portfolio assessment: Sampling student work. *Educational Leadership, 45*(4), 21–26.

Yancey, K. B. (1998a). Getting beyond exhaustion: Reflection, self-assessment, and learning. *Clearing House, 72*(1), 13–18.

Yancey, K. B. (1998b). *Reflection in the writing classroom.* University Press of Colorado, Utah State University Press.

Yancey, K. B. (2004). Postmodernism, palimpsest, and portfolios: Theoretical issues in the representation of student work. *College Composition and Communication, 55*(4), 738–761.

Yancey, K. B. (Ed.). (2019). *ePortfolio as curriculum: Models and practices for developing students' ePortfolio literacy.* Stylus.

Yancey, K. B., & Weiser, I. (Eds.). (1997). *Situating portfolios: Four perspectives.* Utah State University Press.

Yen, W. M., & Ferrara, S. (1997). The Maryland school performance assessment program: Performance assessment with psychometric quality suitable for high stakes usage. *Educational and Psychological Measurement, 57*(1), 60–84. https://doi.org/10.1177/0013164497057001004

Zessoules, R., & Gardner, H. (1991). Authentic assessment: Beyond the buzzword and into the classroom. In V. Perrone (Ed.), *Assessment in schools* (pp. 47–71). ASCD.

Zimmerman, B. J., & Campillo, M. (2003). Motivating self-regulated problem solvers. In J. E. Davidson & R. J. Sternberg (Eds.), *The psychology of problem solving* (pp. 233–262). Cambridge University Press.

Zimmerman, B. J., & Schunk, D. (2001). *Self-regulated learning and academic achievement: Theoretical perspectives.* Erlbaum.

Zimmerman, B. J., & Schunk, D. (2008). Motivation: An essential dimension of self-regulated learning. In D. Schunk & B. Zimmerman (Eds.), *Motivation and self- regulated learning: Theory, research, and applications* (pp. 1–30). Erlbaum.

5

REDESIGNING AND RENOVATING WRITING ASSESSMENT

Engaging teachers and students

Successful remodeling depends on having knowledgeable contractors who understand principles of design, construction, and current codes; who have working knowledge of materials and resources; and who have the supervisory and technical skills to contribute to and implement an effective plan for remodeling. Likewise, educational reform needs teacher-leaders who are knowledgeable across a variety of areas and who can plan and implement changes in ways that improve teaching and learning. In earlier chapters we have suggested several ways we could remodel our current assessment system to enhance its alignment with a complex, socially situated construct of writing and to better serve learning with performance and formative assessments, in particular the learning of higher-order skills. The key to successfully accomplishing these goals, we believe, is the teacher, whether that is a K–12 teacher, a college instructor, or a university professor. State or university policies may aim to develop curricula and systems of performance assessments that promote higher-order skills in writing and complex critical thinking, but their success hinges on the will and skill of teachers to effectively develop, introduce, and implement reforms. As Little (1993) explains, these kinds of reform "demand a greater facility among teachers for integrating subject content, and for organizing students' opportunities to learn" (p. 130). Little argues that the test of effective professional development is "its capacity to equip teachers individually and collectively to act as shapers, promoters, and well-informed critics of reforms" (p. 130). In sum, we need to equip teachers to "play an informed and active role in defining the enterprise of education and the work of teaching" (Little, 1993, p. 132).

DOI: 10.4324/9781003296140-5

Investing in teachers and students

There are many reasons, of course for putting teachers, as Gray (2000) would say, "at the center" of systemic reform efforts. Because teachers enact the curriculum, they are the link between educational policy and students. Because they play the key role in students' learning, they are the gateway to systemic reform. Darling-Hammond (1989), for instance, argues that strengthening the profession of teaching will prove an effective means for meeting students' needs, improving the overall quality of their education, and improving the education system as a whole. And when we refer to "the system," we are not limiting the discussion to the K–12 arena. Rather, we are referring to the educational system as a whole, including higher education. While some studies of systemic reform have been limited to the K–12 level (e.g., O'Day & Smith, 1993), other studies have included higher education. They recognize that systemic reform can involve multiple institutions within a large independent system and that altering any one part of the system will necessarily impact other parts (Swanson, 1995). For example, content requirements for admission to colleges and universities, tests for admission such as SAT and ACT, and bridge programs that offer college credit for courses taught in high school, such as Advanced Placement, have an impact on high school curriculum. And clearly, teachers in both the K–12 and higher education arenas play pivotal roles in implementing intended reforms. Working across the K–12 and college divide is important for literacy teaching and learning because language arts have a significant impact across the curriculum and are often a focus in postsecondary placement assessments, especially given the ubiquity of first-year writing requirements. Gallagher and Turley (2012) make the case that "it is incumbent upon all teachers who have anything to do with student writing . . . to embrace writing assessment" (p. 3). They frame their argument with the revised edition of the *Standards for the Assessment of Reading and Writing*, Standard 2: "The teacher is the most important agent of assessment" (IRA/NCTE, 2010, p. 13, qtd in Gallagher & Turley, 2012, p. 3).

In our view, students should also be at the center of systemic reform efforts along with teachers. Both students and teachers are the ones most affected by the educational system, and yet they often have the least influential voice in the entire enterprise. Although teachers and students are part of an extended social community—schools, neighborhoods, districts, and states—teachers currently have little input into decisions about policies and curriculum, and students even less. All members of the educational community need to be involved in educational reform, but some—teachers and students—are more immediately impacted, and their needs should be primary. If the goal of reform is to improve teaching and learning, especially in communities that have been historically marginalized and underperforming, then it seems critical that those voices are heard.

Investing in teachers' professional development

Because teachers play such a key role in students' learning, we need to ensure that beginning teachers are well prepared to teach writing. A focus of school reform over the last several decades, upgrading the training and licensing requirements for new teachers is one way to advance the level of teachers' knowledge and skill (e.g., National Commission on Excellence in Education, 1983; Darling-Hammond, 1984, 1994; Darling-Hammond & McLaughlin, 1995). We need to add courses on teaching writing to credential program requirements at the K–12 level and to increase writing preparation requirements at the college level as well. Learning in general, and learning to write in particular, is a highly interactive and individualized process, and effective teaching is complex work that requires specialized knowledge of both content and pedagogy. For K–12 teachers, certification requirements are determined by individual states, with most like Maryland, which requires pre-service teachers take methods courses specific to particular areas such as English Language Arts, as well as a designated reading methods course, but nothing specific to the teaching of writing. At the college level, there is no certification process. Instead, instructors typically are required to have an advanced degree in English (where most college writing programs are housed), but that doesn't guarantee the instructor will know enough about teaching writing to be an effective teacher. The Conference on College Composition and Communication (2015a, 2015b) identifies the broad base of knowledge that effective college teachers of writing should have in a wide range of areas, including rhetoric, linguistics, instruction, technical, and research methods. Of course, an advanced degree in other subjects, such as Literature, Critical Theory, or Theater, does not guarantee expertise in the field of writing. All instructors of writing, regardless of the level, should have this broad-based knowledge (see also *Professional Knowledge for the Teaching of Writing*, NCTE, 2016a).

Because learning is a highly interactive process, and because teachers encounter a range of student abilities in any single classroom, individualized, student-centered approaches to teaching are essential. Effective student-centered teachers know the strengths and weaknesses of their students, and they use that knowledge as they engage in complex reasoning about classroom activities and lesson planning (Clark & Peterson, 1986; Shulman, 1987). Recognizing individual differences in learners, student-centered instruction takes development into account, and it builds on and is adapted to each student's skills, interests, and abilities. The teacher acts as a facilitator of learning for individuals instead of simply "delivering" content as instruction to the class as a whole.

Accompanying calls for student-centered teaching are calls for teaching for understanding, an endeavor that requires teachers to develop new knowledge and skills. Not only do teachers need to understand the many different ways in which students learn and develop, they also need to have a deep understanding of their subject matter. Cohen et al. (1993) explain:

> Teaching for understanding promises to enhance the kinds of cognitive outcomes for students that the American system has heretofore been notoriously ineffective at producing. . . . [However], it requires change not only in what is taught but also in how it is taught. . . . Teaching for understanding requires teachers to have comprehensive and in-depth knowledge of subject matter, competence in representation and manipulation of this knowledge in instructional activities, and skill in managing classroom processes in a way that enables active student learning.
>
> *(pp. 2–3)*

Firestone (1993) asserts that many teachers may be unable to teach for understanding in student-centered ways "because they did not experience such teaching as students and were not exposed to it in their teacher training" (p. 9). Moreover, he suggests that collaborative arrangements such as mentor programs, career ladders, and the like in professional development may ultimately do little to change teachers' instructional practices. He argues that more attention should be paid to teachers' pedagogical content knowledge because "Participatory and collegial reforms help teachers use and share what they know. But when the knowledge is not there, very little change will occur" (Firestone, 1993, p. 8).

At the K–12 level, moving toward student-centered instruction and teaching for understanding will, as Firestone (1993) claims, require serious changes in traditional school practices and structures, including "changing how students are grouped for instruction, how time is allocated to subject areas, and how student work is assessed" (p. 11). Firestone asserts that such changes will be possible if a comprehensive package for reform includes "both endeavors to professionalize teaching and the more difficult efforts to improve pedagogy" (p. 11). A comprehensive program to support effective teaching also needs to acknowledge that teaching conditions—such as number of students per class and overall student load and compensation—impact the effectiveness of teaching writing K through college. And, although some see technology "fixes" for teaching and evaluating writing—for example, using automated essay scoring or other automated feedback programs—these kinds of programs cannot replace the feedback and one-to-one work that is required for teaching writing (see *Why Class Size Matters*, NCTE, 2014, and *Statement of Principles and Standards for the Postsecondary Teaching of Writing*, CCCC, 2015b).

Of course, teachers also need to learn about new reading and writing contexts and what that means for teaching, learning, and evaluation. As Gallagher and Turley (2012) explain:

> New ways to write and new kinds of writing require new ways of reading and evaluating. As teachers, we need to help students make sense of their

expanding literacies and texts and images they produce—and we need to make sense of these ourselves.

(p. 6)

For over two decades, writing scholars and teaching experts have echoed the need for writing teachers at all levels to develop greater fluency in multimedia writing (e.g., Selfe & Hilligoss, 1994; Wysocki et al., 2004; Herrington et al., 2009).

Clearly, effective teaching calls for ongoing professional development as the National Council of Teachers of English noted in a 2018 resolution:

> Resolved that the National Council of Teachers of English recommend ongoing, high quality professional learning in the teaching of writing for all teachers across all disciplines at each grade level, K-20.
>
> Be it further resolved that NCTE actively encourage school districts, colleges, and universities in providing high quality professional learning to give teachers the necessary strategies and curricula to deliver effective writing instruction.

NCTE's emphasis on "high quality" professional development is supported by research. For example, research shows that instructors gain new knowledge and skills and employ what they have learned to their own classroom when workshops integrate theory, demonstrations, feedback, and coaching (Joyce & Showers, 1988). In a review of 35 methodologically rigorous studies of teacher professional development initiatives, Darling-Hammond et al. (2017) identified seven widely shared features of effective professional development. Their analysis shows that effective professional development is

> content focused . . . incorporates active learning . . . supports collaboration . . . uses models and modeling of effective practice . . . provides coaching and expert support, offers opportunities for feedback and reflection . . . [and] is of sustained duration.

(p. 4)

Effective professional development programs also put teachers at the center. One example, which grew from a single site in Berkeley, CA (the Bay Area Writing Project), to a national organization of more than 160 sites (the National Writing Project), became well known for its practice of engaging teachers to teach other teachers. Another hallmark of NWP is that it includes K–college teachers, bridging the divide between different levels of education. Similarly, the Instructional Leadership Corps (ILC), a collaborative teacher professional learning project, engages expert teachers who organize local professional development to prompt iterative changes in teaching practices. Like the NWP, the ILC follows a "teachers teaching teachers" model, although it is not limited to teachers of

What teachers say about participating in large-scale assessment

- Three years ago, I despised the idea of assessment. Today, I run the system for my district and work in a new administrative position we didn't even have back then, in addition to my regular teaching duties. The key element that converted me was *teacher involvement*. (emphasis in original, Montgomery, 2004, p. 160, as cited in Gallagher, 2007, p. 68)
- I've always been one who wants to know what's happening and how it's done. So I wanted to get into the scoring at some point so I could know for sure what was expected, not just for students, but also for teachers . . . to make sure I stay current with the expectations for student writing in the state. (as cited in Anderson, 2009, p. 77)
- I felt by participating in the rating process I could better lead the team, especially the new teachers. . . . Even though it's a long three days of scoring. I always have fun. I wish I could do it every year, but it just becomes a matter of time. (as cited in Anderson, 2009, p. 78)
- It allowed me to talk with other English teachers about their ideas for teaching writing and their methods. (as cited in Anderson, 2009, p. 79)
- Every time I go I learn so much from the other teachers, the ones I share the scoring table with and from the trainers, teachers themselves. (as cited in Anderson, 2009, p. 81)
- The main reward of reading a thousand essays was meeting professional and committed teachers from across the country. Meals and breaks were taken up with sharing ideas and stories with other teachers devoted to teaching writing. They represented every possible high school and university setting—public and private, urban and rural, small and sprawling—from across the states and as far away as Switzerland. . . . I left with a greater understanding of education in America from the points of view of teachers devoted to their craft. (Schwartz, 2004, p. 55)
- This inter-institutional project integrated nicely with assessment activities that were being pursued independently at University of Delaware. . . . There was much discussion of how student performance is constrained by assignment design and task conditions, and there were spirited arguments about what such results could tell us about our programs. . . . The ability to benchmark against other campuses helped us think about how our programs and students compare to those on other campuses. Such projects connect us to the larger communities of practice that constitute composition as a field. Working across campuses allowed us to form relationships and to gain perspective because we were able to transcend our local forums of engagement and sites of work. (Pagano et al., 2008, pp. 304–306)

writing. Evaluations of these projects indicate that this model is highly successful (e.g., St. John & Stokes, 2017; Lotan et al., 2019).

While such programs foster the acquisition of new skills through instruction and participatory activities, we also need to provide opportunities for teachers to take active professional roles in curriculum development at the program, school, and district level. As Little (1993) says, "To fit opportunities for professional development to a campaign for the principled redesign of schooling is arguably a different matter indeed from organizing the training and support to implement a program or a set of readily-transferable practices" (p. 132). Teachers acquire important attitudes and skills when they engage in a program improvement process and/or the development of a new curriculum, and they are more likely to buy into a program when they have some say in the process. Involving them in program planning and curriculum design will also position them to participate in larger discussions and decision making about policies, reform, and assessment.

Involving teachers directly in the design, implementation, and scoring of assessments is another important way to support their professional development. Framing assessment as inquiry, Gallagher and Turley (2012) argue that teacher leadership is essential for effective writing assessment:

> [A]ssessment is fundamentally a part of teaching and learning and thus falls well within our professional purview. In fact, because it helps us articulate our values and make sense of and coordinate the various components of our practice, assessment-as-inquiry has the potential to make our work easier, more manageable.
>
> *(p. 13)*

Assessment, they argue, "can help teachers to inspect our own communities' values, to reinvigorate our commitment to our work, and to help us gain more control over our profession" (Gallagher & Turley, 2012, p. 13). While Gallagher and Turley focus in particular on teachers in K–12 public education, we note that their observation holds true for all writing teachers from K–college.

Involving teachers in the development and scoring of assessments

Darling-Hammond and McLaughlin (1995) argue that effective professional development "must engage teachers in concrete tasks of teaching, assessment, observation, and reflection that illuminate the processes of learning and development" (1995, p. 597). Because teachers enact the curriculum, we should restructure our assessment system so that teachers play a substantial role in the planning, decision making, and scoring of assessments at all levels, including school, district, state, and national level assessments as well as across levels. Participating in assessments that are aligned with and model good instruction builds educator capacity. When teachers participate in such assessments, they gain valuable insights about writing and performance standards, about teaching, and about learning. There is even greater value for teachers and, consequently, their students, when teachers from different levels work together across levels, for example, secondary and college writing faculty working together in designing, planning, or scoring a high school graduation or a placement assessment. Darling-Hammond (2017) notes that well-developed systems of performance assessments, such as the system designed by New Hampshire, promote "the use of authentic, inquiry-based instruction, complex thinking, and application of learning . . . [and] incentivize the type of instruction and assessment that support student learning of rich knowledge and skills" (pp. 40–41).

Involving teachers in large-scale assessments has sometimes been challenged on the grounds that their participation might somehow compromise the integrity of the assessment. Some argue that teachers should not be trusted to assess the work of their own students because they might be biased in some way. But that argument is irrelevant in large-scale assessments, where the workflow can be organized so that teachers score the work of students other than their own. Advanced Placement scoring, for example, includes teachers of AP courses, as well as college faculty who teach the post-secondary courses that AP targets, but there is little chance that a teacher would be asked to score an exam written by one of her own students, and in any case, the exams are anonymous for scorers.

The classroom teacher's role in large-scale assessments of classroom portfolios has also been challenged on the grounds that the teacher might somehow manipulate the contents. Holland (2007) quotes a reviewer of the Kentucky assessment system as writing that "policies pertaining to revision of portfolio pieces are highly permissive . . . the writing guidelines note that peers may offer suggestions for revisions and call for teachers to instruct students on how to review each other's writing" (p. 7). The concerns the reviewer expresses reveal the tensions between adopting assessment methods that promote best practices in teaching and traditional efforts to ensure a level playing field. Holland also quotes George Cunningham, a member of Kentucky's School Curriculum and Accountability Council, as claiming that "portfolios have dismal reliability," a claim that has largely been discredited, at least in the case of writing (2007, p. 8).

As we explained in Chapter 4, research has demonstrated that reliable scoring can be brought about through training, moderation processes, and auditing, and further, that reliable scoring was achieved in the Kentucky portfolio assessment program. The writing portfolio required students to write in several major genres, and their work was evaluated with a common set of criteria. Three pieces of writing were required in grades 4 and 7, and four were required in grade 12. The writing included personal expressive writing (e.g., personal narratives, memoirs, vignettes, and essays) and transactive writing for a variety of purposes (e.g., defending a conclusion, explaining a process or concept, telling about a problem) in a variety of forms (e.g., letters, brochures, articles, etc.). The assessment criteria included addressing the purpose and audience for the writing, developing and supporting ideas with relevant details, organizing ideas in a clear and logical manner, composing grammatically correct sentences that vary in length and structure, using correct and effective diction with developing sophistication, and using conventions correctly. Citing a 2007–2008 technical report from the Commonwealth of Kentucky Department of Education, Darling-Hammond (2017) reports that "over time the scores became highly reliable. By 2008, the agreement rate (exact or adjacent scoring) for independent readers involved in auditing school-level scores was over 90 percent" (p. 31).

The benefits of involving teachers in large-scale assessment can be substantial. According to Darling-Hammond (2017), teachers learn significantly from participating in performance assessments and can improve their practice from the scoring process. Darling-Hammond reports, for example, that "Teachers' involvement in orchestrating and scoring the assignments that are part of the portfolio helps them learn about the curriculum standards . . . as well as how to develop curriculum and performance assessments for the classroom" (2017, p. 31). Herman and Linn (2013) report that

> Some states like California, New Hampshire, and New York have required that practicing teachers must be the primary scorers of the performance tasks in statewide assessments and evidence shows that this involvement strengthens teachers' understanding of the standards and the assessments and informs classroom instruction.
>
> *(as cited in Darling Hammond, 2017, pp. 12–13)*

Costs can be reduced when professional development days are allocated for scoring or when teacher scoring is included as part of the test administration contract (Darling Hammond, 2017). And teachers may develop a more positive view of assessments in general. Demailly (2001) observes that in order for assessments to be viewed positively by teachers, "the evaluation must be developed through participation, with extensive teacher involvement" (as cited in Mons, 2009, p. 25).

At the K–12 level, one example of "extensive teacher involvement" is Improving Student's Academic Writing (ISAW), a nationally recognized program that focuses on the improvement of the analytical writing of all students—college-bound, English learners, and struggling writers—and preparing students for college readiness and success. Since its beginning in 1998, ISAW grew to become a year-round professional development program supported at 17 writing project sites, working with "72 low-performing high schools across California" (Marlink & Wahleithner, 2011, p. 2). Stokes (2010) characterizes the ISAW project as an example of the way the NWP operates as a national "improvement infrastructure," defining infrastructure as "the foundational structures that enable necessary work to get done." In ISAW, the work to get done was "building teacher knowledge." Teachers, however, were not "expected to act as recipients of knowledge . . . transmitted to them." Rather, they were "asked to form knowledge relevant to their teaching through thoughtful study and reflection within . . . generative learning experiences" (Stokes, 2010, p. 157).

In the earliest stages of the ISAW project, several California Writing Project (CWP) sites launched new programs that focused on gathering existing knowledge about analytical academic writing. They collected resources from professional development institutes, libraries, high school writing assessment programs, and the like, and they instituted new programs such as year-long teacher research groups focused on academic writing issues (Stokes, 2010). Subsequently, CWP brought teams of high school teachers from the CWP sites together. They participated in discussions led by University of California writing program faculty and shared practices they were developing in their classrooms with one another. They analyzed student work samples and ultimately scored student papers using the University of California's Analytical Writing Placement Exam (AWPE) scoring guide (University of California, 2022, see Chapter 4, Figure 4.1) and a writing prompt from the University's "Subject A" examination, "a quite challenging timed reading-and-writing task that students must pass in order to qualify for freshman English . . . and a rich starting point for dialogue and collaboration among high school teachers and university writing faculty" (Stokes, 2010, p. 153).

In the next stage of the project, teachers began developing a tool to trace "how academic literacy develops across the full span of the high school years":

> To build this knowledge for themselves, the ISAW project leaders led teachers in painstaking analyses of matched pairs of student essays (fall to spring) from the full range of several hundred students in grades 9 to 12 and all language backgrounds. Teachers focused on naming precisely what degree of improvement was exhibited through the year for each of the multiple thinking, reading, and writing skills important to academic literacy and success. These analyses of features of the student writing were ultimately distilled into what became dubbed an "improvement rubric."
>
> *(Stokes, 2010, pp. 154–155)*

The paired comparison approach was based on advice from Haswell (1988), who asserts that paired comparisons provide more information about student progress in a writing course. The outcome of the teachers' work was the ISAW Analytical Writing Improvement Continuum (AWIC; California Writing Project, 2005). Unlike rubrics, which are organized by score point from high to low and which describe several different attributes of writing under the individual score point headings (e.g., see Figure 4.1, the AWPE scoring guide), the ISAW Continuum is organized by "improvement categories" of attributes and multiple "dimensions" of attributes within each category (Marlink, 2009, p. 8). See Figure 5.1.

Instead of using deficit language, as many summative rubrics do, the Continuum describes what the student does, as opposed to what the student doesn't do. Teacher Lara Hoekstra provides an example. Instead of using language such as "Demonstrates little, if any, comprehensive grasp of the text," the Continuum uses language such as "Suggests partial understanding of the text" (Hoekstra, 2021, para 4). Unlike rubrics that move from high levels of performance to lower levels from left to right across the page, the performance levels of the AWIC increase from left to right so that the focus is on improvement. An example of this progression is provided in Figure 5.2.

CWP Director, Jayne Marlink, cautioned that the Continuum shouldn't be read as a "straight line of required steps and stages."

> For us, no straight line meant not expecting students to move across a descriptive band like Understanding the Text, progressing from one box to the next, hitting every one of the four in sequence. Sometimes students' early essays would suggest a "partial understanding of the text," but they learned quickly that . . . what they were working on was an interaction between the ideas in a text . . . and their own. They had no need to spend

---

Response to Essay Topic: The writer responds effectively to the writing task. The writer demonstrates that he or she can present the ideas of the author(s) cogently and develop his or her own ideas in response.

- Responding to the Identified Issue/Subject
- Addressing the Demands of the Essay Topic

Understanding and Use of Text: The writer provides the reader a clear and accurate understanding of the text and effectively uses the ideas in the text to develop the writer's response.

- Understanding the Text
- Summarizing/Recapitulating

Development: The writer develops the essay effectively by analyzing well-chosen examples from passage, experience, observation or other readings in ways that make his or her perspective and claim/assertion compelling.

- Making Own Claims(s) or Assertion
- Developing Examples
- Reasoning
- Using Textual Support

FIGURE 5.1 The categories of improvement used in the Improving Student's Academic Writing (ISAW) program's Analytical Writing Improvement Continuum. Used with permission of the California Writing Project.

Credit Line: California Writing Project (2005). *Analytical Writing Improvement Continuum.* University of California, Berkeley.

Organization: The writer organizes the essay effectively, establishes a focus, and guides the reader through a coherent, well-ordered presentation of his or her ideas. It is clear how each new paragraph advances the writer's response to the essay topic.

- Structuring & Organizing
- Introducing the Essay
- Using Paragraphs and Transitions
- Concluding the Essay

Word Choice and Sentence Structure: The writer uses a wide variety of sentences in ways that help convey and reinforce his or her ideas and chooses words that convey his or her ideas clearly and precisely.

- Choosing Words
- Employing Sentence Structure to Convey Ideas
- Employing Sentence Boundaries

Grammar, Usage and Conventions: The writer makes sophisticated use of grammatical relationships and punctuation to support the effective communication of his or her ideas.

- Using Grammatical Relationships
- Using Punctuation

Anticipating Reader's Needs:
- Anticipating Reader's Needs

FIGURE 5.1   (Continued)

any time in the "general or literal understanding" box because they were already on to "connecting the author's and writer's ideas." . . . Then, of course, as we all remembered from our own writing, a gain in one essay might reverse in the next. The AWIC gave us ways to talk about that with our students and to figure out the reasons why. Were they less sure about the topic? Did they need more help understanding the text? Were they trying something new? We often reminded ourselves that writing improvement and teaching to support it are not a linear, mapped out march to Georgia.

(J. Marlink, personal communication, January 25, 2022)

In addition to looking for progress the students may have made, across the many schools involved in the ISAW project, teachers used the Continuum to "assess

Understanding and Use of Text

The writer provides the reader a clear and accurate understanding of the text and effectively uses the ideas in the text to develop the writer's response.

Understanding the text	Suggests Partial understanding of the text and essay topic, argument and examples.	Shows a general or literal understanding of the text and essay topic.	Presents a specific understanding that connects the author's and writer's ideas.	Explores the relationship between the writer's and author's ideas and demonstrates insight into the implications of the text.
Summarizing/Recapitulating	Summarizes.	Summarizes aptly.	Summarizes with commentary.	Recapitulates with analysis/synthesis.

FIGURE 5.2 Understanding and use of text bands of the Analytical Writing Improvement Continuum. Used with permission of the California Writing Project.

Credit Line: California Writing Project (2005). *Analytical Writing Improvement Continuum.* University of California, Berkeley.

student papers, to design lessons, to talk with their students, and to document students' progress over time" (Stokes, 2010, p. 155). Students, in turn, used the Continuum to self-assess their work and see what they needed to do to improve and obtain higher scores. One teacher, quoted in Stokes (2010) explained:

> When the students get their papers back . . . they would know what it would take to keep moving over [advancing to the next level] because the rubric is elaborate. . . . They can look at it and say, oops, I forgot to counter my argument, oops, I didn't cite any text.
>
> *(as cited in Stokes, 2010, p. 155)*

Besides building knowledge through assessment development and scoring experiences at the school and district level, ISAW teachers participated in program evaluation studies. For example, CWP teachers participated in scoring papers for a two-year ISAW evaluation study described later. Marlink, commented: "By the time of the study, hundreds of high school and community college teachers were part of CWP site sponsored ISAW professional learning communities, so we had a wealth of teachers to draw from" (J. Marlink, personal communication, May 6, 2019). In dozens of school sites across the state, teachers had administered the prompts of the Analytical Writing Placement Exam (AWPE), once in the fall and once in the spring. In the AWPE exam, academic writing involved analyzing a piece of non-fiction text or an idea about an arguable issue, developing a position, and then supporting that position with relevant evidence. A released prompt can be seen on the UC admissions website. After scoring the papers with ISAW's Analytical Improvement Continuum, teachers reviewed their own papers, looked for trends, and met in groups to determine what areas needed attention and to set goals for instruction.

The project coordinators used the AWC and the AWPE (described in Chapter 4) in the evaluation study for scoring because the technical rigor of the exams in use had been well established. The AWC had been used over eight years at NWP National Scoring Conferences. Smith and Swain (2017) report "The inter-rater agreements (consensus among scorers) ranged from 88% to 91% . . ." (p. 103). Similarly, the AWPE had an established record of technical rigor for many years as the writing placement assessment at the University of California.

The two-year quasi-experimental study, funded by the National Writing Project, "Evaluated the performance of 3,600 students in the classrooms of 87 ISAW program and comparison teachers from eighteen low performing high schools, . . . using UC AWPE writing prompts for the pre-post-writing assessment" (Marlink & Wahleithner, 2011, p. 1). The results were positive:

> In both years of the study, ISAW teachers outperformed their comparison counterparts as measured by statistically significant differences in all

seven attributes of student writing evaluated by the NWP's Analytic Writing Continuum assessment and in all 18 attributes of writing measured by the ISAW Analytical Writing Improvement Continuum assessment. These findings hold true for students who are English learners, as well as across racial and ethnic backgrounds, socio-economic status, and gender. Qualitative measures link specific changes in teachers' instructional and assessment practices to students' writing improvement.

(Marlink & Wahleithner, 2011, p. 1)

To gather some additional information about the project, we interviewed two teachers who had participated off and on for a number of years. Their comments suggest that the ISAW project had a powerful impact on participants, in large part because it proved useful and effective in teaching. For example, Marlene Carter, the only English teacher in the math/science magnet school where she taught in Southern California, described how she used it in class:

Let's say I'm teaching how to develop examples. I would give that piece of the Continuum to the students and talk to them about it. Then if the students had written about an example, I'd ask for a volunteer and we would show the paper on the screen in front of the class. And then we would figure out together where the piece of writing fit on the Continuum. Then we would work together as a class and collaborate to figure out how to move it over to the next level. We wanted the students to see that the whole idea of this was improvement. It wasn't just about grading; it's about improving. For the kids it's about "here I am today on a two, and I want to get to a three or four. So let me see if I can work on that to make it a three or four . . ." We worked on the Continuum a line at a time. That's how I broke it down. . . . And it helps when you are reading papers, because I can focus on a couple of things that I want to work on.

(M. Carter, personal communication, November 30, 2021)

Reflecting on the impact of working with the Continuum, Brooke Nichols, English teacher at Grant High School, chimed in:

I really found that the way that I talked about writing, whether I used that improvement Continuum explicitly or not, improvement was always part of the conversation. For example, we would take a student essay, and perhaps that student didn't score well on it. And I would have the kids, working in a group of four, stick it on the left side of a big poster paper. And all around the essay, they listed all the things that they thought needed some work. As a group, they worked on writing a revision of the essay and then attached it to the right side of the poster paper. And then they had to identify all the things they did to improve that writing. Then I would have the kids go around and look at the work of other groups, give their opinion, and say where they saw the improvement . . . so we were always working on revision and improvement.

(B. Nichols, personal communication, November 30, 2021)

The focus on improvement paid off, according to Carter, especially when they took the numbers off the rubric. Carter recalled that her students didn't like being a "one" or a "two." But that year was different:

Yeah, yeah, I remember this young man. He looked at his post-test results. He just yelled it out. 'I improved in 14 areas!' This big basketball player, he was so proud of himself. It was really amazing. It didn't mean that the whole essay was great, by the way, but he improved in 14 areas, which is what you are trying to accomplish.

(M. Carter, personal communication, November 30, 2021)

The road wasn't always smooth. Both teachers indicated that it took time to "get it" and to work it into their curriculum. According to Carter, "you need a multi year exposure to ISAW to really incorporate it":

They showed me pre and post test papers in the beginning, but those were other people's kids. But when I looked at the pre and post papers from my own kids then it clicked. I'm thinking, oh, oh, okay. I get it now. So my kids really needed to do better as a group and that probably means I wasn't really teaching that. . . . And so you kind of hold yourself accountable actually, because you can't blame 30 people for not improving. . . . You might have tried to teach it. But maybe it wasn't effective. So let's try that differently for next time.

(M. Carter, personal communication, November 30, 2021)

Not all teachers at their school sites bought into the program. But the two teachers we interviewed clearly valued the information the assessments gave them about the progress their students were or weren't making. And they valued the opportunities the project gave them to collaborate with like-minded professionals. Nichols said,

I think the collaborative aspect of it was huge. You know, there's a difference between giving someone a rubric. And then you go in your classroom, and you use it in isolation. . . . But the project gave us the opportunity to bring papers, to talk through them, to score them, and

share the stories, like Marlene's student who improved in 14 areas. . . .
Those conversations around that rubric, really, I think, gave us a teaching improvement mindset. So you know it wasn't just moving students
on that continuum. I look at the continuum and I think "where am I on
here in terms of being an instructor and being a teacher of writing?" So
I just really think that it changes your mindset so you are able to look at
improvement in a variety of ways, not just what are your students doing,
but what am I doing?

(B. Nichols, personal communication, November 30, 2021)

The ISAW program exemplifies the benefits to teachers and students, and teaching and learning, when teachers are made central to the assessment process. The
program provided extensive education and ongoing support for teachers over
multiple years focused on teaching and assessing writing. It also helped bridge
the gap between high schools and colleges. By using AWPE prompts, the project
ensured that participating high school teachers and their students understood
the kinds of tasks used in the University of California writing placement exam.
Promising new programs in the NWP are focusing on formative assessment tools
for analyzing students' source-based writing and for evaluating particular genres.
See, for example, "Civically Engaged Writing Analysis Continuum" (National
Writing Project, 2022a) and the "Claim, Reasoning, and Evidence Analysis Protocol" (National Writing Project, 2022b).

Teachers from many states also participate in scoring International Baccalaureate and Advanced Placement exams. While these programs focus on high-stakes
exams, the programs include extensive teacher professional development and rigorous curricula. (Of course, these classes and exams are not required but students
participate by choice.) The professional development for teachers includes the
scoring of the exams. Reporting on their surveys of readers, the College Board
(2021) indicated that "8 out of 10 AP teachers and college faculty who have
participated in more than one AP Reading say that participating in the AP Reading has had a positive impact on their teaching" (para 4). In general, 95% of the
readers "enjoy working together and exchanging ideas and experiences" (para 5).
Readers also report benefits from working with the samples and norming sessions. They "gain valuable insight into the quality and depth of student responses
from a range of AP Exam takers, instead of only being exposed to student work
from a single class or single school" (para 7).

Teachers can be effective at the state and local level if the system allows for
it. Gallagher (2007) documented the role of teachers in the Nebraska statewide
assessment system, the School-based, Teacher-led Assessment and Reporting
System (STARS). STARS involved a system of local assessments, with multiple measures of student performance that used classroom-based assessments for
state reporting and did not include high stakes. While part of STARS involved

standardized assessments, such as a standardized writing exam and some national tests, teachers were integral to the system, as Gallagher (2007) documented:

> The Nebraska Story features teachers and administrators redefining what it means to be a professional educator, schools remaking themselves into professional learning communities, and a state developing lenses for and conversation about the work of schools. . . . put simply, STARS gives us a glimpse into the next generation of standards, assessment and "accountability"—the first 21st-century approach to school improvement.
>
> *(pp. 11–12)*

The approach of STARS, which eventually collapsed under the pressure of NCLB, is in line with the idea that teachers ought to be engaged in and have a voice in developing a new assessment system. It also was in line with priorities for a new assessment system voiced by Darling-Hammond, Pecheone, and their colleagues at the National Conference on Next Generation Assessment Systems:

> Our priorities for what a new assessment system should accomplish are rooted in [the] concern for valid assessment of the deep disciplinary understanding and higher-order thinking skills that are increasingly demanded by a knowledge-based economy. They are also rooted in a belief that assessment must support ongoing improvements in instruction and learning, and must be educative for all members of the educational enterprise: students, parents, teachers, school administrators, members to the public, and policymakers.
>
> *(Darling-Hammond & Pecheone, 2010, p. 5)*

In the view of these scholars, teachers ought to be integrally involved in the development and scoring of assessments, at the state or national level as well as at the level of the school. Doing so, they argue, would "increase the capacity of teachers to prepare students for the demands of college and career in the 21st century" (Darling-Hammond & Pecheone, 2010, p. 6).

Encouraging collaboration across different levels of the system

Clearly, as approaches such as ISAW and STARS demonstrate, engaging teachers in assessment offers valuable opportunities for professional development as well opportunities to bridge the college/secondary divide. The ISAW program provided tailored instruction for meeting college entrance writing requirements. For a somewhat different example of bridging the divide, consider the use of the

Kentucky state-mandated writing portfolio by the University of Louisville as an option for composition placement assessment (Lowe & Huot, 1997; Hester et al., 2007). Students could have their senior portfolio sent to the university, which then had writing instructors evaluate it and place students into the appropriate class based on the portfolio reading.

In yet another effort to bridge the divide, Dixon (2007a) explains how a seven-year collaboration between college and secondary writing faculty began when the English department chair of the local high school knocked on the door at Tidewater Community College to find out "about the college's method of placing students in dual enrollment classes and college remedial composition courses" (Dixon, 2007b, p. 218). That inquiry led to two multiyear projects funded by the Fund for the Improvement of Postsecondary Education (FIPSE) grants that eventually included high schools and college faculty from eight states. In this project, which was titled the Writing Coalition, teachers from middle and high schools and colleges partnered in workshops "to explore innovative approaches to teaching writing, returned to their classrooms to develop and implement strategies, convened regularly to discuss their progress, and refined those approaches to improve their students' readiness for college writing" (Dixon, 2007b, Introduction, p. xiii). A significant focus became writing assessment and portfolios, for both classroom use and then use for placement into college writing (Dixon, 2007b). The entire project hinged on teachers and using professional learning communities to enhance teachers' knowledge, practices, and assessment with the goal of improving student learning.

More recently, Virginia Tech University created a state-wide program, College Access Collaborative, that fosters "partnerships with communities in low high school attainment and low matriculation to post-secondary education," according to the program's homepage. This program is multipronged and includes students, parents, and teachers, and it offers academic preparation and practical support in completing the college application. One component specifically focuses on college faculty working with high school teachers on writing pedagogy and assessment. Carter-Tod (2019) explained that the program worked with high school teachers across the state to provide customized professional development and innovative writing pedagogical practices. They collaborated with specific high schools to provide the kind of high-quality professional development needed for the faculty. She noted that this included activities such as sharing the WPA first-year writing outcomes, sample assignments, activities, and rubrics.

Dual enrollment/concurrent enrollment programs also strengthen the link between secondary schools and colleges. In these programs, students take courses in high school that count toward both their high school graduation requirements and earn them college credit. First-year writing, a common college requirement, is one of the most common courses offered in these programs. The variability in the way such programs work in different states and with different institutions make generalizations difficult, but Stancliff et al. (2017) found assessment in dual enrollment programs helped to bridge the divide between high school and college faculty by developing shared understandings of criteria, an approach that they show also contributed to the professional development of teachers in their state.

Supporting and reinforcing the teacher's role in formative assessment

Because teachers enact the curriculum, and because they have daily contact with students and provide feedback on student writing, we need to prepare teachers to play an effective role in formative assessment. Successful implementation of formative assessment requires extensive knowledge on the part of the teacher. As Trumbull and Lash (2013) explain:

> Teachers must make any act of formative assessment contingent on what has been taught and on how students have responded to the teaching, and they must shape modifications to instruction in ways that make sense for students at different developmental levels within particular domains of study. There is no prescription for how to tailor formative assessment to meet the needs of a particular classroom or student, but this tailoring is what good teaching demands of teachers. Thus, the full burden of implementing formative assessment falls on the teacher.
>
> *(p. 13)*

Students of diverse abilities inhabit most classrooms in public education. According to Biemiller (1993a), "Cognitively advantaged children . . . become able to 'take charge' of their own learning in ways that other children are not observed to do" (p. 10). Among the experiences that advanced students have, Biemiller says, are:

> (a) being taught new academic skills that build on skills they already have; (b) being taught new skills and strategies that do not demand their entire mental capacity to perform; (c) having the opportunity to assist others in using a skill after mastering it themselves; and (d) sometimes having the opportunity to *apply* the skill in meaningful (to them) situations.
>
> *(Biemiller, 1993b, p. 14)*

Cognitively disadvantaged children, on the other hand, "have insufficient cognitive capacity to handle the complexity demands of some or all school tasks as assigned. They constantly require assistance and learn more about how to get assistance than how to do tasks independently" (Biemiller, 1993a, p. 10). One effect of "asking children to do what they can't," Biemiller says, is to "Motivationally create a situation analogous to demanding that all play basketball like 6'6" basketball pros. . . . Most . . . don't 'make the team.'" Asking "children to do what they barely can," says Biemiller, also "deprives students of effective learning":

> When performance requires children to use their full resources, leaving no "surplus capacity" to talk to themselves and others about the task, knowledge about the performance may not be verbalized and may consequently be unavailable when really needed. . . . In short, those who can just "keep up with" curriculum in terms of passing performance tests may also be at risk of not learning skills well enough to use them when needed in new situations.
> *(Biemiller, 1993a, p. 8)*

Successful teaching requires knowledgeable teachers who are adept at designing curriculum and scaffolding particular assignments to fit the needs of individual students. As Slavin (1993) explains, effective teaching requires knowing how to teach heterogeneous groups of students:

> How to choose teaching methods that work for all students, when and how to use cooperative learning most effectively, when and how to individualize, when and how to use tutors or technology to help struggling students, when and how to allow time to vary, when and how to group. Each of these strategies has its own benefits and costs, which are almost certainly different for different types of objectives, students, and settings.
> *(p. 13)*

While Slavin's (1993) description addressed needed research, it applies as well to what teachers need to know and be able to do in the classroom. Although a tall order, teachers make these sorts of decisions routinely, a circumstance that underscores the need for ongoing professional development and genuine support, particularly for the development of teachers' skills in formative assessment. Gallagher and Turley (2012) argue that "teachers' professional judgment *should* be at the center of education" (emphasis in original, p. 13) and that this centering of teachers requires them to understand assessment as inquiry, as integral to teaching not something done in addition to teaching. This approach, which they align with formative assessment, "leads to significant gains for students" and supports teacher learning (Gallagher & Turley, 2012, p. 13).

Turning accountability inside out

Several authors have voiced concerns about the absence of teachers' voices in external, "outside-in" accountability programs that affect them and their students and about the deleterious effects of standardized accountability assessments on teaching and teachers (e.g., Darling-Hammond & Snyder, 1992; Lucas, 1988a, 1988b; McNeil, 1988; Murphy, 1997; Pearson & Valencia, 1987; Smith, 1991; Jones et al., 2003; Gallagher & Turley, 2012). In recent years, experts on assessment and educational policy have singled out the use of high-stakes tests in educational reform as a failed policy. Research on the impact of high-stakes testing, for example, indicates that high-stakes tests, instead of improving motivation and raising student achievement, may actually decrease student motivation and increase the proportion of students who leave school early (Amrein & Berliner, 2003). Amrein and Berliner (2003) investigated the impact of high-stakes testing in 18 states. They reasoned, "If statewide high-stakes testing policies actually improve student learning, we should see that improvement reflected not just in the states' own test scores but also in independent measures" (p. 34). They examined data from highly respected independent achievement measures (SAT, ACT, AP tests, and NAEP) to see if this was the case. Their analysis showed that high-stakes testing policies had resulted in no measurable improvement in student learning. In fact, students in some states with high-stakes tests lost ground compared with students in the United States overall. And the evident growth in NAEP test scores in some states turned out to be "a function of the fact that these states excluded more students from . . . testing than did the other states" (Amrein & Berliner, 2003, p. 36).

Evidence also suggests that when rewards and sanctions are attached to test performance, students become less intrinsically motivated and less likely to become self-directed learners (Sacks, 1999; Sheldon & Biddle, 1998). And as we explained in Chapter 2, standardized assessments can result in a narrowing of the curriculum (Jones, 2007); a concentration of teaching attention on basic skills as opposed to more complex skills, which are less frequently assessed (Mons, 2009); and a reduction in the range of subjects taught (Jones et al., 2003). These effects are often magnified in schools serving disadvantaged students because they are under pressure to demonstrate improvement in their students' scores (Herman, 1992). Standardized assessments with high stakes attached can also have a negative emotional impact on teachers and students (Filkins, 2015).

Scholars have also challenged the use of student scores on high-stakes tests in teacher evaluation. Koretz (2017) notes the several ways test-based evaluation of schools and teachers have become "unmoored from common sense" (p. 145). In one example, he described how some states scrambled to find or develop tests that could be used to evaluate teachers whose students didn't have scores—in subjects like music, art, physical education, and the like, and in some advanced science and math courses. He pointed out that the find-a-test strategy failed because many districts didn't have the capacity to develop good tests or to screen them for quality. In another example he describes how a teacher at an unusually advanced school ended up at the bottom of her district's rankings because the material she taught was years above grade level and didn't appear on the test with which she was evaluated. In another example he describes how a state took scores from teachers who had scores on an appropriate test but used them to

What teachers say about the negative impact of standardized accountability assessments of writing on teachers and students

- When I assess I always talk with students about next steps and help them see assessment as finding ways to keep growing. Test scores, however, calling a kid a "1" or a "3," does the opposite. Kids have cried, thrown up, and the like on test day and after getting scores. Many kids I know are strong learners turn out to be poor test takers and are devastated. (as cited in Filkins, 2015)
- We are under so much pressure to get good results there is little time for anything else . . . I had to cease a lot of projects and other activities and programs in my room to make time for the teaching of test-taking strategies. I felt demoralized and unappreciated by all of the negative press in the newspapers and have doubted myself as an educator for the first time. I'm not sure I would go into this profession if I had to choose all over again. (as cited in Nichols & Berliner, 2007, p. 155)
- We have access to extraordinary technology and travel, rich resources and diverse stories, but we're pressed and we're anxious, and that anxiety shapes every minute of the student experience. Administrators who are worried about test scores produce teachers who are worried about their quarterly benchmark scores, who in turn produce children who are worried about their daily "exit ticket" scores. (as cited in Almagor, 2020, para. 21)
- We only teach to the test even at second grade, and have stopped teaching science and social studies. We don't have assemblies, take few field trips, or have musical productions at grade levels. We even hesitate to ever show a video. Our second graders have no recess except for 20 minutes at lunch. (as cited in Nichols & Berliner, 2007, p. 138).
- I see the downsides of standardized testing with each group of first-year students that comes in the door, as they look at reading and writing overwhelmingly as a means of testing. (as cited in NCTE, 2016b, p. 11)
- Children are "assessed" every day, every week. PLCs [professional learning communities] are really about raising test scores and not about best practices. We are meetinged to death. Constant discussions and pressure about test scores. Teachers cry. They are competitive in a fully unhealthy manner. Black and brown children are treated differently when it comes to gifted and talented identification. We have many Hispanic students who struggle and are also tested ad nauseam for a whole buffet of purposes. Our state is heavy on [major assessment publisher] spending. We still use the antiquated [company-produced curriculum materials] crap! The state's education is in an unholy mess. (as cited in NCTE, 2016b, p. 9)

"evaluate" teachers who didn't have scores. Koretz's evaluation of this practice speaks for itself:

> It's utterly irrational to "evaluate" teachers based on scores earned by students of other teachers, particularly teachers in other schools or who teach other subjects. Imagine, for example, that your own evaluation were based

on the performance of employees in another branch of your employer's firm. Most of us would find this both ludicrous and intolerable.

(Koretz, 2017, p. 145)

Koretz (2017) asserts with good reason that tests "can never be sufficient because they fail to measure so many of the important goals of education" (p. 137). Simply equating poor scores with poor teacher performance without taking into account the students' circumstances, he says, is "much like insisting that doctors treat patients based on one symptom without considering which of its many possible causes is the relevant one" (p. 148).

Since the "outside-in" test-based alternative for promoting increased student learning of higher-order skills has largely failed, are there alternatives? One alternative to using test-based scores to evaluate teachers, as Koretz says, could be a return to observations of teacher performance. But observations only go so far, and they can be subjective. They may provide some feedback to the teacher about their performance, but little if any guidance about how to improve. Another alternative is to turn assessment into inquiry, and to put inquiry into the hands of teachers (Gallagher & Turley, 2012; O'Neill et al., 2002). Teachers can investigate the impact of their teaching and, at the same time, provide useful information for both internal and external evaluators.

In Region 15, the site of the district portfolio project we described in Chapter 4, assessment was transformed into inquiry in the service of learning. Educators in Region 15 created collaborative teaching portfolios. Working in teams, they created purposeful collections "of work selected . . . in an attempt to provide insight into a chosen research question" (Van Wagenen et al., 1996, p. 2). Although the portfolios played a role in the teachers' evaluations, the primary mission of the teacher portfolios was to enhance instruction. Not surprisingly, the "final" reflections in the teaching portfolios weren't really final. As Murphy and Underwood (2000) explained, "Gathering evidence for the portfolio and reflecting on it often generated more questions" (p. 68).

Teachers in Region 15 played an active and generative role in assessment. In the analyses of their portfolios, student work wasn't reduced to grades or scores, nor subjected to any of the usual psychometric tests of rater agreement. Nor were the results used to reward or punish teachers. The primary purpose of the portfolio was to enhance learning; instead of being accountable to external evaluators, the teachers were being accountable to the students. In other words, the traditional model of teacher evaluation, which relies on data collected by external evaluators—the scores of students, or what administrators see during their visits—was turned inside out. The goal of the teacher portfolios was to give the teachers insights about how their own work affected student performance. Thus, the teachers themselves were the portfolios' first and perhaps most important audience. But the portfolios also had a broad range of other audiences, including "other teachers interested in the same research question, beginning teachers, potential employers, administrators, parents, even students" (Murphy & Underwood, 2000, p. 170).

What teachers say about the negative impact of standardized assessments on the teaching of writing

- One administrator suggested that I cut the writing program because "the students take the Idaho Direct Writing Assessment for the last time their freshman year. You teach tenth graders. They don't have to write; they just pick the correct answer." I hoped he wasn't serious. (as cited in Warne, 2006, p. 22)
- Now I will say that our instructional supervisor has a little formula plan that is passed out to teachers in 10th and 11th grade levels and they are to teach this little formula of 5 paragraphs. . . . Say this in your introductory paragraph; put 3 reasons, examples, whatever that you are going to mention. Do a paragraph for each one of those and write a concluding paragraph. (as cited in O'Neill, 2002)
- For the 11th grade college prep we spend two weeks intensively reviewing prompts from the past, writing essays for practice and give it that focus for two weeks right before the test. (as cited in O'Neill, 2002)
- In Michigan, the writing test is hardly draconian, but its demand that students compose an essay in one sitting—and that this single essay be used as an illustration of their total competence as writers—has subverted much of what Elbow and others advocated . . . writing has become an endeavor to appease the invisible reader who will be recruited to evaluate the essay. Process, audience, and the personal investment that is inherent to writing have been expunged. (as cited in Shafer, 2005, pp. 245–246)
- In this high-stakes and decidedly daunting environment, students abandon certain ideas about writing and embrace more reductive and less active approaches. If schools value linear, product-based steps, then students are going to see writing as an act that is quick, devoid of stages, impersonal, and predicated upon the values of a single authority. They are going to cease to see it as a social activity that is read by an authentic audience, and they are going to stop seeing writing as an act of artistic creation. (as cited in Shafer, 2005, p. 241)
- We need to ponder the impact of testing, the way it truncates and supplants genuine, holistic writing and undermines progress. College writing instructors have never been insulated from what happens—or doesn't happen—in high school writing classes, but we are only beginning to appreciate the damage done to students we will someday teach. (as cited in Shafer, 2005, p. 242)
- Most important, college writing instructors must understand that they are not impervious to the problems caused by testing. Area high school students will someday be in our classrooms and their inability to engage in a rich, personal writing process affects their ability to think, compose, and develop into democratic citizens. In the end, we all feel the results of diminishing hope and a depleted understanding of writing process and its efficacy to empower. (as cited in Shafer, 2005, pp. 245–246)

Region 15's portfolio system is an example of an integrated, systemic approach to assessment. The emphasis on self-regulated learning applied to students and teachers alike, and the management fostered a climate in which self-regulation could thrive. It flipped the accountability agenda so that teachers took the lead on evaluating their teaching and student learning with the aim of improvement. In short, it turned the accountability model inside-out. Located in Connecticut, Region 15 benefited from policies that prioritized professional development. Olsen (1999) characterizes two broad camps in the approaches that states take to accountability: "Those that think schools and students will improve if they are given enough resources, support, information, and encouragement; and those that think they need a substantial external push" (Olsen, 1999, p. 8). At the state level, in the time before high stakes became a nation-wide mandate, Connecticut fell into the former camp, putting much of its energy into "honing the skills of its teaching force, drafting new standards for licensure, paying beginning teachers more, and financing a mentoring program for novices" (Olsen, 1999, p. 8). According to Olsen, the state published report cards on schools and gave grants to districts that showed sustained progress over time, but did not explicitly sanction schools that failed to make progress. In those days, prior to the "Race to the Top," Connecticut's policies made room for professional accountability.

Postsecondary educational oversight is different than it is in K–12, although much of it is still of the "outside to inside" variety. There is not, for example, the same mandate to evaluate faculty's performance in the classroom, although there are regular demands to demonstrate student learning. All postsecondary institutions must meet accreditation standards, which includes using direct assessment of student learning. Layered over accreditation standards are state policies and regulations for public institutions. State policies may control, among other things, course descriptions for some of the general education courses, placement testing, proficiency testing, dual enrollment, and transferring of students between institutions. There is a wide variation across states in how much state policy influences particular programs and courses, although writing programs may experience more influence than most because written communication is a common learning outcome, and first-year writing still tends to be a universal requirement with many contingent instructors. In Idaho, for example, the state higher education board mandated the same placement method for all campuses whether a community college or the state flagship university. The writing program faculty across institutions worked with experts in writing assessment, conducted pilot studies, and petitioned the board to allow them to modify the placement method for each college and university so that they could meet the needs of their particular students (Estrem et al., 2018). In Georgia, the Board of Regents of the University System of Georgia, which governs all 26 state colleges and universities, sets the core curriculum, including course descriptions. The board also mandates proficiency exams in writing and reading and has set policies about criteria for exemptions. Passing the reading and writing exams—or satisfying the exemption criteria—is required for graduation. Many other large state systems have some oversight regarding placement and proficiency exams at the college level, although some, such as Washington, might require assessment but leave it to each institution to implement its own.

Private colleges and universities, of course, do not have to follow policies such as those in Idaho and Georgia, although they can institute their own requirements. For example, Hampton Sydney required students to pass a three-hour rhetoric proficiency exam to be eligible for graduation. Some universities, public or private, use portfolios to assess student learning, sometimes at the institutional level, such as Washington State University's Junior Proficiency Portfolio.

Although the demands for assessment vary by state and institution, all institutions are expected to meet external accrediting demands, as we mentioned earlier. These demands, though, allow an institution to privilege teaching and learning in the context of their specific context and mission. For example, Pruchnic et al. (2018) showed how they used a subset of portfolios gathered and scored for a program assessment linked to accreditation to have more in-depth conversation about the curriculum and professional development needs of the faculty. In other words, they were putting assessment in the service of learning. For a subset of already scored portfolio reflection essays, participants listed textual features that they had noticed for each essay without any attempt to focus the group on particular outcomes, rubrics, or textual features. Then in groups, the instructors shared their lists, and the leaders recorded and coded the responses for each essay and compared them across score points.

Other programs have used portfolios collected as part of exit exams or for placement to not only evaluate individual students but also to consider the needs of the program and its instructors. For example, Haswell and McLeod (1997) showed how they used the rising junior portfolio assessment with various constituencies across campus. Walvoord (2010) shared a variety of examples showing how embedded assessments (assessments included as part of a regular course) are used to satisfy accreditation demands for program assessment but also serve as professional development opportunities. The design of the rubric, the evaluation of the student work, and the analysis of the results are done by the program faculty. The results could lead to a change in curriculum, a revision of the assignment, discussions about more effective ways to teach certain goals, and even a revision of program outcomes. These types of assessments put student learning at the center of the institutional assessment requirements, starting with the inside of the classroom and turning it inside out without any kind of high stake for the students whose work is used for the assessment. The low stakes focus the assessment on the effectiveness of the program and institution with the assessment results used to improve teaching and learning, through the shared work of identifying criteria, evaluating student work, analyzing the results, and then using those results to make changes. The assessment is not used to confer rewards or sanctions on a program, or an individual student or teacher, but it is used as part of the institution's evidence for institutional effectiveness and re-accreditation.

In addition to analyzing samples of student performance from classrooms, we can pay more attention to how teachers evaluate student performance and provide more professional development to support them. Providing professional development support around assessment is crucial, since, as Hiebert and Calfee (1989) point out, teachers are already making high-stakes decisions that influence student achievement:

> They decide on group placement: they choose the rate at which new content is introduced to different groups; they grade students on daily, quarterly, and yearly accomplishments. . . . The assessment practices of effective teachers are closely interwoven with instructional decisions.
>
> *(p. 50)*

We should also find ways to integrate teachers' assessments into higher-level decision making. As Hiebert and Calfee (1989) explain:

> [The] ease with which teachers can vary contexts and tasks in classrooms means that the data provide more valid representations of students' performances in a variety of authentic situations.
>
> *(p. 52)*

Although a "teacher cannot claim a Cronbach alpha of .87 or a validity coefficient of .72," assessments based on observations and performance samples can be consistent, and they are repeatable. Such assessments provide insights "often lacking in reports of standardized test results" (Hiebert & Calfee, 1989, p. 82).

Reports based solely on standardized test scores provide a very limited view of the literacy competencies attained by American students. Expanding the role of teachers' assessments in higher-level decision making and making use of the continuous and informed judgments of teachers would provide more comprehensive information about student' competencies.

Locating teachers and students at the center of writing assessment, as we envision it, allows teaching and learning to drive assessment decisions and processes instead of the other way around. This move demands we treat teachers from K–college as professionals and provide them with the support they need to design effective program assessments and engage in effective formative assessments of their students' work, in short, to be professionals. As we explained in Chapter 4, it also means we need to encourage students to set goals and check their own progress, in short, to engage in self-assessment, rather than relying solely on their teacher's judgment. What we are suggesting here is that when we rework our assessment system, we do what we can to turn it inside out. We borrow this idea from Gallagher (2007), who speaks to its possibilities for the future:

> What will this twenty-first century approach look like? For the most part, we can only guess. My hunch—and my hope—is that the new model will turn the old one inside out. It will dismiss accountability as its guiding principle and adopt instead the more robust concept of *engagement*. Its aim will be to nurture mutually responsible partnerships that are not reducible to bottom-line transactions (a compliance approach), but are instead marked by rich and dialogic interactions (a commitment approach). It will return teaching and learning to teachers and students. It will give teachers the tools and the trust they need to practice their art. . . . It will take seriously the notion that schools are not competitive organizations, but rather as Paul Theobold says, agents for the restoration of community.
>
> *(Gallagher, 2007, p. 9)*

In our next chapter, we turn to the metaphor of ecology, focusing specifically on how it has been used in writing studies, and how it can help turn assessment inside out by highlighting the need to attend to the entire educational ecosystem. We also explore the idea of ecological validity to consider the effects an ecological approach to assessment might have on large-scale writing assessment and the ecosystem of education more broadly.

References

Almagor, L. (2020). High stakes tests aren't better—and they never will be. *Boston Review*. https://bostonreview.net/articles/lelac-almagor-testing-still-isnt-better/

Amrein, A. L., & Berliner, D. C. (2003). The effects of high stakes testing on student motivation and learning. *Educational Leadership, 60*(5), 32–38.

Anderson, S. L. (2009). *The instructional practices of teachers who score a state writing assessment: A case study* [Unpublished dissertation, University of Nebraska].

Biemiller, A. (1993a). Lake Wobegon revisited: On diversity and education. *Educational Researcher, 22*(9), 7–12. www.researchgate.net/publication/240801392_Lake_Wobegon_Revisited_On_Diversity_and_Education

Biemiller, A. (1993b). Students differ: So address differences effectively. *Educational Researcher, 22*(9), 14–15.

California Writing Project. (2005). *Analytical writing improvement Continuum*. University of California.

Carter-Tod, S. (2019, March 19). *Bridging the gap: Supporting students in the transition between high school and college writing* [Conference presentation]. Conference on College Composition and Communication.

Clark, C., & Peterson, P. (1986). Teachers' thought processes. In M. Wittrock (Ed.), *Handbook of research on teaching* (3rd ed., pp. 256–274). Macmillan.

Cohen, D., McLaughlin, M., & Talbert, J. (1993). *Teaching for understanding: Challenges for policy and practice*. Jossey-Bass.

College Board. (2021). *Become an AP reader*. https://apcentral.collegeboard.org/pdf/become-ap-reader.pdf

Conference on College Composition and Communication. (2015a). *Statement on preparing teachers of college writing* [Position Statement]. http://www2.ncte.org/statement/statementonprep/

Conference on College Composition and Communication. (2015b). *Statement of principles and standards for the postsecondary teaching of writing* [Position Statement]. http://www2.ncte.org/statement/postsecondarywriting/

Darling-Hammond, L. (1984). *Beyond the commission reports: The coming crisis in teaching*. Rand Corporation. www.rand.org/content/dam/rand/pubs/reports/2007/R3177.pdf

Darling-Hammond, L. (1989). Accountability for professional practice. *Teachers College Record, 91*(1), 59–80.

Darling-Hammond, L. (1994). *The current status of teaching and teacher development in the United States*. Paper prepared for the National Commission on Teaching and America's Future. https://eric.ed.gov/?id=ED379229

Darling Hammond, L. (2017). *Developing and measuring higher order skills: Models for state performance assessment systems*. Learning Policy Institute Report, Council of Chief State School Officers. https://learningpolicyinstitute.org/sites/default/files/product-files/Models_State_Performance_Assessment_Systems_REPORT.pdf

Darling-Hammond, L., Hyler, M. E., & Gardner, M. (2017). *Effective teacher professional development*. Learning Policy Institute. https://learningpolicyinstitute.org/sites/default/files/product-files/Effective_Teacher_Professional_Development_REPORT.pdf

Darling-Hammond, L., & McLaughlin, M. W. (1995). Policies that support professional development in an era of reform. *Phi Delta Kappan, 76*(8), 597–604.

Darling-Hammond, L., & Pecheone, R. (2010). *Developing an internationally comparable balanced assessment system that supports high quality learning*. Educational Testing Service. www.ets.org/Media/Research/pdf/Darling-HammondPechoneSystemModel.pdf

Darling-Hammond, L., & Snyder, J. (1992). Reframing accountability: Creating learner-centered schools. *Teachers College Record, 93*(5), 11–36.

Dixon, C. (Ed.). (2007a). *Lesson plans for teaching writing*. National Council of Teachers of English.

Dixon, C. (Ed.). (2007b). Appendix A: Why institutions need to cross-pollinate. In *Lesson plans for teaching writing* (pp. 217–238). National Council of Teachers of English.

Estrem, H., Shepherd, D., & Sturman, S. (2018). Reclaiming writing assessment. *WPA: Writing Program Administration, 42*(1), 56–71.

Filkins, S. (2015). *NCTE assessment story project: What we have learned* [Conference Presentation] National Council of Teachers of English Annual Meeting.

Firestone, W. (1993). Why "professionalizing" teaching is not enough. *Educational Leadership, 50*(6), 6–11.

Gallagher, C. (2007). *Reclaiming assessment: A better alternative to the accountability agenda*. Heinemann.

Gallagher, C., & Turley, E. (2012). *Our better judgment: Teacher leadership for writing assessment*. National Council of Teachers of English.

Gray, J. (2000). *Teachers at the center: A memoir of the early years of the national writing project*. National Writing Project.

Haswell, R. (1988). *Contrasting ways to appraise improvement in a writing course: Paired comparison and holistic.* [Paper presentation] Annual Meeting of the Conference on College Composition and Communication, St. Louis, MO.

Haswell, R. H., & McLeod, S. (1997). WAC assessment and internal audiences: A dialogue. In K. B. Yancey & B. Huot (Eds.), *Assessing writing across the curriculum: Diverse approaches and practices* (pp. 217–236). Ablex.

Herman, J. L. (1992). What research tells us about good assessment. *Educational Leadership, 49*(8), 74–78.

Herman, J. L., & Linn, R. L. (2013). *On the road to assessing deeper learning: The status of smarter balanced and PARCC assessment consortia.* University of California, National Center for Research on Evaluation, Standards, and Student Testing (CRESST).

Herrington, A., Hodgson, K., & Moran, C. (Eds.). (2009). *Teaching the new writing: Technology, change, and the assessment in the 21st-century classroom.* Teachers College Press.

Hester, V., O'Neill, P., Neal, M., Edgington, A., & Huot, B. (2007). Adding portfolios to the placement process: A longitudinal perspective. In P. O'Neill (Ed.), *Blurring boundaries: Developing writers, researchers and teachers: A tribute to William L. Smith* (pp. 61–90). Hampton Press.

Hiebert, E. H., & Calfee, R. C. (1989). Advancing academic literacy through teachers' assessments. *Educational Leadership, 46*(7), 50–54.

Hoekstra, L. (2021, October 31). *Instead of seeing students as far below basic or advanced, we see them as learners.* Guest Post, Larry Ferlazzo's Websites of the Day. https://larry ferlazzo.edublogs.org/2012/10/31/instead-of-seeing-students-as-far-below-basic-or-advanced-we-see-them-as-learners/

Holland, R. (2007). *Portfolios: A backward step in school accountability.* Lexington Institute. https://lexingtoninstitute.org/wp-content/uploads/2013/11/holland_portfolio_assessment_8_29_07.pdf

Jones, B. D. (2007). The unintended outcomes of high—stakes testing. *Journal of Applied School Psychology, 23*(2), 65–86.

Jones, G. M., Jones, B. D., & Hargrove, T. Y. (2003). *The unintended consequences of high-stakes testing.* Rowman & Littlefield Publishers, Inc.

Joyce, B., & Showers, B. (1988). *Student achievement through staff development.* Longman.

Koretz, D. (2017). *The testing charade: Pretending to make schools better.* University of Chicago Press.

Little, J. W. (1993). Teachers' professional development in a climate of educational reform. *Educational Evaluation and Policy Analysis, 15*(2), 129–151. https://lsc-net.terc.edu/do/paper/8063/show/use_set-teacher_pd.html

Lotan, R. A., Burns, D., & Darling-Hammond, L. (2019). *The instructional leadership corps: Entrusting professional learning in the hands of the profession.* The Learning Policy Institute, Stanford University.

Lowe, T., & Huot, B. (1997). Using KIRIS writing portfolios to place students in first-year composition at the University of Louisville. *Kentucky English Bulletin, 46*(2), 46–64.

Lucas, C. K. (1988a). Toward ecological evaluation. *The Quarterly of the National Writing Project and the Center for the Study of Writing, 10*(1), 1–3, 12–17. https://eric.ed.gov/?id=EJ390373

Lucas, C. K. (1988b). Toward ecological evaluation: Part two. Recontextualizing literacy assessment. *The Quarterly of the National Writing Project and the Center for the Study of Writing, 10*(2), 4–7. https://archive.nwp.org/cs/public/download/nwp_file/1781/Toward_Ecological_Evaluation_-_Part_1.pdf?x-r=pcfile_d

Marlink, J. (2009). Improving students' academic writing: Developing new knowledge about teaching and assessing for improvement. *California English, 15*(2), 6–9.

Marlink, J., & Wahleithner, J. (2011). *Improving students' academic writing: Building a bridge to success.* Final Report for the National Writing Project Local Sites Research Initiative. California Writing Project. https://archive.nwp.org/cs/public/download/nwp_file/15419/ISAW_LSRI_final_report.pdf?x-r=pcfile_d

McNeil, L. M. (1988). Contradictions of control, part 3: Contradictions of reform. *Phi Delta Kappan, 69*(7), 478–485.

Mons, N. (2009). *Theoretical and real effects of standardised assessment.* Education, Audiovisual & Culture Executive Agency. https://citeseerx.ist.psu.edu/viewdoc/download?doi=10.1.1.174.4813&rep=rep1&type=pdf

Murphy, S. (1997). Teachers and students: Reclaiming assessment. In K. Yancey & I. Weiser (Eds.), *Situating portfolios: Four perspectives* (pp. 72–89). Utah State University Press.

Murphy, S., & Underwood, T. (2000). *Portfolio practices: Lessons from schools, districts and states.* Christopher Gordon Publishers.

National Commission on Excellence in Education. (1983). *A nation at risk: The imperative for educational reform.* https://edreform.com/wpcontent/uploads/2013/02/A_Nation_At_Risk_1983.pdf

National Council of Teachers of English. (2014, April 1). *Why class size matters today.* http://www2.ncte.org/statement/why-class-size-matters/

National Council of Teachers of English. (2016a, February 28). *Professional knowledge for the teaching of writing.* http://www2.ncte.org/statement/teaching-writing/

National Council of Teachers of English Assessment. (2016b). *The assessment story project: What we learned from teachers sharing their experiences with literacy assessment.* National Council of Teachers of English Assessment.

National Council of Teachers of English. (2018, February 20). *Resolution on professional learning in the teaching of writing for inservice teachers.* https://ncte.org/statement/resolution-professional-learning-teaching-writing-inservice-teachers/

National Writing Project. (2002a). *Civically engaged writing analysis Continuum.* https://cewac.nwp.org/

National Writing Project. (2022b). *Claim, reasoning, and evidence analysis protocol.* https://sites.google.com/site/nwpcollegereadywritersprogram/formative-assessment-tools/the-claim-evidence-and-reasoning-protocol

Nichols, S., & Berliner, D. C. (2007). *Collateral damage: How high-stakes testing corrupts America's schools.* Harvard Education Press.

O'Day, J. A., & Smith, M. S. (1993). Systemic reform and educational opportunity. In S. Fuhrman (Ed.), *Designing coherent education policy: Improving the system* (pp. 250–312). Jossey-Bass.

Olsen, G. (1999). Toward a post-process composition: Abandoning the rhetoric of assertion. In T. Kent (Ed.), *Post-process theory: Beyond the writing process paradigm.* Southern Illinois University Press.

O'Neill, P. (2002, November). *The impact of state-mandated writing assessment on high school curriculum, teachers, and students' preparation for first-year college writing.* National Council of Teachers of English Annual Convention.

O'Neill, P., Schendel, E., & Huot, B. (2002). Defining assessment as research: Moving from obligations to opportunities. *Writing Program Administration, 26*(1–2), 10–26.

Pagano, N., Bernhardt, S. A., Reynolds, D., Williams, M., & McCurrie, M. K. (2008). An inter-institutional model for college writing assessment. *College Composition and Communication, 60*(2), 285–320.

Pearson, P. D., & Valencia, S. W. (1987). Assessment, accountability, and professional prerogative. In J. E. Readence & R. S. Baldwin (Eds.), *Research in literacy: Merging perspectives* (pp. 3–16). National Reading Conference.

Pruchnic, J., Susak, C., Grogan, J., Primeau, S., Torok, J., Trimble, T., Foster, T., & Barton, E. (2018). Slouching toward sustainability: Mixed methods in the direct assessment of student writing. *Journal of Writing Assessment, 11*(1). www.journalofwritingassessment.org/article.php?article=125

Sacks, P. (1999). *Standardized minds: The high price of America's testing culture and what we can do to change it*. Perseus Books.

Schwartz, J. (2004). Reflections of an AP reader. *English Journal, 93*(4), 53–57.

Selfe, C. L., & Hilligoss, S. (Eds.). (1994). *Literacy and computers: The complications of teaching and learning with technology* (Research and scholarship in composition, Vol. 2). Modern Language Association of America.

Shafer, G. (2005). Standardized testing and the college composition instructor. *Teaching English in the Two-Year College, 32*(3), 238–246.

Sheldon, K. M., & Biddle, B. J. (1998). Standards, accountability, and school reform: Perils and pitfalls. *Teachers College Record, 100*(1), 164–180.

Shulman, L. (1987). Knowledge and teaching: Foundations of the new reform. *Harvard Education Review, 57*(1), 1–23.

Slavin, R. E. (1993). Students differ: So what? *Educational Researcher, 22*(9), 13–14.

Smith, M. A., & Swain, S. S. (2017). *Assessing writing, teaching writers: Putting the analytic writing Continuum to work in your classroom*. Teachers College Press.

Smith, M. L. (1991). Put to the test: The effects of external testing on teachers. *Educational Researcher, 20*(5), 8–11.

Stancliff, M., Whittig, E., McIntyre, L., Rose, S., & Roen, E. (2017). Collaborative assessment of dual enrollment: The view from Arizona. *Journal of Writing Assessment, 10*(1). www.journalofwritingassessment.org/article.php?article=117

St. John, M., & Stokes, L. (2017). *NWP: A national infrastructure that helps improve student writing*. Inverness Research, Inc.

Stokes, L. (2010). The national writing project: Anatomy of an improvement infrastructure. In C. E. Coburn & M. K. Stein (Eds.), *Research and practice in education: Building alliances, bridging the divide* (pp. 147–162). Rowman & Littlefield.

Swanson, J. (1995). Systemic reform in the professionalism of educators. *The Phi Delta Kappan, 77*(1), 36–39. https://www2.ed.gov/pubs/SER/ProfEd/bkgd.html

Trumbull, E., & Lash, A. (2013). Understanding formative assessment. Insights from learning theory and measurement theory. *WestEd*. www.wested.org/resources/understanding-formative-assessment-insights-from-learning-theory-and-measurement-theory/

University of California. (2022). *About the exam. Entry Level Writing Requirement*. https://admission.universityofcalifornia.edu/elwr/about-the-exam/

Van Wagenen, L., Nelson, D. M., & Hibbard, K. M. (1996). *Creating an educator's collaborative portfolio: Documenting classroom strategies to enhance learning*. Regional School District 15.

Walvoord, B. E. (2010). *Assessment clear and simple: A practical guide for institutions, departments, and general education* (2nd ed.). Wiley.

Warne, B. M. (2006). Teaching conventions in a state-mandated testing context. *English Journal, 95*(5), 22–27.

Wysocki, A. F., Johnson-Eilola, J., Selfe, C. L., & Geoffrey Sirc, G. (2004). *Writing new media: Theory and applications for expanding the teaching of composition*. Utah State University Press.

6

AN ECOLOGICAL APPROACH TO WRITING ASSESSMENT

Throughout this book, we have considered ways to remake the educational accountability system. We have drawn on extensive scholarship focused on learning, writing, and writing assessment to argue for turning the system inside out, with the goal of improving teaching and learning to write. To achieve this goal, we have argued that educators and designers of writing assessments should pay close attention to current scholarship about:

- Construct and consequential validity and the roles these aspects of validity play when assessments are created and interpreted, especially when stakes are attached to the results;
- Evolving theories of writing, which now cast writing as a socially situated, meaning-making activity that varies in complex ways across contexts and discourse communities;
- The central role that teachers play in the development of student writers by engaging in formative assessment and providing developmental feedback; and
- The need to include teachers as active participants and decision-makers in assessment development and scoring.

To help us think through the ways we might remake the writing assessment system so it better serves teaching and learning, we initially used the metaphor of a house renovation. Using this metaphor helped us consider ways we could flip the system—much as a contractor might flip a house. We identified features of the existing accountability system that needed renovation, for example, the misuse of single-sample assessments for making claims about overall writing proficiency and the damaging effects of high-stakes testing. In this chapter, we turn to the

DOI: 10.4324/9781003296140-6

metaphor of ecology because it encourages thinking beyond the features and effects of individual assessments to thinking about the health of the educational ecosystem as a whole as well as the ways that systems within it are interrelated and interdependent.

The term *ecosystem*, as introduced by Tansley (1935), referred to the system resulting from the integration of "all the living and nonliving factors of the environment" (Van Dyne, 1966). The concept of an ecosystem was originally tied to the idea of a biological community of plants, animals, insects, and the like encompassed within a spatial boundary and interacting within an environment that includes physical conditions such as wind, rain, and temperature as well as soils, water, air, and so on. The general idea is that controlling factors of an ecosystem (e.g., macroclimate, geological materials, including water, and organisms) are more or less independent of each other and in turn are composites of many separate elements that are variable in time or space. The dependent elements of the ecosystem, on the other hand, are things like the microclimate, soil, vegetation, consumer organisms such as herbivores and carnivores, and decomposer organisms such as bacteria, fungi, and the like. According to Van Dyne (1966), "Each change in a controlling agent in the ecosystem produces in time a corresponding change in the dependent elements of the ecosystem" (p. 5). In other words, changes in some elements of the system promote changes in other elements of the system.

Although originally used in reference to the natural world, the concept of ecosystem has been useful in sociology and the study of human ecosystems that include social elements. In relationship to society and humans, ecosystems consist of:

1. social institutions: collective solutions to universal and particular social challenges;
2. social cycles: temporal patterns for allocating human activity; and
3. social order: cultural patterns for organizing interactions among people and groups (Burch & DeLuca, 1984; Machlis et al., 1997).

(Redman et al., 2004, p. 163)

Current frameworks now view ecosystems as even more inclusive, bringing together the social and biological components of the environment and exploring the complex networks of relationships and interactions in what Redman et al. (2004) refer to as the social-ecological system because it encompasses both social and biological aspects:

1. a coherent system of biophysical and social factors that regularly interact in a resilient, sustained manner;
2. a system that is defined at several spatial, temporal, and organizational scales, which may be hierarchically linked;

3. a set of critical resources (natural, socioeconomic, and cultural) whose flow and use is regulated by a combination of ecological and social systems; and

4. a perpetually dynamic, complex system with continuous adaptation (Burch & DeLuca, 1984; Machlis et al., 1997).

(Redman et al., 2004, p. 163)

In sum, a social-ecological ecosystem is made up of an interconnected network of biological, physical, and social components. It recognizes the complexity of the relationships among the inhabitants and their environment. Thinking about the role played by educational assessment in this complex, interconnected way means taking into account all aspects of the educational system, including the people involved and their health and well-being, the physical and material conditions of the schools, the social relationships among participants, and, as we have argued, factors such as policies, processes, and practices in the system.

Ecology in writing studies

In writing studies, the use of "ecology" and various forms of the term (e.g., eco-system, ecological, eco) is common. For example, Cooper, in her influential 1986 article, proposes "an ecological model of writing, whose fundamental tenet is that writing is an activity through which a person is continually engaged with a variety of socially constituted systems" (p. 367). Cooper goes on to explain that "ecological" is not just another way to refer to context: "an ecological model encompasses much more than the individual writer and her immediate context" and examines the dynamic systems (p. 368). "In place of the static and limited categories of contextual models, the ecological model postulates dynamic interlocking systems which structure the social activity of writing" (p. 368). In her explanation, Cooper (1986) emphasizes, among other things, that an ecological model for writing focuses our attention "on the real social context of writing" not general, idealized, or abstract contexts (p. 371), with the "focus on readers as real social beings" (p. 372). She concludes by contending, "Writing is one of the activities by which we locate ourselves in the enmeshed systems that make up the social world. It is not simply a way of thinking but more fundamentally a way of acting" (Cooper, 1986, p. 373).

Cooper, of course, is not the only scholar in writing studies to use the metaphor of ecology or ecosystems. Ecocomposition, "a post-process theory of writing that attempts to delineate the places, environments, and ecologies of writing" (Jones, 2018, p. 1), has been taking root for the last 30 years. It highlights place and the material context that gives rise to writing. In this framework, context and situation cannot be adequately represented by simplistic, static models such as audience, purpose, genre, and message because situations are dynamic. Edbauer (2005) explains, drawing on theorists such as Phelps (1988), Warner (2002), Vatz

(1973), and Bitzer (1968), that the rhetorical situation is dynamic with the writer or rhetor constructing the context in real time. The emphasis on the particular situation, the location of the writer in a particular place and time, is a key assumption of ecocomposition. Jones (2018) summarizes it this way:

> [W]riting emerges out of the reciprocal interaction of writers and places in complex rhetorical ecologies. Place is more than content for writing; it constitutes the conditions of writing itself. Examining specific places allows ecocompositionists to delineate and locate ecologies of writing.
>
> *(p. 25)*

Dobrin and Weisser (2002) argue for the importance of the "intersections between discourse, place and environment" in the teaching of writing (p. 567). They explain that "ecocomposition attempts to provide a holistic, encompassing framework for studies of the relationship between discourse and environment" (p. 572). The central focus of the pedagogy of ecocomposition should "directly assist students in becoming better producers of writing in a variety of writing environments . . . encouraging students to recognize their experiences in all environments as affecting and being affected by their writing" (Dobrin & Weisser, 2002, p. 582). This approach "encourages political activism, public writing, and service learning, and student writing can be directed beyond scope of classroom assignments to address larger, public audiences" (Dobrin & Weisser, 2002, p. 580). Ecocomposition is aligned with the contemporary construct of writing we have discussed in earlier chapters—a socially mediated activity that varies in important ways across different cultures, discourse communities, contexts, and purposes for writing—as well as best practices for teaching writing with an emphasis on context, and authentic writing tasks and audiences, all of which would demand students learn a variety of genres and processes in meeting the demands of different audiences and purposes.

Writing assessment ecologies

Wardle and Roozen (2012) propose an " 'ecological' model of writing assessment," basing the need for ecological assessment on a conceptualization of literate development that goes beyond only "vertical" development within a single context, discourse community, or activity system to encompass "a broad range of literate experiences over lengthy periods of time" (p. 108). They argue that an ecological model "reflects the shift toward a broader, more multidimensional view of expertise . . . that recognizes persons' engagement with and movements between activities in multiple settings" (p. 109). "The basic goal" of the assessment model they envision "is to offer students, teachers, departments, institutions and other stakeholders a fuller, richer account of the kinds of experiences with writing that are informing students' growth as writers throughout the undergraduate years"

(p. 107). Their model is thus closely aligned with our own views about the need to align writing assessment with current understandings of writing as a complex cognitive and socially situated meaning-making activity that varies in significant ways across contexts and purposes for writing and of curriculum that supports the development of rhetorical dexterity. Their discussion of ecological assessment, however, is limited to writing assessment conducted in colleges and universities and does not address the complex challenges faced in the K–12 educational context, where power relationships play an outsized role and where the range of stakeholders extends beyond a classroom, program, or institution.

Inoue (2015) takes up issues of power in his description of a writing assessment ecology at the classroom level, and like Wardle and Roozen (2012), he focuses on the postsecondary context. He identifies the elements of a writing assessment ecology as "power, parts, purposes, people, processes, products and places" (p. 10). Ecological *power* is expressed, he says, in the ways teachers control and design assignments such as portfolios "what [students] write, how portfolios are put together, how many pages or documents to include, what students should reflect upon, etc." (p. 121). Ecological *parts* "refer to the artifacts, documents, and codes that regulate and embody writing . . . it is the instruments, scores, grades, portfolios, essay prompts, students' and teachers' responses, or scoring rubrics that we often refer to" (p. 125). Ecological *purposes* vary for different stakeholders in the ecology. For example, purposes typical for teachers and writing program administrators are

> to check for students' comprehension of material or proficiency in writing, to place students in courses, to predict future performance in college generally, to motivate students to do work in a class, or to provide feedback for revisions and future practices.
>
> *(pp. 133–134)*

For students, purposes may be "to get a good grade in the class, to follow orders (like a good student would) or because that's what you do in school, to get feedback for revisions for future writing practices" (p. 134). Ecological *people* "bring their own abstractions and values that can shape their purposes in the environment, their responses to it, and create various, uneven consequences" (p. 146). Ecological *processes* include the writing process or processes that are taught and students' engagement or lack of engagement in the assessment processes of their work. Inoue (2015) asserts "that writing teachers should carefully construct the writing assessment ecology of their classrooms both theoretically and materially" (p. 3).

While Inoue's discussion is focused on anti-racist pedagogy and is directed at ways teachers can create an anti-racist writing assessment ecology in their college classrooms, his overall formulation of the elements of an ecology provides a way to consider and analyze elements of writing assessment ecologies at other levels of the educational system as well. For example, individuals with ecological power may change from level to level of the educational system, but the idea that power plays an important role in assessment ecologies remains relevant across its different levels, from the classroom to the national arena. More often than not, in the larger, "institutional" arena of writing assessment, especially at the K–12 level, elected or appointed officials are the ones who exercise power. Agencies far from the classroom specify standards at the K–12 national level about what should be taught, and sometimes how. At various points in time, local, district, and state level agencies have also promoted (or required) or ignored different approaches to the teaching of writing. In this arena, power typically comes from the outside in. Nevertheless, the idea that power plays an important role in ecologies remains central to the health of the educational system as a whole because ecologies are dynamic with interconnected relationships. What affects one element of an ecology affects others.

One important element in assessment ecology not specifically identified by Inoue is policy. Testing policies decided by people outside of classrooms have had a disproportionate impact on the educational ecosystem as a whole as well as the ecologies of individual sites—classrooms, programs, schools, districts, and states— from elementary school through college. Because large-scale assessments impact educational decisions made at all levels, they influence what teachers teach and what students learn. In short, they impact teaching practices, another element not distinctly identified in Inoue's list. Effects of assessments, especially those with high stakes attached, ripple throughout the classroom ecology and the ecosystem as a whole because they influence teaching practices. They impact—and are impacted by—larger structural issues such as racism, sexism, and classism. Gere et al. (2021) address the historical injustices associated with writing assessment and argue for ways to move toward a more just approach:

> Because assessment ecologies are shaped by broader policy infrastructures, the work of justicing requires not only attention to curricular and testing policies (e.g., Jeffery, 2009), but also to the social, institutional, and economic "policy regimes" (Kynard, 2013, 225–230) that shape broader structural inequalities. Already, assessment scholars have drawn attention to the fact that assessment ecologies can be affected by "food or housing insecurities" (Poe and Inoue, 2016, p. 125)—just as they are affected by policies that regulate immigration, discrimination, labor conditions, and school access, accessibility, and affordability.
>
> *(pp. 403–404)*

Gere et al.'s approach acknowledges the complex relationships between all aspects and actors involved in the teaching and assessing ecosystem.

Not all policy decisions bring about positive results. For example, Gere et al. (2021) explain, "Standard language ideologies and racism figured prominently in the establishment of writing assessment in schooling in the United States" (p. 388). As we have explained in earlier chapters, the focus on standardizing writing assessment can undermine the development of the very skills that will allow a student to become an effective writer who is prepared to meet a variety of writing challenges in a variety of situations because teachers' classroom practices are influenced by the assessments. Teachers who feel pressured to teach to the test may narrow the strategies they use for teaching as well as the writing curriculum in their classrooms, focusing on a particular genre or format because of the test. In some districts, test prep is mandated. Reductive test prep materials and practices include the exclusive use of prompt formats used on a test, limiting tasks to the specific writing genres or structures (such as the five-paragraph essay) associated with the test, or using the test rubric not to teach students about key components for evaluating a text, but to mimic the scoring of the test when responding to peers, self-evaluating, and grading. They may focus on correctness and conventional uses of language instead of a critical understanding of language. In such cases, policies can have a negative effect on the writing ecology as a whole—the power, parts, purposes, people, processes, products, and places.

The dilemma, however, can be addressed. In ecological terms, we need to develop policies that would promote a healthy ecosystem, which includes promoting practices that research shows are effective. We offered recommendations in Chapters 4 and 5, based on research, about some of the ways we could promote a healthier ecosystem for the learning of writing:

- Promoting formative assessment;
- Engaging students in self-assessment;
- Investing in teacher development;
- Involving teachers in designing, developing, and scoring large-scale assessments;
- Creating joint assessment programs that bridge K–12 and college;
- Turning assessment into inquiry; and
- Engaging teachers and students in the joint development of criteria for a variety of writing tasks.

We also need to develop assessment practices that would promote a healthier ecosystem for the learning of writing. For example, portfolios and extended authentic tasks, which have a positive impact on teaching writing, can be used in large-scale assessment as well as the classroom. Researchers have already demonstrated that these types of assessments are more aligned with a contemporary understanding of writing as a complex construct, allow for more authentic tasks, have more positive than negative consequences for teaching and learning, and can meet traditional psychometric standards, especially in terms of reliability and validity. Recommendations we made in Chapters 4 and 5 were aimed at promoting positive outcomes:

- Redesigning assessments to align with a complex cognitive and social construct of writing;
- Broadening the range of situations and conditions for writing in large-scale assessments;

- Limiting the scope of conclusions drawn from large-scale assessment;
- Integrating reading and writing;
- Collecting classroom writing samples;
- Assess multimodal literacy; and
- Assessing collaborative writing tasks.

These recommendations, as research reviewed in earlier chapters has shown, can satisfy the psychometric standards advocated by educational measurement organizations such as the American Education Research Association and the National Council on Measurement in Education in the *Standards for Educational and Psychological Testing* as well as literacy organizations such as the National Council of Teachers of Writing.

As we explained in Chapter 2, validity is critical in educational measurement. We argued that construct and consequential dimensions of validity are of particular importance when considering contemporary large-scale writing assessment. However, there is another aspect of validity to consider as we think more broadly about the ecology of writing and writing assessment.

Ecological validity

To create better writing assessments in the classroom and beyond, we cannot ignore psychometric theories and practices; nor can we ignore what we now know about the construct of writing. To achieve a balance, we argue that we need to rethink our approach to validity. Educational testing, especially in the case of writing assessment, needs to include ecological validity in validity inquiry. We are drawn to this dimension of validity, common in some areas of social science but not in educational measurement, because of the way it prioritizes the context of the construct being tested. Social psychologists define ecological validity as

> the extent to which research findings would generalize to settings typical of everyday life. As such, ecological validity is a particular form of external validity. Whereas external validity refers to the overall extent to which findings generalize across people, places, and time, ecological validity refers more specifically to the extent to which findings generalize to the settings and people common in today's society.
>
> *(Wegener & Blankenship, 2007, p. 275)*

Wegener and Blankenship (2007) further explain that in terms of ecological validity, researchers "ask whether research results represent what happens in everyday life" (p. 276). This kind of question resonates with writing given the wide range of factors that influence a writer. According to Schmuckler (2001), "a key issue regarding the ecological validity of the research setting is its representativeness and naturalness," and he notes "a primary consideration" that "the environment contain crucial features of naturalistic settings" (p. 421). He further explains that "the relevance of the environment is also critical in that it must be functionally central in producing and observing the behavior in question; it must be a true environment in which actors behave on a regular basis" (Schmuckler, 2001, p. 421).

While social psychologists associate this aspect of validity specifically with research, it doesn't appear to be a dimension of validity explored in educational assessment. After all, it isn't addressed in the last two editions of the *Standards* (AERA et al., 2014; 1999). However, it is a widely used concept in research related to psychology as evidenced by its coverage in the *Encyclopedia of Social Psychology* (Baumeister & Vohs, 2007) as well as journal articles in a range of fields including neuroscience and neuropsychology. In a research setting, ecological validity relates to differences in the conditions in a laboratory or controlled setting versus the natural environment. The controlled setting of psychological experiments is analogous to the controlled setting of standardized testing. Both create threats to validity.

The natural environment of writing, as documented by researchers, is far different than the timed and solitary context that is enforced in standardized assessments, where students write in isolation, with limited access to other resources, and often on impromptu topics. The writers in the world outside of school that Brandt (2015) studied write in different contexts, with different purposes, audiences, genres, and standards, and use a wide range of processes and technologies. After summarizing the complexity and nuances of writing in the everyday experiences of workaday writers and writing-intensive youth, Brandt concluded that "writing presents its greatest challenge to the educational enterprise, which is growing increasingly out of step with the wider world" (p. 165). A gap exists between the writing of assessment and writing in the world of work, although, for decades, researchers have documented the collaborative, iterative processes of writing in many workplaces and the challenges students have as they move from school to the workplace (e.g., Droz & Jacobs, 2019; Stanton, 2017; Dias & Pare, 2000; Barchilon, 1998; Cornett, 1998; Katz, 1998; Cross, 1994, 1997; Reynolds et al., 1995; Schreiber, 1993). In workplace writing, more focused, time-limited tasks are not cold topics, and writers can draw on resources, including peers.

A gap also exists between the writing in standardized assessments and writing in the world of college. Given the most recent focus in K–12 education on "college and career readiness," it seems that ecological validity should be a central concern in the design of writing assessments. If one of the roles of the accountability agenda is to ensure students are prepared for college, then the assessment should be aligned with the writing tasks and environment the students will encounter in college. Yet, standardized writing assessments are out of alignment with much of the writing that happens in school, and especially in college classrooms. When writing for examinations, students have a sense of the material covered; the assignment isn't a cold topic. Typically, the writing is closely tied to the subject matter of the class, and students have had time to read, ask questions, and study before sitting down to write a timed essay on a discipline-specific topic. When writing outside of a formal testing situation, students frequently are encouraged to use a writing process that extends across days or weeks and includes research, feedback, revision, and collaboration. Writing tasks that engage students in meaningful ways enhance learning and contribute to personal and social development (Anderson et al., 2015). The contrast between the writing that people experience in natural settings (including school, college, and career) and the writing that students are asked to do in the context of standardized writing assessments highlights the need to consider validity in a different way than the traditional psychometric approach the educational measurement community has promoted. Ecological validity prompts us to consider whether the performance on an assessment—a controlled setting—aligns with the writer's performance in an authentic, naturalistic context.

Taken together, we suggest that ecology (the study of ecosystems) and ecological validity provide the frameworks we need to turn writing assessment inside out. By including ecological validity in validity inquiry, we would examine the results of an assessment in terms of authentic contexts in the ecosystem as a whole, both in school and out.

Taking an ecological approach to validity

Our understanding of writing as a complex, socially situated endeavor reminds us that a student's performance on an assessment tells us relatively little—apart perhaps, from the degree to which the student has mastered a certain kind of grammar and a particular set of conventions when writing in a specific context—about how well the student can perform when writing for different purposes under different conditions in different social situations, disciplines, and discourse communities. Can the writer perform effectively when writing formal and informal classroom-based writing tasks and discipline-specific exams as well as tasks outside of school—e.g., self-sponsored, social, and/or job-related tasks? Can the writer perform effectively in different disciplines and discourse communities? The results of traditional standardized assessments may be accurate in terms of how a student performs in response to a single specific type of task in a single specific context, but the results do not necessarily reflect how that same student may perform when other tasks and contexts are in play. An ecological dimension of validity would thus call for test developers and those who require tests to have a better understanding of how writing varies across different kinds of tasks undertaken in different conditions as well as how writers work outside of the controlled, artificial environment of the assessment context.

Can we create writing assessments—in the classroom and in large-scale situations—that reflect more closely the places, purposes, and conditions that writers will encounter? We have recommended some first steps in this direction, such as assessments that include multiple genres, multiple modes, and authentic tasks and audiences, including portfolios and extended collaborative projects. Tasks such as these encourage authentic writing processes and can support the development of rhetorical dexterity and critical language awareness. Students need to develop a repertoire of processes, rhetorical knowledge, and metacognitive skills as well as knowledge of language and genre conventions to be successful in college, career, and their personal endeavors. Improving students' overall abilities to write thus requires multiple assessment tasks that collectively represent writing in a variety of authentic contexts under various conditions. It goes without saying that this is a goal that cannot be accomplished by a single-sample test.

Taking an ecological approach to assessment would require considering the construct, the tasks, the stakes, and the intended and unintended consequences but also the relationships among all of these factors. It would include investigating the way the test impacts teaching and learning. It would highlight the dynamic nature of writing and provide support for assessments that include multiple genres written in multiple conditions. It would support formative assessments to support learning, and it would require that teachers and assessors have an understanding of writing that aligns with literacy scholarship. An ecological approach goes far beyond simply using statistical formulas to claim generalizability or future success. It would require a more fully developed and sophisticated understanding of what students need to know and be able to do so they are prepared for writing that comes next—in college, careers, and beyond. It would encourage assessment developers to provide validity arguments that encompass the relationships among different components of teaching, learning, and the goals of education.

An ecological approach would also encourage assessment designers and policy makers to strengthen relationships across educational levels, for example, between elementary school and secondary school or between secondary and post-secondary institutions so they can create teaching, learning, and assessments that prepare students for the writing challenges they will face when they leave one classroom or school for another. Teachers across levels will need to be more aware of what the tasks and demands at other levels will be so they can support students when they make the transitions. In other words, if high school is preparing students for college or career, then teachers need to know what the writing demands of college and career will be.

College writing instructors and their K–12 counterparts will need to establish more consistent means for sharing information and techniques that flow both ways. When information is shared across educational levels and contexts, high school teachers will develop better understanding of what students will encounter as they move to college, and college instructors will develop a better understanding of the experiences students have before they come to college. And all teachers need to understand the writing activities and ecologies students encounter beyond school. Creating this kind of extended network will make for healthier connections across different levels and institutions as students move from one educational environment to another. The challenge is to create sustainable networks that survive beyond particular individuals or special projects. This requires policies that prioritize these kinds of connections. An ecological approach to assessment allows us to align contemporary constructs of writing, learning, and assessment while also thinking about the relationships among all of the components of the system.

An ecological approach also gives us a strong argument for putting and keeping teachers at the center of student assessment. Teachers are critical for student learning. They are essential to creating authentic classroom learning environments that prepare students for what they will experience beyond the classroom. They are conduits between the larger educational system and the classroom. They translate curricular goals and educational policies into learning activities. They need policies that support their professional development and increase their knowledge about effective formative and summative assessment. Accountability systems should be designed to help teachers prosper—to gather knowledge, develop effective practices, to grow and thrive—so they can in turn be accountable to their students. Assessments can support this approach if they are an organic part of professional learning, and if they make teacher and student learning the primary goal, as we saw with several of the examples in Chapter 5. This redesigning and refocusing of writing assessment should also align with what we, as a field, have learned about writing and learning. It needs to happen in the classroom, and at other levels of the educational systems, including schools, districts, and states—even at the national level—with teachers contributing to decision making at all levels.

Redesigning writing assessment practices on such a broad scale is a formidable challenge, and we are well aware that the real challenge will be in figuring out how to put into action the policies needed to develop and successfully implement a well-structured, coherent, and technically sound assessment system that works across multiple levels, that reflects contemporary understandings of the complexities of writing, and that promotes best practices in teaching. We are hopeful that our ideas may serve as a springboard for action by the many stakeholders involved in writing assessment.

References

American Educational Research Association, American Psychological Association, & National Council on Measurement in Education. (1999). *Standards for educational and psychological testing*. American Educational Research Association.

American Educational Research Association, American Psychological Association, & National Council on Measurement in Education. (2014). *Standards for educational and psychological testing*. American Educational Research Association.

Anderson, P., Anson, C. M., Gonyea, R. M., & Paine, C. (2015). The contributions of writing to learning and development: Results from a large-scale multi-institutional study. *Research in the Teaching of English, 50*(2), 199–235, A1–A3.

Barchilon, M. G. (1998). Writing for engineering fields. In J. A. Lutz, A. Jean, & C. G. Storms (Eds.), *The practice of technical and scientific communication: Writing in professional contexts: ATTW contemporary studies in technical communication* (Vol. 4, pp. 37–48). Ablex.

Baumeister, R. F., & Vohs, K. D. (2007). Ecological validity. In *Encyclopedia of social psychology* (Vol. 1, pp. 276–276). Sage Publications. https://doi.org/10.4135/9781412956253.n167

Bitzer, L. F. (1968). The rhetorical situation. *Philosophy and Rhetoric, 1*(1), 1–14.

Brandt, D. (2015). *The rise of writing: Redefining mass literacy.* Cambridge University Press.

Burch, Jr., W. R., & DeLuca, D. R. (1984). *Measuring the social impact of natural resource policies.* University of New Mexico Press.

Cooper, M. (1986). The ecology of writing. *College English, 48*(4), 364–375.

Cornett, P. L. (1998). Writing in medical and health care environments. In J. A. Lutz & C. G. Storms (Eds.), *The practice of technical and scientific communication: Writing in professional contexts, ATTW contemporary studies in technical communication* (Vol. 4, pp. 151–186). Ablex.

Cross, G. A. (1994). *Collaboration and conflict: A contextual exploration of group writing and positive emphasis.* Written Language Series. Hampton Press.

Cross, G. A. (1997). Writing through the grapevine: The influence of social network clusters on team-written texts. In C. Kirklighter, V. Cloe, & J. M. Moxley (Eds.), *Voices and visions: Refiguring ethnography in composition* (pp. 66–76). Boynton/Cook.

Dias, P., & Pare, A. (Eds.). (2000). *Transitions: Writing in academic and workplace settings.* Hampton Press.

Dobrin, S., & Weisser, C. (2002). Exploring relationships between discourse and environment. *College English, 64*(5), 566–589.

Droz, P. W., & Jacobs, L. S. (2019). Genre chameleon: Email, professional writing curriculum, and workplace writing expectations. *Technical Communication, 66*(1), 68–92.

Edbauer, J. (2005). Unframing models of public distribution: From rhetorical situation to rhetorical ecologies. *Rhetoric Society Quarterly, 35*(4), 5–24.

Gere, A., Curzan, A., Hammond, J. W., Hughes, S., Li, R., Moos, A., Smith, K., Van Zanen, K., Wheeler, K. L., & Zanders, C. J. (2021). Communal justicing: Writing assessment, disciplinary infrastructure, and the case for critical language awareness. *College Composition and Communication, 72*(3), 384–410.

Inoue, A. B. (2015). *Antiracist writing assessment ecologies: Teaching and assessing writing for a socially just future.* The WAC Clearinghouse, Fort Collins, CO and Parlor Press.

Jones, M. P. (2018). Writing conditions: The premises of ecocomposition. *Enculturation: A Journal of Writing, Rhetoric and Culture.* www.researchgate.net/publication/327103999_Writing_Conditions_The_Premises_of_Ecocomposition

Katz, S. M. (1998). Learning to write in organizations: What newcomers learn about writing on the job [Part I]. *IEEE Transactions on Professional Communication, 41*(2), 107–115.

Machlis, G. E., Force, J. E., & Burch, W. R. (1997). The human ecosystem Part I: The human ecosystem as an organizing concept in ecosystem management, *Society & Natural Resources, 10*(4), 347–367. https://doi.org/10.1080/08941929709381034

Phelps, L. W. (1988). *Composition as a human science: Contributions to the self-understanding of a discipline.* Oxford University Press.

Redman, C., Grove, J., & Kuby, L. (2004). Integrating social science into the long-term ecological research (LTER) network: Social dimensions of ecological change and ecological dimensions of social change. *Ecosystems, 7*(2), 161–171. https://doi.org/10.1007/s10021-003-0215-z

Reynolds, J. F., Matalene, C. B., Magnotto, J. N., Samson, Jr., D. C., & Sadler, L. V. (1995). *Professional writing in context: Lessons from teaching and consulting in worlds of work.* Routledge.

Schmuckler, M. A. (2001). What is ecological validity? A dimensional analysis. *Infancy, 2*(4), 419–436.

Schreiber, E. J. (1993). From academic writing to job-related writing: Achieving a smooth transition. *IEEE Transactions on Professional Communication, 36*(4), 178–184.

Stanton, R. (2017). Do technical/professional writing (TPW) programs offer what students need for their start in the workplace? A comparison of requirements in program curricula and job ads in industry. *Technical Communication, 64*(3), 223–236.

Tansley, A. G. (1935). The use and abuse of vegetational concepts and terms. *Ecology, 16,* 284–307.

Van Dyne, G. M. (1966). *Ecosystems, systems ecology and systems ecologists.* Oak Ridge National Laboratory, Health Physics Divisions.

Vatz, R. (1973). The myth of the rhetorical situation. *Philosophy and Rhetoric, 6*(3), 154–161.

Wardle, E., & Roozen, K. (2012). Addressing the complexity of writing development: Toward an ecological model of assessment. *Assessing Writing, 17*(2), 106–119.

Warner, M. (2002). Publics and counterpublics. *Public Culture, 14*(1), 49–90.

Wegener, D. T., & Blankenship, K. L. (2007). Ecological validity. In R. F. Baumeister & K. D. Vohs (Eds.), *Encyclopedia of social psychology* (Vol. 1, pp. 275–276). Sage. https://doi.org/10.4135/9781412956253.n167

INDEX

Page numbers in *italics* indicate a figure on the corresponding page.

Pearson, P. D. 15
Pecheone, R. 165
pedagogical diversity 40
peer review 79–80, 110, 127
Pelz, K. 62
performance assessments, designing
  128–136
Perin, D. 72, 77, 80
Perl, S. 61
Perry, K. 63
Phelps, L. W. 183
Pianko, S. 82
Porter, J. 73
portfolio assessment 116, 118–119, 125
portfolios, designing 128–136
practices that align with a social
  perspective on writing; building genre
  knowledge and rhetorical capacity
  76–77; integrating modes of literacy
  in instruction 75–76; writing for
  a purpose 72–73; writing to real
  audiences 73–75
Prior, P. 57, 64
providing feedback on writing 79
Pruchnic, J. 174
psychometric approach to assessment
  27–28, 136, 188, 190

Ramaprasad, A. 98
rating scales in instruction 81
Ravitch, D. 18
reading and writing, integrating 119–122
Redman, C. 182
reflection 82–85, 122, 130–133;
  constructive reflection 81, 83;
  reflection-in-action 80–81, 83;
  reflection-in-presentation 81, 83
reliability 27–28; acceptable level of
  45; alternate form 27; AWPE strong
  record of 103; at college level 119;
  coefficient 27; hermeneutic approach to
  28; internal consistency 27; interrater
  27, 161; inter-reader 28; in large-scale
  assessments 27–28; portfolio 118;
  psychometric approach to 187; scores
  for Kentucky portfolios 118; scores for
  Vermont portfolios 118; test-retest 27;
  traditional psychometric approach to
  27; validity versus 28
Robertson, A. 120, 127
Robinson, K. 61
Roozen, K. 184–185
Rosenblatt, L. M. 65

Rosinski, P. 75
Ross, J. A. 81
rubric: genre-specific rubric
  105–106, 108; rubric-referenced
  self-assessment 81
Ruth, L., 44
Ryan, M. 82

Sanchez, C. 80
Scardamalia, M. 131, 133
Schmidt, A. E. 15
Schmuckler, M. A. 188
Schon, D. 82
School-based, Teacher-led Assessment and
  Reporting System (STARS) 164–165
Schoonen, R. 45
Schunk, D. 100
self-assessment 80–82, 99
self-regulated strategy instruction 81
Sfard, A. 69
Shavelson, R. J. 44
Shepard, L. A. 10, 33, 97, 136
Sills, E. 125–126
Slavin, R. E. 168
Slomp, D. H. 33–34, 39
Smarter Balanced Assessment Consortium
  (SBAC) 121
Smith, M. A. 105, 108–109, 117, 161
Smith, M. L. 10
Smith, W. L. 32, 120
social constructivism 68
social perspective on writing 58–62
Spalding, E. 39
Stancliff, M. 167
standardized tests 16–17
standard language ideologies 15
*Standards of Educational and Psychological
  Testing* 29
Stecher, B. M. 9
St. Martin's Handbook 72
Stokes, L. 156, 161
Street, B. V. 57
student-centered teaching 150
summative assessment *see* assessment of
  learning (summative)
Swain, S. S. 105–106, 108–109, 161
Swales, J. 76
systematic error 42

Tansley, A. G. 182
"teachers teaching teachers" model 152
test-based accountability 14–15